DAVID LAT

SUPREME AMBITIONS

A NOVEL

Cover design by Elmarie Jara/Ankerwycke.

Printed in the United States of America

18 17 16 15 14   5 4 3 2 1

Library of Congress Cataloging-in-Publication Data

Lat, David.
  Supreme ambitions / David Lat.
    pages cm
  ISBN 978-1-62722-046-0 (alk. paper)
  I. Title.
  PS3612.A8684S87 2014
  813'.6--dc23

                         2014029863

Discounts are available for books ordered in bulk. Special consideration is given to state bars, CLE programs, and other bar-related organizations. Inquire at Book Publishing, Ankerwycke, American Bar Association, 321 N. Clark Street, Chicago, Illinois 60654-7598.

www.ShopABA.org

For my parents and for Charlene.

"High status is thought by many (but freely admitted by few) to be one of the finest of earthly goods."

—*Alain de Botton*

"If nothing else, there's applause... like waves of love pouring over the footlights."

—*All About Eve*

"I'm tough, I'm ambitious, and I know exactly what I want. If that makes me a bitch, OK."

—*Madonna*

SUPREME AMBITIONS

I

The walk from the law school to Yorkside was short. This was good; I wanted this to be a short conversation. As a dutiful daughter, I felt the need to update my mother on important developments, but I didn't want to get caught up in a long argument about my life and career choices.

"Hi Mom. What's up?"

"Nothing much. Waiting for your father to come home from a job so we can have dinner. And your sister is coming over from the Center. Almost done cooking—I made *sinigang*, one of your favorites. Too bad you're not here. How are you?"

"Oh, fine. I just wanted to let you know—I'm going to be in Los Angeles next week. For a clerkship interview with a judge."

"You're flying out to L.A.? Next week? How much is your ticket?"

"Five hundred or so," I said (rounding down, and excluding taxes and fees).

"Five hundred? That's a lot. Why aren't they paying? Like the law firms?"

"I had to buy on short notice. And this isn't a law firm. It's for a clerkship. With a federal judge. It's the government."

My mother sighed, in Queens. I heard her, in New Haven.

"Audrey, I don't understand why you want to do this 'clerky' thing. Your cousin Vincent works as a clerk."

"At a Shoe Mart in the Philippines. This is completely different."

"So you went to Harvard and Yale, and your dad and I borrowed all this money, and you borrowed all this money, so you could get a job as a clerk? Like your cousin Vincent?"

"This is a *law clerk* position, with Judge Christina Wong Stinson. A federal judge. A federal *appeals court* judge. One level below the Supreme Court. And some say Judge Stinson herself might be nominated to the Supreme Court someday."

"Audrey, it's up to you—your life, your career. I'm just a nursing assistant, I don't know anything about this law-law stuff of yours."

"I've explained this before, Mom. A clerkship with a federal appellate judge is an amazing experience for a young lawyer, a chance to see litigation from the point of view of a judge. And it's very prestigious. Top law students from around the country would kill for a Ninth Circuit clerkship."

Well, maybe not *any* Ninth Circuit clerkship; it would have to be with the right judge. The Ninth wasn't as uniformly prestigious as, say, the D.C. Circuit. But I wasn't about to try and explain this to my mother.

"So this job is prestigious," she said. "Is prestige going to pay your rent? Or your student loans?"

Actually, it could. But I did not feel like explaining to my mother, a nurses' aide whose interaction with lawyers was mercifully limited, the complex process by which the legal profession generates, fetishizes, and monetizes prestige.

"I can live on a law clerk's salary," I said. "I'd be making at least $60,000 a year . . ."

"Ay, *susmariosep*! Sixty thousand a year? Why don't you just go back to that Cravath place? You'd be making over $150,000, right? Now *that's* good money. Your father and I have never made that much in a year—combined."

Now it was my turn to sigh. Maybe I would try and enlighten my mother. I had an idea about how to put a stop to her carping.

"Cravath pays $160,000," I said, referring to Cravath, Swaine & Moore, where I had worked as a summer associate (and which I had an offer to return to after graduation). "But what if I could get about twice that much—just as a signing bonus, on top of a six-figure salary?"

I could sense my mother's ears perking up. She was not a greedy woman and did not have extravagant tastes. But as an immigrant who had come to the United States with practically nothing, who had slowly scrimped and saved her way into the bottom rung of the middle class, she did not take money for granted. She had been dazzled by my job last summer at Cravath—a job that paid me more than $3,000 a week, while wining and dining me at Manhattan's best restaurants—and couldn't stop bragging about it to her friends.

"So . . . how does that signing bonus work?" she asked. "I thought you said this clerk thing pays about $60,000?"

"Yes, that's right," I said. "But if I get this clerkship and impress Judge Stinson, she could recommend me for a clerkship with a Supreme Court justice. And Supreme Court clerks, when they leave the Court and go to law firms, get huge signing bonuses—as high as $300,000. On top of a base salary of about $200,000."

My mother was momentarily silent—not her usual state.

"Well," she said, "that sounds pretty good. That could pay off your student loans instantly. And help out with the costs of your sister's care. And maybe send your mom and dad on a cruise, ha! You should become a Supreme Court clerk."

I laughed—loudly—and then immediately felt guilty. But that was my spontaneous reaction to my mother's comment. She might as well have said, "You should become an international luge champion."

"Mom, these positions are almost impossible to get. Supreme Court clerks are the best and the brightest young lawyers in the country."

"Audrey," said my mother, in an almost lecturing tone, "you graduated magna from Harvard for college. Now you're at Yale for law school, and you're on law review. You worked over the summer at Cravath. How many are better and brighter than you? How many law students get profiled in the *Filipino Reporter*?"

I was touched by my mother's pride in me. And in the *Filipino Reporter*, the New York–area newspaper for the Filipino American community

("Fair, Fearless, Factual"). But I had to dispel her illusions.

"There are hundreds of law students out there with résumés just like mine. There are 40,000 new law school graduates each year—and about 40 Supreme Court clerks. It is literally a one-in-a-thousand opportunity."

"But you are one in a million—and so pretty, too! *Mestiza* beauty, as they say back home. Of course a supreme judge will want to hire you. Like that black one, the one who likes the dirty movies. Ha!"

My mother started to laugh at her own joke, an old habit of hers. I felt myself blushing. (Due to my Irish heritage on my father's side, I could pass as white and was quite capable of blushing.)

"Mom, I have to go. I'll talk to you later."

"Okay, *hija*. Be a good girl!"

When I arrived at Yorkside, a casual pizza-and-diner-type eatery just down the street from the law school, Jeremy was already standing outside. He pretended to peruse the menu, even though he'd get the same thing he always got: a cheeseburger, with Swiss and lettuce and tomato, no bun. His near-pathological aversion to carbs helped him stay extremely thin. I was a size two, in good shape, but hanging out with Jeremy made me feel fat.

A waitress, neither surly nor friendly, seated us in a roomy booth near the back, then took our drink order. I was grateful for the relatively private table. We decided to meet at Yorkside precisely to avoid the law school cafeteria (and not just because of its hummus of dubious provenance). The Yale Law School dining hall in early September —the height of clerkship application season for third-year law students, pursuant to the Law Clerk Hiring Plan—was a hive of anxiety and competitiveness.

My friendship with Jeremy Silverstein dated back to our first year of law school, when we were in the same 1L class section. We frequently found ourselves on opposite sides of classroom debates: I was a moderate, which passed for conservative at the law school, while Jeremy was very liberal. But we bonded over a shared love of good Indian food and bad television. Now, as 3Ls, we served together as articles editors for the

Yale Law Journal, spending many late nights arguing over which pieces to accept for publication.

The waitress brought us our Diet Cokes and took our food order: cheeseburger sans bun for Jeremy, a chicken Caesar salad (dressing on the side) for me. Jeremy and I engaged in small talk—classes, journal submissions, gossip about a potentially philandering professor—before tackling the topic we had come to Yorkside to talk about: which clerkship interviews we had scored. Due to our different political views, we were applying to different slates of judges, meaning that we weren't competing head-to-head for the same jobs. This allowed us to discuss clerkship applications without freaking each other out.

"So, Miss Audrey," said Jeremy, squeezing lemon into his drink with a chemist's precision, "tell me which judges you're interviewing with."

"Well, Mr. Silverstein, why don't you tell me about your interview schedule?"

"I asked you first," he said—and he was correct. The playground rule has a legal counterpart: first in time, first in right.

I smiled flirtatiously. Jeremy was a little too skinny, but cute. I sometimes wondered what our relationship would be like if he weren't gay.

"Right now I have four interviews," I said, in as matter-of-fact a way as possible. But I knew four was impressive—and so did Jeremy, whose eyes grew wide.

"Very nice," he said. "I kind of hate you right now. So who are you seeing?"

"Let's see," I said, pretending to search my memory, when actually he could have woken me up at three in the morning and I could have blurted out these names instantly. "Barbara McDaniel."

"You applied to a *district* judge?"

"You're such a snob! District court clerkships are often better learning experiences than circuit court clerkships. And it's not just any district— it's the Southern District of New York, the best trial court bench in the country, with the best cases. Judge McDaniel handled Enron, World-Com . . ."

"Sure," Jeremy said, "but district court is district court, and circuit court is circuit court. In district court, you'll spend all your time dealing with crap like motions practice and discovery disputes. Trust me—I interned for a district judge after 1L year. Wouldn't you rather be clerking for an appeals court, drafting opinions on big sexy issues of law?"

Jeremy was a good person and one of my best friends, but he could be a horrible snob. In his defense, he was a product of his environment. A clerkship with a district judge, a trial-level judge in the federal system, was enormously prestigious and hard to get. But some people at Yale, both professors and students, quietly looked down upon district-court clerkships. There were some exceptions to this rule—it was okay to go district if you really wanted to be a trial lawyer, if you clerked for the right judge on the right district, if you followed it up with an appeals-court clerkship—but it generally held true.

"All of my other interviews are circuit," I said. "Michael DeConcini, Third Circuit. Steven Collins, Eighth Circuit."

"Ugh . . . Isn't Collins in, like, Iowa?"

"It's only a year," I said. "I could live anywhere for a year. I'm more focused on judges than geography. Collins has a great reputation. He graduated from here, clerked for the Supreme Court, served as U.S. Attorney. I could learn so much from him. And he could become a big feeder judge in a few years. In fact, he's already fed a few of his clerks into Supreme Court clerkships."

"I could not live in Iowa for a year," Jeremy said. "Geography aside, Collins is too conservative for me. Who's your last interview?"

"Judge Stinson, Christina Wong Stinson. Former district judge in Los Angeles, now on the Ninth Circuit?"

"Hello! You don't need to say that as a question! Stinson is *major*. Possible SCOTUS nominee in a Republican administration. She'd be the first Asian American on the Court. Feeder judge to the Dark Side—um, I mean, the conservative justices. Is she your first choice?"

"I feel very lucky to have these interviews, and each judge has his or her own strengths . . ."

Jeremy gave me a withering look.

"Okay," I said, "Stinson is my top choice."

I didn't want to admit how badly I wanted to clerk for Judge Stinson. Articulating a desire and pursuing it avidly makes it so much worse when you fail. I thought of the William James quotation: "With no attempt there can be no failure; with no failure, no humiliation." But there was no sense in hiding such things from Jeremy.

"So," he asked, "I assume you've scheduled her first? So you can bag on the others if she makes you an offer?"

"Yup."

"Well, feeder judges move fast, and Stinson is a feeder. Nicely done, girl."

Jeremy raised his Diet Coke with lemon in my direction; we clinked glasses.

"Stinson is a feeder judge," I said, "but not a top, top feeder. Out of her four clerks each year, she feeds maybe one of them. It's not a done deal that her clerks go on to the Supreme Court. You have to excel."

"That's fair," Jeremy said. "You probably have to be her favorite clerk in your year. She's no Polanski."

Ah yes, the Honorable M. Frank Polanski—a colleague of Stinson's on the Ninth Circuit, an indisputably brilliant jurist, and a possible Supreme Court nominee (handicapped mainly by his white-maleness, and partly by his reputation for being difficult). He was also, far and away, the top feeder judge in the country. Landing a Polanski clerkship was tantamount to landing a Supreme Court clerkship, since he had an almost perfect record of feeding his clerks to SCOTUS (with the help of the vast network of his former clerks, the Polanski Mafia).

"Judge Polanski, I kind of hate him sometimes," I said. "He and his clerks hog all the Supreme Court clerkships. It's not fair."

"If only you had won the editor-in-chief job," said Jeremy. "Then you might have gotten a Polanski interview."

"Stop torturing me! I'd be a lock for a Supreme Court clerkship as a *Yale Law Journal* EIC with a Polanski clerkship. And Polanski is an amazing judge who's written some great opinions."

"Great if you oppose the Ninth Circuit's efforts to bring justice and a progressive agenda to the western United States!"

I laughed. The Ninth Circuit was the nation's most left-leaning appeals court, known for issuing decisions that were embraced by the ACLU and NPR crowds (before getting overturned by the Supreme Court). And Polanski was one of a handful of conservative judges who could get in the liberals' way (unless he happened to side with them, which he did from time to time).

The waitress arrived with our dishes, placing them before us unceremoniously, and asked us if we needed anything else. We did not.

"So," I asked Jeremy, as I added trace amounts of dressing to my salad, "those are all my interviews. Now tell me all about yours."

"I have three interviews," Jeremy said. "First up is James Kenote."

"You applied to a *district* court judge?"

"I'm willing to make an exception for the first openly gay man appointed to the federal bench."

In addition to serving as an articles editor, Jeremy was president of OutLaws and a cheerleader for all things gay.

"Fair enough," I said. "Who else are you interviewing with?"

"Sheldon Gottlieb, in Pasadena."

"Congrats! Your hero. The liberal lion of the nation's most far-left appeals court."

We toasted again. Gottlieb was too old and too liberal to ever be nominated to the Supreme Court, so he did whatever the heck he wanted—and got away with it, thanks to lifetime tenure for federal judges. Jeremy idolized Sheldon Gottlieb for his outspokenness—on the bench and off, in opinions and in speeches—on behalf of various oppressed groups. But to many others, including myself, Gottlieb was a left-wing judicial activist who used the law to achieve goals he couldn't accomplish through the ballot box.

"And," Jeremy said, "last but not least, Marta Solís Deleuze."

"Ugh. You applied to her? I didn't know you were a masochist. I don't know if all the stories are true, but if even half of them are . . ."

"Yeah, I know, some say Deleuze is a raging beeyatch," said Jeremy. "But she's a champion for criminal defendants who have been railroaded, immigrants facing deportation, victims of police brutality. And she's a wise Latina, young enough and ethnic enough to someday get traction as a Supreme Court nominee. She's wicked smart—a former SCOTUS clerk herself, natch. I could learn a shitload from her. And she's in San Francisco, which would be a *fabulous* place to live for a year."

"And she's starting to become a feeder judge, even though she's new to the Ninth."

"True. But in terms of feeding, my best bet is probably Gottlieb."

"Yeah. He's about at the level of Judge Stinson."

Jeremy referred to judges so casually—"Gottlieb" or "Deleuze," as opposed to "Judge Gottlieb" or "Judge Deleuze." When you grow up as the son of the managing partner of Jenner & Block and a tenured professor at the University of Chicago Law School—Jeremy's mother, Judy Silverstein, was a leading tax law scholar—you're more likely to see federal judges as part of your family social circle, as opposed to gods and goddesses (which is how I viewed them).

I pushed my plate away, even though it still held about a third of my salad.

"That's all you're eating?" Jeremy asked.

"You know how I eat," I said. "I have no desire to return to my childhood chubbiness. Being an overweight biracial girl with a disabled sister was no recipe for playground popularity. Anyway, I hope you get Gottlieb, and I get Stinson. It would be fun to clerk on the Ninth Circuit together."

"It would! But we'd probably end up working against each other on a lot of cases. Since, you know, you'd be working for the forces of darkness."

"The forces of darkness? Judge Stinson and her allies just want to interpret the law faithfully, to apply the law as written. It's not a matter of pushing an agenda, from the left or the right. It's about the text of the

Constitution, the statutes, and the precedents. The job of the judge is to apply the law to the facts."

"Oh, Audrey, don't be so naïve. 'The law' isn't some pure thing floating out there in the ether. What ends up being 'the law' is affected by a million things other than the text. It's affected by how the case is argued by the lawyers. It's affected by how the judges interact with the lawyers, and with each other. And yes, like it or not, it's affected by the political beliefs and policy preferences of the judges. Hell, as the old saying goes, sometimes the law depends on what the judge had for breakfast."

"I completely disagree. There *is* such a thing as 'the law,' and it's not just based on the political preferences of the judges. And anyway, if anyone is working for the forces of darkness, it's your side. I can imagine you and Judge Gottlieb trying to do something crazy, like flinging open the doors to the California prisons to let those poor misunderstood criminals roam the streets. And when you do, Judge Stinson and I will do our best to stop you."

"Two liberal Jewish guys versus two conservative Asian girls," said Jeremy. "Is that a fair fight? I think you judicial divas would kick our pale white-boy asses."

"You make us sound like a pair of right-wing dragon ladies! We're moderates. I'm a 'conservative' only here at crazy-liberal Yale, and she's a 'conservative' only on the crazy-liberal Ninth Circuit. Our views are probably where the average American's are. And, not to be too technical, we're each half-Asian."

I flashed my best million-dollar smile at him. I have my physical flaws, but my teeth are gorgeous. And sharp.

2

I ended up with a window seat on my flight out to Los Angeles. Since I had booked on short notice, I wound up near the back of the plane, close enough to smell the lavatories' mix of cleanser and other substances. But at least I wasn't in a middle seat; in fact, the middle seat next to me was empty, a rare thing these days. The relative comfort allowed me to concentrate for most of the flight, reading printouts of newspaper articles about Judge Stinson, her most noteworthy opinions, and the generally glowing clerkship reviews from the Yale career services office written by former Stinson clerks. Sample line: "The worst part about clerking on the Ninth Circuit and for Judge Stinson is that I probably won't have a job that's this interesting, and a boss who's this awesome, until much later in my legal career—if ever."

After landing at LAX, I stopped at a Starbucks in the terminal for a tall coffee—inside a grande cup, so I could fill up the empty space with milk—and a (low-fat) blueberry muffin, which I deemed unlikely to give me stomach trouble before an interview. I had learned, from past experience, not to interview on an empty stomach. During my senior year of college, while I was being interviewed for the Rhodes Scholarship, my stomach growled—loudly—and I didn't get the fellowship.

To this day I blame my audible stomach rumblings for changing the course of my life. Had I gotten the Rhodes, everything would have been different. Have you ever had an experience where, had things turned out just a little bit differently, your entire life would have been transformed?

The time a talent scout was supposed to visit your college athletic practice, but canceled at the last minute? The time you almost got asked out by a celebrity? The time you came in second place at a prestigious musical performance competition? For me, that time was my failed Rhodes interview. Like a Supreme Court clerkship, a Rhodes Scholarship gets mentioned in your obituary.

After polishing off the coffee and muffin, I made my way to the terminal exit. I stepped outside, into brilliant sunshine and a perfect temperature in the low seventies, and headed for the taxi line. Unlike New York cabs, which are all yellow and made in a limited number of styles, cabs in Los Angeles lack uniformity of appearance; they instead come in an unregulated jumble of colors and styles. Welcome to the jungle.

I wound up in a patriotic minivan: red, white, and blue. The driver was thin, cheerful, dark-skinned, and of indeterminate age. His driver identification card said his name was Pervez Hamadani; I guessed he was Pakistani.

I thought about how an immigrant cab driver was about to drive me to my clerkship interview with a federal judge who was herself the daughter of an immigrant cab driver. As my airplane reading had reminded me, Christina Stinson (née Wong) was the daughter of a taxi driver who came to the United States from Shanghai and an American-born nursing assistant. The future judge grew up in modest circumstances, in a working-class neighborhood in the Inland Empire.

I was struck by the similarities in our backgrounds. We were both biracial women. We both grew up without much money. We both had mothers who were nurses' aides. After doing well in college (Stinson graduated summa cum laude from UCLA), we both went straight through to law school (in her case, Boalt Hall, aka UC Berkeley).

The driver, Pervez, made eye contact with me using his rearview mirror and asked me my destination. I told him the address, feeling self-conscious as I said it due to its regal ring: 125 South Grand Avenue, Pasadena.

"What is that?" he asked, as he entered the address into a GPS device.

Again, a difference between Los Angeles and New York cabbies: the latter wouldn't be caught dead using GPS (even though, truth be told, some of them could use it, especially in the West Village).

"A federal courthouse," I said. "The Ninth Circuit courthouse."

"In Pasadena? Isn't the courthouse downtown?"

"That's the district—er, the trial—court. I'm going to the appeals court."

"What's the difference?" he asked, pulling away from the curb. I wondered whether he was trying to be polite or was genuinely interested.

"The trial court is where most of the action is—where trials are held, where criminals get sentenced—that sort of thing."

"Ah, like O.J. Simpson!" The driver's face brightened with recognition. "My first year in the United States! The white Ford Bronco!"

"Yes, like O.J.," I said, "except that was state court, and I'm going to federal court."

"What's the difference?"

I felt like a law professor teaching a 1L civil procedure class. Was this fellow preparing for his citizenship test?

"State versus federal depends on the law involved," I said. "Some areas of law are mostly state law, like family law and divorces and that sort of thing. And some areas of law are mostly federal—like immigration, say."

Mentioning immigration seemed to dampen Pervez's enthusiasm for legal discussion. He turned the radio on to NPR. I looked out the window at the passing neighborhoods of Los Angeles, which reminded me of the cab queue at the airport, chaotic and clashing. The city seemed squalid and seedy. At least L.A.'s infamous traffic wasn't bad: there was plenty of volume, but we moved at a decent clip. I was surprised at the hilly, wooded terrain; I always thought of Los Angeles as sprawling, flat, and denuded.

As we passed through a series of tunnels fringed with lush vegetation, Pervez lowered the volume on the radio and made eye contact with me through the rearview mirror.

"Young lady, where are you from?"

When my Asian-looking mother got asked this question, it was a national-origin inquiry; for me, it was a simpler query.

"New York."

"And you are going to a trial in a court?"

There was something courtly in his demeanor. I decided I liked Pervez.

"Oh no, I'm going to the appeals court," I said. "The court that reviews what the trial court did to make sure it's okay."

"So you're a lawyer?"

"Not yet . . ."

Pervez turned around and grinned.

"You are too young—and too pretty!—to be a lawyer."

I laughed. His grin was sweet, not lecherous.

"Thank you," I said, "but I hope to be a lawyer someday. Right now I'm in my last year of law school. I'm here to interview for a job as a law clerk."

"You came all the way from New York for a clerical job?"

I was about to laugh again but stopped myself. I didn't know much about clerkships until I started law school. And misconceptions about a law clerk's role—from Pervez, from my mother—were a healthy and humbling reminder that clerks play a behind-the-scenes role in the justice system.

"Actually, law clerks don't do much clerical work," I explained. "They assist judges in deciding cases—helping the judges prepare for court, and researching and drafting opinions."

"Sounds important! I bet it pays well."

"Not particularly. But it's great experience, it looks good on a résumé, and you can get a high-paying job at a law firm afterwards."

"And where do these cases come from? All over?"

I was starting to feel like a Wikipedia entry. I rattled off some facts about the Ninth Circuit: the largest federal appeals court, jurisdiction over cases coming from nine western states, about 30 active judges, headquarters in San Francisco.

"You are a very knowledgeable young lady! Good luck in your interview."

We exited the highway and turned onto a broad boulevard lined with orange trees. It was a stately street, with large and tasteful homes on either side, all bathed in a golden light. It reminded me of exclusive neighborhoods back east. As my mother rode the 7 train back to Woodside, the doctors she worked for would drive their Mercedeses and BMWs back to towns like this, in Westchester or Fairfield or Bergen County.

Pervez noticed me craning my neck to take in the scenery.

"This is one of the nicest parts of the city," he said. "We're almost there. If you get the job, you'll see this every day."

We turned left on to a shadeful side street, then quickly turned right. Seemingly out of nowhere, a pink palace materialized. Standing about six stories tall, with a bell tower, it loomed over the low-slung residential neighborhood. Said the female voice on the GPS: "You have reached your destination."

"This is it?" Pervez asked. "Are you sure this is a courthouse? It looks like a hotel."

"Actually, it used to be a hotel," I said, as the research I had done about the building came back to me. "It started off as a resort called the Hotel Vista del Arroyo. During World War II, it was used as an army hospital. After the war, it fell into disrepair, until it got converted into a courthouse."

Pervez pulled the car up a bit, and we saw a large rectangular sign on the lawn, in a shade of pink that perfectly matched the stucco of the building: "Richard H. Chambers United States Court of Appeals Building—125 South Grand Avenue."

The taxi fare came to a little under $80 on the meter. I gave Pervez five crisp $20 bills, hoping that tipping generously would bring me good luck for the interview—the superstitious Filipino in me.

"If you ever need a taxi, call me," he said, handing me his card. "This is L.A., you can't just walk out into the street and wave for a cab."

I got out, my briefcase-like purse slung over my shoulder, and looked up at the building. The courthouses I was familiar with were grim concrete affairs, coldly beautiful neoclassical structures, or sleek and sterile towers of stone and glass. They embodied the power and greatness of government, but at the cost of aesthetic appeal or architectural originality. The Richard H. Chambers Courthouse in Pasadena looked nothing like these other courthouses; it was splendid and welcoming, in large and equal measure. I could understand why one amateur photographer, who had taken pictures of the courthouse and posted them online, dubbed it "the most beautiful courthouse in America," adding that "law clerks who work elsewhere should feel cheated."

The courthouse was set back a good distance from the street. I walked through an arbor, lined with gently weathered wooden benches and flowering white rosebushes, and reached two ornately carved wooden doors, each with three diamond-shaped, leaded-glass panes. Through one of the panes, I could vaguely make out a high-ceilinged, light-filled foyer—an entrance hall that could have belonged to one of the million-dollar homes down the street.

I pulled open one of the (surprisingly heavy) doors. No automatic glass doors here. This was no ordinary courthouse.

Three courthouse security officers lounged in chairs next to a metal detector, looking profoundly bored. This was an ordinary courthouse after all.

The guard closest to the entrance, a stout, bald man, rose out of his chair.

"How can we help you, young lady?" His tone sounded slightly patronizing, as if I had wandered into the wrong building and he would soon have to give me directions.

"I'm here for an interview with Judge Stinson."

The bald guard nodded and asked me for a photo ID. I handed him my passport—like many New York City kids, I had never acquired a driver's license—and he wrote my name down in a ledger. His two colleagues stood up and exchanged strange glances.

"Into the lioness's den," said a tall guard with short gray hair, as he took my bag and placed it on the conveyor belt for the x-ray machine.

The lioness's den? Would Judge Stinson be a tough interviewer? Many interviews for legal jobs consist of a schmoozy, conversational rundown of the candidate's résumé. As a "learned profession," law likes to think of itself as more genteel than, say, a ruthlessly data-driven enterprise like management consulting, with its "case study" interviews that amount to hazing with math. But every now and then you get grilled. I willed the blueberry muffin to remain still in my stomach.

I passed through the metal detector without setting it off, thanks to my decision to refrain from jewelry (except for two small faux-pearl earrings), and collected my purse from the x-ray machine. The bald guard pointed out the elevator to me and directed me to the fifth floor.

The courthouse elevator had just a single door, made of wood and carved in the same elaborate manner as the two front doors. The narrowness of the doorway unnerved me. I sometimes find signs in random everyday phenomena, a habit acquired from my mother, and I took the narrowness of the elevator as a commentary on the narrowness of my chances of landing the job. I opted for the stairs. As I ascended the wide and inviting staircase, with a wrought iron banister and colorful Mission-style tiles between each step, I congratulated myself for picking kitten-heel pumps; they had enough of a heel to be femininely elegant, but were perfectly comfortable for climbing stairs.

Upon reaching the fifth floor, I had no trouble locating the chambers. A handsome brass nameplate read: "Chambers of the HON. CHRISTI-NA WONG STINSON." I pressed a buzzer, as softly and politely as I could—I hate loud and obnoxious buzzers—and opened the door after being buzzed through.

The elegance of the courthouse's public spaces prepared me for something nice, but not for Judge Stinson's jewel box of a chambers. The waiting room, decorated in harmonized shades of beige, yellow, and gold, could be described as modern French provincial meets California country. It looked straight out of a coffee-table book of Napa Valley estates, not like any space owned by the federal government. I certainly hoped the American taxpayer hadn't paid for the hardwood floors, a sharp departure from the wall-to-wall nylon carpet commonly seen in government offices, or the vase full of fresh-cut orchids, sitting on a low table of pale wood.

At the far end of the room, in front of two high windows that admitted copious amounts of sunshine, stood a secretary's station, with cabinets and desk space built into the corner. It was standard-issue in design, except it was made of the same ivory-colored wood as the coffee table. I then realized: this was all custom work, including the coffee table.

I introduced myself to the pleasingly plump, conspicuously chipper woman behind the desk. She rose out of her chair to shake my hand.

"Audrey, it's wonderful to meet you. I'm Brenda Lindsey, Judge Stinson's judicial assistant. Welcome to Pasadena!"

She gestured, mock-grandly, by raising both of her arms. But given the beauty of the courthouse, the gardens, and the chambers, claims to grandeur had a basis.

"Thank you," I said. "It's great to be here."

"Please, have a seat. Can I get you something to drink?"

"I'm fine, thank you."

"The judge is in the middle of an interview, but she should be done very soon. Just make yourself comfortable."

Brenda's warmth allayed my jitters—slightly. I perched myself on the edge of a supremely comfortable beige couch, which was built into the wall like a banquette. Everything was so beautiful and expensive-looking, I felt like I was disturbing the space with my presence.

A door shut. A harried young brunette in a black pantsuit emerged into the waiting room from somewhere deeper within chambers. She scanned the room; our eyes met. She looked at me with an impolitic intensity, for a few seconds too long, almost hungrily. Was she trying to intimidate me?

She must be from Harvard Law School, where they learn the dark arts of cutthroat competition that we were never taught at kinder, gentler Yale. She had the grim aggressiveness of an HLS student, as well as the lack of fashion sense. (Sorry to disappoint you, but *Legally Blonde* was just a movie.)

Harvard Girl's botched pixie cut made her look mannish, as did her poorly fitting pantsuit. The color black, while interview-safe, was uninspired.

I smiled a half-smile and raised my hand in tentative greeting at Harvard Girl. I was about to stand up and introduce myself, the polite thing to do—but before I could say or do anything, Harvard Girl pulled a BlackBerry out of her pocket, checked the time, and strode out of the room.

I wasn't sure what to do with myself while waiting to see Judge Stinson—normally I'd check email on my iPhone, but that seemed vaguely disrespectful—so I turned my attention to the offerings on the coffee table. There was a reprint of an article by Judge Stinson from the *Virginia Law Review*, "The Role of the Federal Judge in Our Constitutional System," which was odd coffee-table fare. I had already read it, so I set it aside in favor of a book of California country-style houses. Feeling my typical pre-interview anxiety, I welcomed the distraction of "seaside estates, canyon villas, and courtyard bungalows."

I began by admiring the ocean views from the terrace of a Malibu mansion. Then I lost myself in the architectural ingenuity of an ultra-modern barn-style house in the Russian River Valley.

"You're reading my favorite book, I see!"

I startled and looked up. Standing in front of me, looking amused, was a petite, stunningly attractive Eurasian woman: the Honorable Cristina Wong Stinson. With her ambiguously exotic good looks, she looked like a shorter Catherine Zeta-Jones.

I scrambled to my feet. The book, still open to the Malibu estate, dropped with a thud on the table—I had forgotten I was holding it! Did I just damage federal property?

What to do first: shut the book and restore it to its proper place, or shake hands with the judge? I went with people over property.

"Judge Stinson, it's an honor to meet you," I gushed, flustered. "I'm

Audrey Coyne."

"And I'm Judge Stinson," she said, smiling and extending her hand. "But you already knew that."

I shook her hand and chuckled at her quip. The one thing I remembered from Trial Practice class was to always laugh at a judicial joke (or anything resembling one).

Then I remembered the book, splayed out helplessly on the coffee table. I imagined the spine creasing from where I had left it open. Every time she saw that crease, the judge would think of me.

"Your Honor, I'm so sorry about your book," I said, rushing to close the book, with exaggerated delicacy, and replacing it on the table. "I forgot I was holding it, you see, and then when I stood up . . ."

"Don't worry about it," she said. "I have a dozen copies at home. I wasn't joking about that being my favorite book—my house is featured in it, and the author gave me plenty of courtesy copies."

"Well, Judge, if your house is as beautiful as your chambers . . ."

"That's very kind of you, Audrey, but let's be honest—this old place? I did the best I could. Unfortunately, the people at GSA—the General Services Administration, they manage government property—have all of these restrictions. And they didn't give me much of a budget. I had to, well, supplement it . . ."

She smiled, and I smiled back. Perhaps what they said about Californians was true: everyone I had met so far, from Pervez to Brenda to the judge, was so affable.

"Did Brenda offer you something to drink?" Judge Stinson asked. This made me feel like a client at her husband's talent agency. The judge was married to Robert Stinson, one of Hollywood's most powerful agents—and the reason she lived in a mansion fit for a coffee-table book, despite earning a federal judge's relatively modest salary. They met as associates at Gibson Dunn & Crutcher, before he left for the entertainment world and she made partner.

"I'm fine, thank you," I replied. "I had something at the airport."

"Very well. Let's get started, shall we?"

Judge Stinson led me down a short, wainscoted hallway. Tokens of power and prestige adorned the walls: a group portrait of all the Ninth Circuit judges; a group portrait of all the judges of the Central District of California, back when Judge Stinson was a trial judge; a glass-encased commendation from a women's bar association, given to her when she was an up-and-coming litigation partner at Gibson Dunn; and, most impressive of all, a photograph of Judge Stinson and her husband with President George W. Bush, who had appointed her to the bench, and Laura Bush. Trailing a few diplomatic steps behind the judge, I admired how the cut of her pearl-gray knit suit flattered her body—a body that, despite the judge being almost old enough to join the AARP, didn't need much flattering.

I suppressed a gasp upon entering Judge Stinson's private office. It was flooded with sunlight, thanks to a bank of windows that offered spectacular views of a high-arched bridge that spanned a deep ravine. The room's overall aesthetic could still be described as modern California, but with Asian accents: a handmade Oriental rug, faded enough to be antique; two blue-and-white vases, made of Chinese porcelain, that were the size of small children; and red lacquered end tables, flanking a tan couch. Judge Stinson directed me to the couch—which was, like the one in the anteroom, far more comfortable than it looked—and seated herself in a round tufted club chair.

Intimidated by such surroundings, I would have picked at my cuticles, had my manicure left me anything to pick. But Judge Stinson quickly put me at ease. Going over my résumé, she asked me standard questions—how I liked Harvard for college, what were my favorite classes in law school, what articles I was currently editing for the law review—and I gave standard, enthusiastic answers. Having been through such interviews during the law firm hiring process, I knew the drill.

As an Asian (or part-Asian) woman of a certain age, with a warm and chatty manner, Judge Stinson reminded me of my mother—except with better hair, an unlined face (Botox?), and unaccented English. And, of course, an intricate knowledge of the legal profession's elaborate hierarchies. She nodded approvingly upon seeing that I had summered at Cravath, murmured "very nice" upon seeing that I had made the finals of the moot court competition in the spring of my 2L year, and raised her eyebrows (in a good way) at my membership on the articles committee of the law review.

"I noticed your impressive grades," Judge Stinson said, without even fishing out my transcript from the pile of materials on her lap. "But we receive, through diversity jurisdiction, a fair number of complex commercial cases here in the Ninth Circuit. Your mediocre grade in Business Organizations jumped out at me. How can I be confident that you'd handle these cases competently?"

"Well, Judge Stinson," I said, "I don't know that I'd call a Pass a 'mediocre' grade. It wasn't a Low Pass . . ."

Yale Law School has grades, contrary to popular belief, but the scale is spare: Honors, Pass, Low Pass, Fail. My single grade of Pass, on a transcript otherwise filled with Honors, was Business Organizations—"Corporations" at most other schools—with the fast-talking, hard-grading Regina Ranieri.

"Audrey, you're cute," said Judge Stinson, smiling. "But don't get cute with me. You're in your third year of law school. Have you heard of any of your classmates receiving a Low Pass?"

"No . . ."

"I've seen dozens of Yale transcripts over the years. How many Low Passes do you think I've seen in total?"

"Ten?"

"One," she said, pointing a single, meticulously manicured fingernail toward the ceiling. "I was so amazed, I called the professor. The student was living in San Francisco that semester, working on a startup, and showed up twice—for the first class, and for the exam. And he got a Low Pass, not a Fail."

I shifted on the couch. I felt the blueberry muffin in the pit of my stomach. I noticed the nails of my right hand digging into a throw pillow.

"So," Judge Stinson said, sitting back in the club chair, "why don't you tell me about your Business Organizations grade?"

I remembered what I had learned while preparing for the moot court finals: take a moment to collect your thoughts before answering a judge's question. So I did.

"Biz Org was actually one of my favorite classes," I said. "I learned a tremendous amount. My grade on the final resulted mainly from an error I made on a question regarding hedge fund regulation. So this past summer, at Cravath, I sought out a partner who practices in this area, worked on a fund formation with him, and helped him write a law review article. And this semester I'm taking Regulation of Financial Instruments with Professor Ranieri. I'm working very hard and hope to redeem myself with a better grade this time around."

Judge Stinson nodded intently, a hint of a smile playing across her lips. I felt like an Olympic gymnast who had just nailed a landing. Having covered my résumé and transcript, which Judge Stinson set down on one of the end tables, we turned to more substantive matters.

"I am not, shall we say, the typical Ninth Circuit judge," she said. "I assume you are familiar with my judicial philosophy?"

"Absolutely, Judge Stinson. You stand out on the Ninth Circuit for your commitment to judicial restraint, set forth very powerfully in your opinions—*Grant*, for example, where your theory of harmless-error analysis was eventually adopted by the Supreme Court. And your dissent from the denial of rehearing in *Upton*, a major qualified-immunity case, where you were once again vindicated by the high court . . ."

"Audrey, you flatter me!" Judge Stinson chuckled. "Please continue."

I felt the beginnings of a blush in my cheeks—yes, I was being sycophantic—but I wanted this job very badly. And the judge seemed not to object. I had learned when interviewing for law firm jobs to tell the difference between interviewers who hated suck-ups and interviewers who enjoyed compliments, and I could see that Judge Stinson fell into the second camp.

"I also admire your academic writing," I said. "Your *Virginia Law*

Review piece on the role of judges in our constitutional system—it takes the familiar subject of judicial restraint and makes it fresh, infusing it with your practical insights as a sitting judge."

I was glad to sneak in mention of the UVA article. That way Judge Stinson would know I was reading a coffee-table book instead of her law review piece because I had already read the latter.

"Again, that's very nice of you. But my own feeling is that it's not my best work, despite its excellent placement. I prefer my article in the *Harvard Journal of Law and Public Policy*, about jurisdiction as a limit on judges' power. People tend to see jurisdiction as a series of dry, technical questions. What is the legal basis for jurisdiction? Is it federal question jurisdiction, under section 1331? Is it diversity jurisdiction, under section 1332? Is it supplemental jurisdiction, under section 1367? Was the case filed in the trial court within the statute of limitations? Was the notice of appeal timely filed, to create proper appellate jurisdiction?"

Some might have found this recitation pedantic, but I was impressed. Some judges become removed from the details of judicial craft after they've been on the bench for a while, but Judge Stinson struck me as someone still very much in touch with the finer points of the law.

"But jurisdictional limits are not mere technicalities," she continued. "Constraints on the power of judges are an important and valuable thing. Don't get me wrong, I love having power"—here she smiled wide, and I admired her teeth—"but I'm unelected, here for life, and not very accountable to the people. And that's not necessarily a good thing."

"Judge, I wouldn't mind having you as a benevolent dictator!"

"Ha! Tell that to my husband. Or my kids. I can't get them to do anything!"

I laughed—and this time it was genuine. We went back and forth about judicial restraint for a few more minutes. Judge Stinson cited Justice Frankfurter's dissent in *West Virginia v. Barnette*, arguing that a judge's personal opinion about the wisdom or evil of a law is irrelevant when he is deciding a case. I cited a *Harvard Law Review* article by Justice Holmes, in which he famously wrote, "We do not inquire what the legislature meant; we ask only what the statutes mean." She in turn quoted Chief Justice Marshall from *Marbury v. Madison*: "it is emphatically the province and duty of the judicial department to say what the law is"—what it "is," not "should be."

It felt like a religious revival, with Judge Stinson and me quoting our favorite passages back and forth to each other and saying "Amen" in response. But instead of citing Bible verses, we were quoting from the greatest hits of judicial restraint, textualism, and related theories.

"Of course, this court isn't the only battleground in the struggle against judicial activism," Judge Stinson said. "There are other fronts that are even more major. Are you planning to apply for Supreme Court clerkships?"

I was expecting this question, based on the clerkship write-ups of former Stinson clerks.

"Yes, Judge," I said. "It is a dream of mine to clerk for a justice of the Supreme Court."

"Excellent. I encourage—*strongly* encourage—all of my law clerks to apply to the Court. It reflects well on me as a judge to send my clerks on to the Court. And I like to be thought well of. I like to be a judge who's going places."

"You have a lifetime appointment to a federal appeals court! That's pretty great, you know! Who else do you have to impress? Where else is there to go?"

Judge Stinson's eyebrows arched electrically. What had come over me? I couldn't believe my excited utterance—in a raised voice, fraught with emotion, and without a prefatory "Judge" or "Your Honor." It was far too casual, if not downright disrespectful, and far from the proper way to address a member of the federal judiciary.

The judge stared right at me. I braced myself for her reprimand.

"Excuse me, Your Honor," I said before she could respond, modulating my voice. "I meant no disrespect. I was just, well, I was thinking, you have such an amazing position . . ."

"Audrey," Judge Stinson said, shaking her head and sighing. "There is *always* somewhere else to go. Always."

She paused, touching a bejeweled finger to her perfect chin, and looked off into space for a few moments. Then her gaze returned to me.

"So you're interested in clerking for the Court," she said. "Of the current justices, who are your favorites, and why?"

"I have two. I admire Justice Keegan for his focus on the text and for articulating the theory of originalism so cogently. And I admire Justice Wilson for his close attention to history, and for his open-mindedness—his willingness to reconsider doctrinal questions that other judges view as settled. I would apply to all nine justices, which I understand is protocol, but I would most love to clerk for either Justice Keegan or Justice Wilson."

"I am lucky enough to call both of them my friends," said the judge, gesturing toward a wall where I could make out photographs of her with both justices. "And several of my clerks have gone on to clerk for them. I'm glad you have such good taste in justices. I never know what to expect from you Ivy League types!"

"Please, Judge, don't lump me in with everyone else! We're not all wild-eyed judicial activists."

"Oh, Audrey, I'm just kidding. I went to Boalt Hall for law school, and I can assure you that UC Berkeley is not a hotbed of judicial restraint. Nor is the Ninth Circuit. I sometimes feel like the lone voice crying out in the wilderness when I argue in favor of deciding cases based on, you know, *the law* . . ."

I laughed. Yes, this interview was a game, and I was determined to play by the rules.

"One last question," said the judge. "I have received over one thousand clerkship applications for this cycle, from the very best students at the nation's leading law schools. With over one thousand applicants, why should I hire *you*?"

The question's directness floored me. And flustered me.

"Your Honor," I blurted out, "I'm you."

What had I just uttered? Where had that come from? Why was I intent on sabotaging myself?

"Excuse me?" Judge Stinson's impeccably groomed eyebrows were raised so high that I no longer suspected Botox.

"Judge Stinson, I'm you. I'm smart, I'm ambitious, and I'm relentless. I came up from a humble background and made something of myself. Some people underestimate me—they expect me, as an Asian American woman from modest means, to be some sort of wallflower—but then I prove them wrong. Big time."

I was too nervous to stop and gauge the judge's reaction. I plowed ahead. I had no choice.

"I work hard, extremely hard, until I get the job done. I learned all about hard work from my mother, a nursing assistant, who has worked long hours for years. I've inherited the immigrant work ethic from my parents—my mother, an immigrant from the Philippines, and my father, the descendant of Irish immigrants. I take nothing for granted. If selected for the high honor of clerking for you, I will not disappoint. You have my word."

Judge Stinson stared at me. I let the silence linger. Normally I hate conversational breaks, but I had said my piece.

I realized at that moment where the "I'm you" had come from. A few years ago, a Senate candidate in Delaware responded to accusations that she dabbled in witchcraft by running television ads that started out with her saying, "I'm not a witch. I'm you." After watching this video endlessly on YouTube (because I found it hilarious), the phrase "I'm you" seeped into my subconscious—from where it burst forth during a moment of great stress.

"Audrey," Judge Stinson said, after a silence that seemed to last forever, "I don't normally do this . . ."

What was she about to do? Throw me out of chambers? The Yale clerkships adviser would be thrilled to learn how I mouthed off to a Ninth Circuit judge, who would probably refuse to hire Yalies for the next five years in retaliation for my rudeness.

"I prefer to wait until I've finished all my interviews before making offers," said Judge Stinson. "But I feel a special connection with you. I would love to have you as my clerk."

I felt nauseous. I felt elated. This was actually happening.

"Judge Stinson," I said, trying to imbue my voice with maximum gravitas, "I would be honored to have you as my judge."

We shook hands again. Her handshake was firm, but her hand was impossibly soft. Pearl cream?

"Excellent," the judge said. "I look forward to our working together."

3

Before I knew it, it was a sweltering Sunday afternoon in August 2012. Upon landing at LAX, I called my old pal Pervez, who had driven me to and from my interview with Judge Stinson a year earlier. After my two suitcases were stashed securely in the back of the minivan, we drove off to Pasadena.

"So," Pervez asked, "why did you decide to live in Pasadena?"

"I'm going to be working long hours as a clerk, and I don't drive. So I need to be close to the courthouse."

"Ah yes, the courthouse I took you to—beautiful courthouse. Anyone who works in that building must be very important!"

Although I was glad that Pervez no longer viewed my clerkship as purely clerical, I responded to his impressed-sounding tone with humility. I emphasized that law clerks simply assist the judge, who is the ultimate decision maker, and that everything coming out of chambers would go out under the judge's name. As clerks, we were like Santa's elves—essential but unseen contributors to the process.

This limited responsibility was something I actually appreciated, at least some of the time. I had just graduated from law school (and not a very practically oriented school at that), and I was not even admitted to the bar (New York bar exam results wouldn't come out until November). What did I know—about law, or life, or anything? It gave me comfort to know that I would just be doing research and making recommendations, which my judge was free to ignore or override as she saw fit.

On other days, of course—like, for example, the day that I got the clerkship—I felt excited by my proximity to power, and confident that I would be an amazing law clerk. But today I felt anxious, like a third grader about to start a new school year. I suspected that this vacillation between anxiety and minimization of one's role, on the one hand, and confidence and exaggeration of one's influence, on the other, was common among law clerks.

There wasn't much traffic on this Sunday, so it didn't take long for us to arrive at my new home: a nondescript, run-down, low-rise apartment complex a few blocks from the courthouse. I had taken the small studio without visiting it in person (because I couldn't afford another flight out to Los Angeles), so I had seen it only in pictures. Like someone you've seen only in an online dating profile, it looked dumpier in person.

Pervez took my heavy suitcases all the way to my door, on the second floor of the open-air building. Once again, as I had done when he drove me to my clerkship interview, I gave him $100 on an $80 metered fare. I was happy to be generous, especially given how nice he was and how much he had to fight with my bags, but I did feel a twinge of money-related worry as I fished the twenties out of my wallet.

Money worries were why I had gone with this apartment, a unit passed down among several cycles of Stinson clerks, along with IKEA furniture on its last legs. So I wasn't that troubled after I opened the door and surveyed the cramped, borderline grim-looking quarters, which looked like a motel room where a down-on-his-luck movie outlaw might hole up while on the lam. This was what I had expected. This was what it looked like to be living on a law clerk's salary with more than $150,000 in student loans. And this was not where I'd be spending most of my time anyway; former Stinson clerks had joked about how chambers was their real home.

At least Michael Nomellini, the prior tenant, had left the apartment very clean (especially for a guy). It didn't take me long to unpack and tidy up the place. Since it was still bright outside, I decided to check out the apartment's small swimming pool, located in the central courtyard.

I just wanted to take a quick look, so I didn't bother changing into a swimsuit.

The pool itself was well maintained but empty. There was only one resident sitting next to the pool, and she was hard to miss: a young, large African American woman who reminded me of Gabourey Sidibe from *Precious*. She wore a red bikini with white polka dots. And she was reading a copy of . . . the *Stanford Law Review*?

I stood at the edge of the pool area, behind the white metal gate. My neighbor, deeply engrossed in her reading, did not notice my presence. Should I go over and say hello?

Intrigued by my neighbor, I didn't notice how much I was leaning into the gate—which swung open with a loud creak. I fell forward before regaining my footing. The young woman looked up, and our eyes met.

"Girl, what you looking at?"

Her confrontational tone rendered me speechless.

"What," she said, "are your ears as small as your tiny white ass?"

I tried to defuse her hostility with warmth. I walked over to her, put on a big smile, and extended my hand.

"Hi," I said. "I'm Audrey. I just moved into the building."

"Harvetta," she said, rising to her feet and shaking my hand. "Harvetta Chambers."

"I'm sorry, I didn't mean to, startle you. I was just, well, you know . . ."

"Oh, I know, all right! You were just checking out my big black booty!"

She slapped her prodigious thighs and laughed. I joined in, feeling relieved; Harvetta's belligerence was playful. Was she going to be my Sassy African American Friend?

"Actually," I said, "I noticed your reading material. No offense to the *Stanford Law Review*, but I go with *Us Weekly* when working on my tan."

"You kidding? I *love* law review articles. I can get interested in almost any type of law. For my job I'm a state law kinda gal, but today I'm reading on the federal side, about the effect of the SEC's new proxy access rule on shareholder value for small companies. Next up is a linguistic analysis of ERISA preemption. Followed by an empirical assessment of dissentals—you know, dissents from denial of rehearing en banc in the circuit courts. Right now I'm like a pig in shit!"

I didn't quite know what to say to that.

"So," I said, "did you go to Stanford Law?"

"Naw," Harvetta said, "Stanford? That place is for rich bitches. I keep it *real*—I went to McGeorge. You a lawyer too?"

"Well, almost, kind of," I said, as I frantically tried to recall what I even *knew* about McGeorge. "I took the bar a few months ago, but I haven't gotten the results yet, so I'm not yet a lawyer. Right now I'm clerking for a judge."

"Get the fuck outta here! Me too. Who you clerking for?"

"Judge Stinson? Ninth Circuit?"

"Is that a statement, or a question? Because I've heard of the Ninth Circuit. Isn't that the crazy liberal court that's always getting smacked down by the Supreme Court?"

I felt myself blushing. Even though I hadn't started work yet, I wanted to defend the honor of the court, or at least of my judge.

"My boss, Judge Stinson, is one of the more conservative judges . . ."

"Yeah, look, you don't need to explain yourself to me," Harvetta said. "I'm just clerking for a state judge, not one of those fancy federal judges."

"For whom are you clerking?"

"Sherwin Lin, California Supreme Court."

I didn't know *that* much about state court clerkships, but I had a vague recollection of the California Supreme Court using long-term staff lawyers rather than law clerks.

"Oh," I said, trying my best to sound politely confused, "I thought that the California justices didn't have law clerks?"

"Yeah," Harvetta said, "the Cal Supremes usually roll with permanent staff attorneys. But Lin is trying something new—a mix of staff attorneys and term clerks. His staff attorneys are up in San Fran with everyone else. We're his first two clerks, working with him here in Pasadena, where he lives. He got permission from the court to keep chambers down here for now because his dad is real old and sick and lives here. It's an experiment. Hope we don't fuck that shit up for everybody else!"

My strict Filipina mother did not tolerate profanity, so people who cursed a fair amount—like Jeremy, and definitely like Harvetta—sometimes threw me for a loop. My face must have betrayed my discomfort.

"What, is my potty mouth freaking you out, girl? Don't you worry. I am like the president," Harvetta said, raising her arms skyward before adopting a markedly different tone, straight out of the evening newscast. "I am extremely talented at calibrating my manner of speaking to my audience. Do you think I obtained a clerkship with the Honorable Sherwin Lin by cursing up a blue streak during the interview?"

Once again, Harvetta left me speechless. She liked to read law review articles for fun. She could oscillate seamlessly between gangster and grande dame. Who *was* this bizarre woman?

"So," she asked, as I tried to collect my dropped jaw from the pool deck, "where did you go to law school? Some fancy-ass place?"

"Um, Yale?"

"Yeah, I figured," she said, smacking my forearm—surprisingly hard. "Don't worry, I won't player-hate. My boss went to Yale, so I have mad respect."

That's right: Harvetta's judge, Sherwin Lin, was still renowned at Yale for his brilliance. He served as executive editor of the law journal, won a slew of prizes at graduation, and clerked on the D.C. Circuit (of course) followed by the U.S. Supreme Court (of course). He was nominated to the Ninth Circuit before the age of 40, but some of his controversial speeches and academic writings as a UCLA law professor derailed his nomination. After the Republicans successfully filibustered his Ninth Circuit appointment, the governor appointed him to the California Supreme Court.

Despite (or perhaps because of?) my puzzlement at Harvetta, I wanted to get to know her better. She seemed friendly, beneath the tough-talking veneer, and she was without a doubt an interesting character. We exchanged contact info and agreed to hang out sometime.

As I headed back to my apartment, I continued to think about Harvetta. I would have expected someone who liked to read law review articles for pleasure to have attended a higher-ranked law school than McGeorge (whose rank I looked up on my iPhone almost immediately after we parted ways; it wasn't even in the *U.S. News* top 100). And I wondered about where her whole "street talk" thing came from. If I had to guess, she was from an upper-middle-class African American family but was trying to "keep it real" by sounding like someone from a more modest background.

Based on the fact that she had landed a clerkship with Justice Lin, Harvetta must have done fairly well in law school. But even a clerkship on the California Supreme Court, the highest court of the largest state, was less prestigious than most federal court clerkships. As for U.S. Supreme Court clerkships, I wondered: did Harvetta even know about them?

4

I was nervous when I arrived at the Ninth Circuit courthouse for my first day at work. My pale gray Theory skirt suit, a pricey splurge from my summer at Cravath, wasn't giving me the usual jolt of confidence. I don't sweat very much, but by the time I arrived at work, I was sweating—and not from the seven-minute walk from my apartment to the courthouse, in a still-cool California morning.

This Monday marked the start of my Legal Career. And because I went straight though to law school from college, this was also the first day of my first Real Job. This was a Big Deal.

When I reached the door to Judge Stinson's chambers on the fifth floor, I pressed the buzzer tentatively, just as I had when I came for my interview. Instead of being buzzed in, the door flew open before me.

"Audrey! So wonderful to see you! Welcome!"

Before I knew what was going on, I was being hugged by the judge's secretary, Brenda Lindsey—*all* of Brenda Lindsey. I tried my best to return the hug, although I feared I was doing so too stiffly. Brenda and I had met just once, but as the outgoing clerks had told me, Brenda viewed the clerks like her children.

"The judge is out of town this week for a conference," Brenda said, "but let me show you to your office and introduce you to the other clerks."

I was the last of my clerk class to arrive, a position I had chosen to give myself time to decompress after taking the bar exam in late July. The downside of arriving last meant I got the one windowless office, while my co-clerks enjoyed views of the Arroyo Seco valley and the Colorado Street Bridge. I consoled myself by telling myself this would be an advantage: a windowless office meant fewer distractions from work. (And I could always go work in the chambers library—yes, the chambers had its own private library, in addition to the main courthouse library on the first floor—if I wanted sunlight and a view.)

As for my co-clerks, we had already met each other online—i.e., over email and Facebook—but meeting them in person still felt momentous. Would we become fast friends, foxhole buddies in the Ninth Circuit's jurisprudential war? Would we wind up as rivals for the favor of Judge Stinson, constantly trying to outdo and one-up each other? Or maybe a bit of both? The legal profession, stocked with competitive overachievers, was rife with such "frenemy" relationships.

Something made me uncomfortable about Amit Gupta, a graduate of Columbia Law, where he had served as executive managing editor of the *Columbia Law Review*. (He didn't mention that when we met, but of course I had looked up all my co-clerks on Google prior to arriving in chambers.) Amit seemed intense, energetic, and high-strung; he bowed slightly when he shook my hand and said, in a manner that bordered on fake, "It is a pleasure to meet you!"

We had some things in common—minorities, both from New York, both from Queens, even—but I felt there was something Amit was hiding from me, something that made me uneasy. I resolved to keep an eye on him. Maybe I just felt threatened by him because I viewed him as my biggest competition for Judge Stinson's favor. Amit had won the National Spelling Bee as a child. Would that kind of quirky honor catch the eye of a justice or a clerk skimming through Supreme Court clerkship applications?

I felt more at ease upon meeting James Hogan, who had a firm but not crushing handshake and a bright, easy smile. He could also be in the running for a SCOTUS clerkship, as a graduate of Boalt Hall, the judge's alma mater. His impressive height and striking good looks certainly wouldn't hurt him. It seemed to me, based on anecdotal observation, that Supreme Court clerks tended to be better-looking than average; perhaps the justices, faced with so many excellent résumés, used looks as a tie-breaker.

For whatever reason, I didn't feel as immediately competitive with James as I did with Amit. Maybe it was because James and I were so different; he seemed so relaxed, so Californian, and so tall. Compared to James, Amit and I looked like dark neurotic dwarfs.

I didn't know what to make of my third co-clerk, Larry Krasner. Maybe I was reading too much into the fact that he graduated from a less highly ranked law school—Loyola Law School, based here in Los Angeles—but he didn't have a very academic air. Maybe he was having a bad day or something, but he greeted me with so little enthusiasm, it seemed like he didn't even want to be in chambers.

I spent the rest of my first day with Janet Lee, the outgoing clerk that I would be replacing. Janet, whom I had briefly met when I interviewed with the judge, was also originally from New York, although she had gone to law school at Stanford. She was now moving back to New York to work at Wachtell Lipton.

Janet described my specific duties as a clerk, which could be divided up into three broad areas. First, in advance of each oral argument "calendar," or one-week period in which Judge Stinson would hear cases in court, I would help the judge get ready for the arguments. This would involve writing a "bench memorandum," a memo summarizing the facts and legal issues of a case and offering a recommendation for how the case should be decided, and preparing a "bench book," a binder containing the memo and various key documents relevant to the case. (Janet referred to the making of the bench book—which involved highlighting the documents, putting them in a particular order, and sticking colorful tabs all over them—as "arts and crafts.") I would also meet with the judge to discuss the cases orally during "review week," the week immediately prior to the calendar week.

"Here's one thing you *must* remember," Janet said. "When you first get a new case, you need to make sure the court has jurisdiction to hear it. Judge Stinson is very particular about jurisdiction."

I knew this from having talked about it with the judge during my interview and from the judge's writing in the area. Jurisdiction concerns the court's authority to hear a particular case. There are all sorts of reasons, some quite technical, as to why a court might lack jurisdiction—and if there's a "jurisdictional defect," the case must be dismissed.

"For example," Janet added, "take the notice of appeal—the statement filed by the losing party in the trial court indicating it plans to appeal. If the notice of appeal is not timely filed, then the Ninth Circuit can't hear the case, no matter how important the legal issues at stake. It must dismiss for lack of jurisdiction."

I nodded; this was all familiar to me. A few years ago, the Supreme Court had decided a case making clear that a late-filed notice of appeal deprives the appellate court of jurisdiction, full stop. When we discussed the case in law school, the policy struck some of my classmates as unduly harsh—shouldn't there be some sort of "good cause" exception?—but it made sense to me. Allowing exceptions to the deadline would completely undermine the policies underlying the doctrine.

Second, Janet explained, after the completion of each oral argument calendar I would work with Judge Stinson on the opinion in the case. How much work this would involve would vary depending upon the judge's role in the case—writing the majority opinion, dissenting, or merely offering editorial suggestions on the opinion of a colleague—and whether the opinion was published or unpublished. Published opinions constituted official precedents of the Ninth Circuit, which would bind the court in future cases, and they tended to be formal and polished pieces of writing. Unpublished opinions or "memorandum dispositions," involving just the case at hand, tended to be short and even cryptic.

Third, I would assist Judge Stinson with "en banc" matters, an area where the judge was fairly active. This would involve reviewing the opinions generated by other Ninth Circuit three-judge panels to see if they were problematic—for example, inconsistent with Ninth Circuit or Supreme Court precedent. If so, the judge might want to call for rehearing

en banc, or a rehearing by a larger group of judges. Working on en banc matters with the judge included advising her on which cases to call en banc, helping her issue en banc calls (which involved drafting a "call memo" explaining why the case should be reheard), and also defending the judge's own opinions against en banc calls from other colleagues. Because Judge Stinson was more conservative than many of her Ninth Circuit colleagues, she participated actively in the en banc process, either calling for rehearing in cases where the panel reached a result she viewed as unjustified (read: unacceptably liberal), or defending her own opinions against en banc calls by ideological opponents like Sheldon Gottlieb and Marta Deleuze.

In the final part of the orientation, Janet reviewed the specific cases I was inheriting from her. I was stuck by how many different areas of law they involved—criminal procedure, bankruptcy, intellectual property, sentencing, immigration—and all the different procedural stages they were at. It felt overwhelming, like a buffet at a casino hotel—except filled with things for me to mess up rather than consume.

"I've never taken intellectual property or immigration law," I confessed. "Is that going to be a problem?"

"You'll figure it all out," Janet said. "Read the briefs and cases, do extra background reading if you have to. The main library downstairs has every treatise you could imagine."

"And I can always go to the judge with questions, right? She must know all these areas cold by now."

Janet paused.

"I wouldn't bother the judge with the small stuff," she said.

At the end of the orientation, Janet presented me with a document entitled "Janet Lee Departure Memo," which summarized the training she had given me in written form.

"This memo contains pretty much what you need to know," Janet said. "You'll have to prepare a similar departure memo when you finish the clerkship. The judge is big on clerks training their successors and transitioning their cases."

"Thanks! This looks great," I said, thumbing through the tome. "And can I call or email with questions too?"

Janet paused again. Was she frowning?

"Well," she said, "I'm going to be pretty busy once I get to the firm . . ."

I could tell she was looking for a graceful out, so I quickly jumped in.

"Oh, I totally understand. I'm sure your hours will be brutal. Do you think you'll miss clerking?"

More hesitation. Pursed lips.

"I've learned a lot working here," Janet said in a careful, measured way, "but I'm ready to move on. And to collect a salary with another zero in it."

Janet slung her handbag over her shoulder and extended her hand for a farewell handshake.

"You'll find clerking for Judge Stinson to be very . . . interesting," she said. "Good luck."

5

I spent Tuesday morning reading the briefs and doing research for *Hamadani*, an immigration case involving a Pakistani journalist seeking political asylum in the United States. To establish entitlement to asylum, the applicant must demonstrate a "well-founded fear of persecution" back in his home country on account of his political opinion. Ahmed Hamadani, a journalist and ethnic activist in the province of Baluchistan, claimed that his advocacy of autonomy for Baluchistan would put him in grave danger if he were forced to return to Pakistan, where other supporters of Baluchi nationalism have been persecuted and even killed over the years. But the legal standard for granting asylum is stringent, and Immigration and Customs Enforcement (ICE), opposing Hamadani's request, noted various inconsistencies in his asylum application. ICE also claimed that Hamadani was exaggerating his fear of persecution and his role in the Baluchi nationalist movement. It was an interesting and difficult case.

So immersed in my reading, I didn't realize it was half past noon until James's tall, slender figure materialized in the doorway of my windowless office.

"Lunch?"

How could I say no to a sandy-haired boy with blue-green eyes, flawless skin, and great teeth?

"Sure, thanks."

I had brought my lunch to work, and so had my co-clerks. Not only was that the economical thing to do, but there weren't many dining options in the courthouse's residential neighborhood. Fortunately, the chambers had a small but well-equipped kitchen. After collecting my salad from the refrigerator and microwaving my tomato soup, I joined my co-clerks around a conference table in the library.

"So," James said to me, "are you working on any interesting cases?"

"I've just started reading the briefs in this immigration case . . ."

"Audrey," interrupted Amit, "he said *interesting* cases."

Larry guffawed at Amit's bitchy quip. Amit seemed pleasant enough when we met yesterday; what was his problem today?

"I never took immigration law," I said, "so I'm finding it interesting, since it's new to me."

"Then you'll find almost all of your cases interesting," Amit said. "You went to Yale, right? The Ninth Circuit doesn't get *that* many 14th Amendment cases. Or constitutional-law cases. Or cases about feminist post-structuralist legal theory."

"Yale does have some incredible theoretical offerings," I said, "but you can take many black-letter courses as well. I took Admin, Antitrust, Biz Org, Crim Law, Crim Pro, Legislation, Sentencing. Plus lots of statutory classes: Securities Regulation, Tax, Advanced Tax. And I really enjoyed Bankruptcy . . ."

James was trying—unsuccessfully—to suppress a grin. Amit was staring at the ingredients list on his bag of potato chips; was the former spelling bee champ looking for more words to memorize? I realized my response was somewhat aggressive, but I wanted to show, early on, that I wasn't a pushover.

"Yeah, but those were the *Yale* versions of those classes," Larry said. "At Loyola, we learned *the law*. Like, the kind you find *on the books*. Not all your airy-fairy crap."

I nodded politely, feeling no need to argue with Larry. I tasted a spoonful of my soup, found it too hot, and made a mental note to knock ten seconds off the microwave time in the future.

"It sounds like you learned a lot at Loyola," James said to Larry, managing to sound friendly rather than patronizing. "Did you enjoy law school?"

In order to land a Ninth Circuit clerkship, Larry must have blown the roof off of Loyola. And people who graduate at the top of the class tend to look back fondly on their law school years, like schlubby, middle-aged former jocks looking back at senior year of high school.

"Actually, no," Larry said. "I kind of hated it."

Larry was weird. He wasn't making eye contact with us, nor was he looking down at his food. He seemed to be staring at the far wall of the library.

After letting that response hang in the air for a while, Amit asked what we were all thinking.

"But you must have done very well in law school, right? To land a Ninth Circuit clerkship with Judge Stinson?"

Larry laughed, loudly—too loudly. This was still a library, even if we had temporarily converted it to a cafeteria.

"Not really," Larry said. "I wasn't on law review. I graduated in the middle of the class. I got this job through my dad. My last name is Krasner—as in Jonathan Krasner."

Ah, Jonathan Krasner—the two-time Oscar-winning director, whose critically acclaimed films also managed to make tons of money. One of the biggest clients of Robert Stinson, the Hollywood super-agent married to my boss.

"My dad and the Stinsons go way back," Larry continued. "Bob has represented my dad his whole career. So when I went into my third year of law school without a job lined up for after graduation, my dad called the judge and got me this gig. I don't think I'm going to be that into clerking—I really want to go into entertainment law—but hey, a job's a job. And clerking's supposed to be great for the résumé, even if you don't go into litigation. Pretty awesome, huh?"

My first thought was not awesome: the rest of us would end up doing Larry's work for him. Nor was my second thought: one of my colleagues in this coveted job got the post through connections, not merit.

But my third thought actually *was* awesome: there was no way Larry was getting a Supreme Court clerkship. Judge Stinson hired him as a favor to his dad, but she wouldn't pick him as her favored clerk, the one she would push to the justices. Cronyism might get you to the Ninth Circuit, but it couldn't get you to One First Street.

My competitors for Judge Stinson's favor were Amit and James. I had nothing to fear from Loyola Larry. One down, two to go.

On Friday afternoon, shortly after I returned to my desk after another lunch with the co-clerks, my office phone rang.

Who could it be? Who had this number? Who still used landlines, anyway?

It rang a second time. How was I supposed to answer? Janet hadn't said anything about that during orientation.

After the third ring—I didn't want to let it ring a fourth time, especially if it was the judge—I picked up.

"Hello, chambers of Judge Stinson, Audrey Coyne speaking."

"Bitch, you've been in the building a week, why haven't you stopped by? Or called?"

"Hi Jeremy," I said. "Sorry, I've been swamped. I've been staying late every night. I'm getting killed here."

"Last time I checked, girlfriend, you weren't the only one with a Ninth Circuit clerkship. We have cases to read and bench memos to write here in Gottlieb's chambers too. Don't let this job turn you into a crappy friend."

"I am not a crappy friend! And friendship is a two-way street. Why haven't you called me?"

"I've been trying to reach you this entire week. You haven't responded to my texts. You haven't answered your cell. I thought of leaving you a voicemail, before remembering that nobody has checked their voicemail since, like, 2005. So I finally decided to try your work phone—I looked you up in the courthouse directory—because I figured you wouldn't *dare* let your office phone go unanswered."

"You're right," I said. "Sorry, I'm so overwhelmed. I have a million bench memos to write. I have a big ERISA case—I never took ERISA in law school—and I have a bunch of immigration cases, and I don't know anything about immigration law. There's so much I don't know."

"You'll get it all done. You always do. What are you up to this weekend?"

"Working. My judge"—I hadn't even finished my first week of work, and Judge Stinson was already "my" judge—"is coming back from out of town. I have a bunch of things I need to give her on Monday. And they need to be perfect. I'll be here all weekend."

"Yeah, I'm working too. Gottlieb comes into chambers every day except Sunday, and he expects us to be here when he's here. From nine in the morning to nine at night usually."

"For such a champion of labor, he's quite the taskmaster."

"But he works as hard as we do. I'm learning so much. He's brilliant. He calls me into his office to talk multiple times a day. We read the cases together. We edit the drafts together, line by line, until the wording is just right. We work so closely."

"That's great," I said. "Just what a clerkship should be."

"So I'm free on Sunday, at least Sunday night. How about dinner and a movie?"

"I don't know, I have so much work. And on Monday morning, we have our weekly meeting, which is a big deal in chambers. It's my first one. I need to be prepared."

"Come on, you're like a damn Boy Scout—always prepared. You've worked late every night this week. You're working over the weekend. Taking one night off won't kill you."

"Monday is my first time seeing the judge since our interview. I have to be at my best. You know what they say: first impressions are everything!"

"You know what they say," Jeremy said. "All work and no play makes Audrey a dull girl!"

I could afford to take one night off this week. Right?

"Okay, fine," I said. "But let's meet up early."

"Deal. I'll come by Stinson's chambers around six to pick you up. Any excuse for me to see that hot co-clerk of yours."

"James? He's straight."

"How do you know? Have you asked him? You've been here, what, a week?"

"I just *know*. I have a feeling."

"And I have a feeling too. There's a gay in every chambers in this court. And in the Stinson chambers, James is the best bet."

"You're projecting. You did this all the time in law school. You think that every guy is gay. Especially if he's attractive."

"So you think James is attractive, do you?"

I was glad Jeremy wasn't there to see my cheeks turning pink.

"He's attractive by conventional standards," I admitted, "but that's not necessarily my type."

"Because you're just *so* unconventional. Let's make a wager. I will bet you a nice dinner that one of your co-clerks is gay."

I couldn't afford a "nice" dinner as easily as Jeremy could. He had no debt from law school, thanks to the generosity of his parents (who were also helping him out during the clerkship with a sizable "allowance"). But thinking over the bet, I liked my odds. As the best dressed and most in-shape of my co-clerks, James was arguably the most likely to be gay, at least based on stereotypes. But I just *knew* he couldn't be gay—meaning that, *a fortiori*, nobody was gay.

"That's a bet," I said.

"Great," Jeremy said. "I'll start thinking about what I want to eat. Other than James."

6

Monday morning. It was only five minutes to nine, and I had already cursed Jeremy Silverstein ten times.

We had met early on Sunday night, as planned. After tasty and affordable Mexican food at El Cholo on Colorado Boulevard, we saw a documentary, *The Queen of Versailles*, at the Laemmle Playhouse down the street. After the movie, Jeremy convinced me to grab a "quick drink" at Bodega Wine Bar (which, despite having the word "bodega" in its name, is quite upscale). That "quick drink," singular, turned into several rounds, plural, since we had so much catching up to do. We polished off a round of cocktails and a bottle of a strong Petite Sirah from McManis, a California vineyard. I didn't get home until one in the morning, and I didn't get to bed until two—much, much later than I had planned. Jeremy had been kind enough to pay for the drinks (which made me feel less guilty for having to pay for a cab home). But I was paying the price now, with a brutal hangover.

I folded my arms in front of me on my desk, rested my head on my arms, and closed my eyes. I just wanted my little windowless office to stop spinning.

"Clerkadees!" Brenda sang out from the short hallway connecting the four clerks' offices. "It's Monday morning meeting time!"

"Clerkadees," Brenda's preferred nickname for the four of us, was sweet and endearing, just like Brenda. But at that moment, I wanted to herd Brenda and my co-Clerkadees into my office, lock the door, flee the courthouse, and go home to sleep.

I lifted my head up from my desk. Ugh. Still spinning.

"Good morning," James said, leaning lankly in the doorway to my office.

"Hi," I said feebly.

"Don't take this the wrong way, but you're not looking so hot today, Coyne."

"Thanks. I'm not feeling so hot right now either."

"Did you and Jeremy have a late night?"

"You could say that."

Brenda appeared next to James and poked her head into my office.

"Clap clap, Clerkadees," she said. "The judge doesn't like being kept waiting."

I dragged myself to my feet and immediately tottered in my three-inch heels. I had chosen them because I wanted to look good for my first Monday meeting with the judge, but I now regretted the decision. I followed Brenda and my co-clerks across the chambers, stepping gingerly, as if walking through a minefield.

We entered the judge's private office, as elegant as ever, and took our seats around a marble-topped table in the conference area. An antique mantel clock on a side table showed it was exactly 9 o'clock.

The judge was sitting at her desk in the center of the room, reading a brief. She read for what seemed like forever, while the rest of us sat in awkward silence. Finally, she set aside the brief, walked over, and seated herself at the head of the table.

"Good morning," she said with a smile, looking around at everyone. "Audrey, welcome to chambers."

I wasn't sure if I was expected to say anything, so I just smiled and nodded. I wanted to keep my mouth shut as much as possible—fearing that if I opened it, I might vomit.

"So how were your weekends?" the judge asked. She turned to Amit, who had taken the seat directly to her right (of course).

"I spent most of the weekend working," Amit said. "I made excellent progress on my bench memos for the upcoming sitting. I think I'll be ready to discuss my cases ahead of schedule, Judge."

Even though this was true—Amit and James and I all saw each other in chambers on both Saturday and Sunday—Amit said it so sycophantically. I could see him waiting for a pat on the head from the judge. But that wasn't what he got.

"Amit, my chambers is not a sweatshop! I appreciate your diligence, but you really should get out on the weekends. There are so many wonderful things to see and do, both in Pasadena and in Los Angeles. Promise me that you'll do something fun next weekend."

I half expected Amit to say work *was* fun, but he simply nodded, chastened. Perhaps his predecessor clerk hadn't explained the Monday morning meeting to him as well as Janet had explained it to me. Janet had told me that the judge would ask about our weekends at each Monday meeting and wanted to hear that we had outside interests and got to enjoy some of what L.A. had to offer. It struck me as a sign that the judge cared about her chambers staff, seeing us as more than mere workhorses.

The judge turned her gaze to James, sitting to Amit's right.

"I had a great weekend," said James, omitting mention of the many hours he spent working. "I checked out the new postwar sculpture exhibit at the Norton Simon."

"I'm glad to hear that," the judge said. "A lovely museum, right here in Pasadena. Robert served on the board for a number of years."

"I also went for long runs in Arroyo Seco Park on both days," James added. "And on Sunday I had dinner with a friend from law school."

"Larry," said Judge Stinson, "what about you?"

"Went out to my parents' place in Malibu. A barbecue for some of their friends. Pretty sweet."

So that's where Loyola Larry was while the rest of us were toiling over our bench memos—out at his famous father's Malibu beach house.

"Please thank your parents for the invitation," said the judge. "We had hoped to stop by, but I was feeling so exhausted on Saturday after getting back from my trip."

After Brenda recounted her weekend spent gardening, everyone turned to me. James had taken the high road in not bragging about working, but I couldn't resist.

"I joined Amit and James here in chambers over the weekend," I began, wanting the judge to know that Amit wasn't the only one with a work ethic. "But I took last night off for dinner and a movie with a friend."

"What did you see?" the judge asked.

"*The Queen of Versailles*," I said, starting to explain the somewhat obscure movie—Jeremy's pick. "It's a documentary . . ."

"About the woman who builds the huge mansion?"

"Yes, Judge. Supposedly the largest single-family house in the United States."

"And how did you like it?"

"I thought it was great—entertaining, topical, a meditation on marriage and money . . ."

"Nicely put. I will cite your recommendation when I try to get my husband to go see it. Robert and I are both big movie buffs. He favors Hollywood fare—it's how he makes his living, after all—but I prefer documentaries and foreign films. Audrey, you have good taste."

The judge smiled at me. I beamed back at her. Amit shuffled his papers.

We then moved into the meeting proper. Together we reviewed a series of different lists: pending cases, cases needing draft opinions, possible en banc cases, cases on the six-month list. As Judge Stinson moved through the lists, she fired off questions to all four of us. Which other judge still needs to send us comments on our draft opinion? What is the status of this potential en banc call? Why is this case on the six-month list? The judge's questions didn't touch on the merits of any of the cases, so I couldn't gather much about her jurisprudence, but I could tell she was a skilled manager.

I had been nervous about the meeting before it started, especially given my hangover—but once we started talking about the cases, I forgot my discomfort and focused on what was before me, like a seasoned athlete on a playing field. I stumbled the least in answering the judge's queries, followed by Amit and James in a rough tie, followed by the hapless Larry.

At the end of the meeting, Judge Stinson collected her papers and stood up, resplendent in a cerulean suit that looked like Chanel (or my idea of Chanel, since I didn't own one myself).

"Excellent work, everyone," she said. "Audrey, it's wonderful to have you on board."

7

A few weeks later, on a Wednesday in September, a cab dropped off my co-clerks and me in front of the James R. Browning United States Courthouse. We were in San Francisco for the annual Ninth Circuit law clerk orientation.

The cab ride to the courthouse wasn't long; we could have walked. And we would have, if the doorman at the Union Square Hilton hadn't grimaced when we asked him for directions to Seventh and Mission. He suggested we take a cab. Before the four of us could discuss, Amit had already hopped into one—taking the front passenger seat, of course. As we drove past boarded-up buildings, payday-loan providers, and Chinese takeout places featuring photos of their dishes above the counter, I could see why the doorman counseled against walking.

The Browning Courthouse looked like a courthouse should: just as magnificent as the Ninth Circuit's courthouse in Pasadena, but less inviting and more imposing. Even through the thick morning fog, apparently unusual for this time of year, we could make out balustrades, cornices, and pediments—hallmarks of Beaux-Arts design that I remembered vaguely from an architecture class I took in college. It made sense to me that this majestic building, clad in white granite and brick, was the official headquarters of the Ninth Circuit. It made less sense to see the structure surrounded by seediness, sticking out like a wealthy widow who had wandered into a strip club.

"Did you know," Amit said, reading something off his iPhone, perhaps a Wikipedia entry, "that the courthouse's design was inspired by Italian Renaissance palazzos? That skilled artisans had to be brought in from Italy to do some of the work? That when it opened for service as a federal government building in 1905, it was praised as 'the post office that's a palace'?"

"I did not know all that," James said, shooting me a sly smile. "But it sounds about right. It's a beautiful building."

"I dunno," Larry said. "It looks kinda . . . old. And some of these old buildings are totally crap on the inside."

But what we encountered on the other side of two gigantic bronze doors was anything but "crap." After passing dutifully through the metal detector and security checkpoint, we found ourselves in a vast entry hall whose air felt cold due to all the marble it contained—panels of classic white marble trimmed in green marble, a double-barrel-vaulted ceiling with marble mosaics, and more mosaic tile on the floor. Each end of the hall featured a rotunda with a stained-glass dome ringed with eagles that appeared to be made of more marble mosaic tile.

Standing in the majestic foyer of the James R. Browning Courthouse, I shivered—partly from the marble-cooled air, and partly from the glory of it all. I hadn't had this feeling when I first entered the Richard Chambers Courthouse in Pasadena, but that building, while no less beautiful, exuded an intimate, residential feel. The Browning Courthouse sent a different message, emphasizing the power and impersonality of the law. Marveling at the marble, I thought to myself: this is a temple to the law, my boss is one of the law's high priestesses, and I am one of her acolytes.

We made our way to the library atrium, the main site for the orientation sessions. Each clerk received an orientation packet that contained the Code of Conduct for Judicial Employees, a pamphlet called "Ethics for Federal Judicial Law Clerks," and different handouts on assorted topics of importance—immigration law, habeas corpus law, and the ever-important subject of jurisdiction.

The most interesting item in the packet was the law clerk "facebook," a compilation of capsule bios of all the other law clerks, including education and employment histories, career plans, and hobbies. As we waited for the orientation to start, I flipped through it, looking for the clerks with the most high-powered backgrounds—the clerks most likely to be interested in clerking for the Supreme Court. I was dazzled by many of them: a winner of the Purple Heart, a master scuba instructor, a certified sommelier, a reader of ancient Greek poetry, a former Olympic diver. Who *were* these people? I felt like an impostor among them.

I turned to the bios for the clerks to Judge M. Frank Polanski, the biggest feeder judge on the court. Three men, one woman. Their bios contained sly jokes about how hard the notoriously demanding Judge Polanski was making them work. Under "Future Plans," one of them listed "sleeping for a very long time." Under "Travel," another wrote "to and from chambers," while a third wrote "yes please, preferably somewhere without a fax machine."

The woman clerking for Judge Polanski looked familiar. I stared at her picture, then realized where I recognized her from: she was the unfriendly brunette whom I spotted in Judge Stinson's waiting room back when I interviewed for my clerkship. As I had guessed from her frumpy attire, she had gone to Harvard Law School:

Lucia Aroldi
Law Clerk to Judge M. Frank Polanski
Place of Birth: Topeka, KS
Date of Birth: April 15, 1986
Hometown: Lawrence, KS
College/Degree/Year: Princeton, AB, 2007
Law School/Degree/Year: Harvard, JD, 2012
Other Post Grad/Year: Cambridge, M. Phil., 2009 (Marshall Scholar)
Prior Employment: Summer Associate, Sullivan & Cromwell.
Hobbies/Interests: Hobbies? What hobbies?
Future Plans: World conquest.
Travel: Extensive.
Stories/Items of Interest: First woman to win the Fay Diploma in ten years.

That bio had "future Supreme Court clerk" written all over it. Noting that she won the Fay Diploma, the prize for graduating from Harvard Law with the highest GPA, was gauche. But someone in Lucia's position didn't have to worry about social niceties.

Of course I flipped over to my own bio to review it against the others (and to check out my photo, which thankfully was fine):

Audrey Coyne
Law Clerk to Judge Christina Wong Stinson
Place of Birth: Far Rockaway, NY
Date of Birth: June 19, 1988
Hometown: Woodside, NY
College/Degree/Year: Harvard, AB, 2009
Law School/Degree/Year: Yale, JD, 2012
Other Post Grad/Year: None listed.
Prior Employment: Summer Associate, Cravath Swaine & Moore.
Hobbies/Interests: Running, movies, reading (mostly fiction).
Future Plans: Practicing law to the best of my ability.
Travel: Canada, Mexico, Philippines, United Kingdom, United States.
Stories/Items of Interest: None listed.

Looking at my bio, I felt poor, boring, and small. There was nothing tony about my towns; Far Rockaway and Woodside were both solidly working-class. I had no other postgraduate education; many of the other clerks, like Lucia, had master's or even PhD degrees. My travel paled in comparison to that of many of the other clerks, who had lived and worked all over the world. Sure, there were some nice names on my résumé, like Harvard, Yale, and Cravath, but those institutions cranked out thousands of people each year. Amit at least had the distinction of being *the* National Spelling Bee champion. There was nothing in my bio that felt similarly special.

Needing to feel better about myself, I turned to Loyola Larry's entry:

Larry Krasner
Law Clerk to Judge Christina Wong Stinson
Place of Birth: Los Angeles, CA
Date of Birth: September 26, 1985
Hometown: Beverly Hills, CA
College/Degree/Year: University of Southern California, BA, 2007
Law School/Degree/Year: Loyola (Los Angeles), JD, 2012
Other Post Grad/Year: None listed.
Prior Employment: Krasner Productions; Summer Associate, Gang Tyre Ramer & Brown.
Hobbies/Interests: Movies, TV.
Future Plans: Lawyer to the stars.
Stories/Items of Interest: Yeah, my dad is Jonathan Krasner.

Larry's bio didn't give me the ego boost I had hoped for. It showed he belonged here—in California, where he was born and raised, and in these corridors of power, as someone who grew up in Beverly Hills. Sure, it reeked of nepotism—he probably got into USC because his father had given millions to its film school, and his work experience was for his father's production company and for Gang Tyre, his father's law firm—but at least it was different and interesting. He certainly was the only law clerk who could claim that his father was a famous film director.

The day passed in a blur of speeches, tutorials, and panel discussions on topics like habeas corpus law, en banc procedures, and standards of review. I finally got the guidance on immigration law that I was seeking. At a panel on jurisdiction, we were reminded of the importance of double-, triple-, and quadruple-checking whether the court has jurisdiction. Does the court have jurisdiction over the parties? Does the court have jurisdiction over the issues? Was the notice of appeal filed on time?

In the evening, we gathered at the Sir Francis Drake, a small and stylish hotel in Union Square, for cocktails and dinner. At the reception, my co-clerks and I huddled together in a corner. We hadn't been great about networking, so we didn't know a huge number of clerks other than people we had gone to law school with. I looked for Jeremy and watched him working the room, chatting comfortably with one judge after another. My co-clerks were drinking—Larry had a beer, James had a glass of red wine, Amit had some fruity-looking cocktail—but I just nursed a Diet Coke. I had learned from past experience to avoid alcohol before dealing with federal judges.

Suddenly I felt a chill wind. Had I walked into excessive air conditioning? Actually, no—it was Judge Marta Solís Deleuze, liberal lioness of the Ninth Circuit, heading straight for us. She was short, had no make-up, and wore a hideous orange pantsuit that didn't flatter her dark skin tone—truth be told, it made her look like a prison inmate.

"I'm Judge Deleuze," she said, extending her small, bony hand. We introduced ourselves by name and shook hands with her. Her hand was cold, her grip fierce. I suppressed a shudder.

"And where are you all clerking?" she asked.

We all paused, for a few seconds too long, before James stepped up to the plate.

"In Pasadena," he said cheerily. "It's such a beautiful courthouse, the way they did the restoration is just . . ."

"*For whom* are you clerking?"

"For Judge Stinson," he mumbled, in the way one might greet an acquaintance whose name you think you know but aren't sure about.

Deleuze frowned.

"Have a good year," she said, before turning on her heel and walking briskly away.

Larry brayed loudly. I shot him a look of death. Deleuze might be lacking in social graces, but she was still a federal judge.

"What's her problem?" Larry asked.

I looked around to confirm that Deleuze was out of earshot.

"She and Judge Stinson are at opposite ends of the Ninth Circuit ideologically," I whispered. "And for Judge Deleuze, the political is personal."

Larry shrugged. "Whatever."

A fork clinked against a glass, and the room quieted. Attention turned toward the front of the room, where a gray-bearded man with kind eyes was speaking into a microphone.

"Good evening," he said. "My name is Stanley Runyan, and I'm the chief judge of the Ninth Circuit, with chambers in Billings, Montana. I'm pleased to welcome you all to tonight's dinner, the highlight of the law clerk orientation."

Applause—and it sounded genuine. Word on the street was that the chief judge was well liked and respected, even by the conservatives who were his jurisprudential opponents.

"During dinner, we'll be treated to a panel discussion featuring three of my colleagues, who will share their reflections on serving on our wonderful court. I hope you'll find their conversation stimulating and enjoyable."

"Tonight we have almost the entire court in attendance," Chief Judge Runyan said. "More than 40 judges from nine states, including senior judges, and almost all of the law clerks—120 strong. This evening is an opportunity to get to know people from other parts of our great and far-flung court, people you wouldn't otherwise meet."

"We have not done assigned seating," he continued. "I've learned from my time as chief that federal judges don't like being bossed around."

Polite laughter. Always laugh at a judicial joke.

"But as you head into dinner, please distribute yourselves so that there are no more than two judges at each table, and no law clerks sitting with their own judge. If we follow those two rules, everything should work out right. Thank you, and enjoy the evening."

More applause, followed by the crowd breaking up and drifting toward the doors leading to the dining room.

"Who should we try and sit with?" James asked.

"I don't know about you guys," Amit said, "but I'm going to sit with the chief judge. He's the boss of this place, and I want to find out what makes him tick."

"Good idea," Larry said.

Amit hurried off in the direction of the chief judge, without waiting for anyone else, and Larry tagged along after him. James and I turned to each other.

"Well, Coyne, I guess it's just us. Anyone you're targeting?"

"I'm tired of all the jockeying," I said. "Let's take a break from the rat race. Let's just pick a table, sit down, and see who joins us."

We wandered into the ballroom, found a table in the middle of the space, and stood behind two seats, side by side. Protocol seemed to call for waiting for a table to fill up before sitting down. I turned to my left and chatted nervously with James as we waited for our fellow guests. I spied Jeremy at Chief Judge Runyan's table near the front of the room, along with Amit and Larry.

"Hello! And aren't you a lovely creature?"

The voice, bearing a heavy Eastern European accent, came from a short, plump man with gray hair.

"Hello," I said. "I'm Audrey Coyne, and this is my co-clerk, James Hogan. We're clerking for Judge Stinson."

"Of course you are! A beautiful clerk for a beautiful judge. I'm Frank Polanski."

So *this* was the legendary Frank Polanski—the brilliant, difficult, colorful Frank Polanski. A huge feeder judge to the Supreme Court, as well as a possible Supreme Court justice himself.

"It's an honor to meet you, Judge Polanski," I said.

"And it's a pleasure to meet you, flower of my heart."

Flower of my heart? A beautiful clerk for a beautiful judge? These weren't things you'd expect a federal judge to say to someone he was meeting for the first time—which was part of his undeniable charm.

As we ate our salads, I chatted with Judge Polanski. He was funny, engaging, and focused; I was impressed by his attentiveness, especially given his prominence and power. James, meanwhile, spoke with two law clerks who had flown down from Alaska for the orientation. The other judge at our table was a senior judge from Seattle who looked ancient, seemed hard of hearing, and rarely opened his mouth (not counting a few burps).

Conversation subsided when the entrees arrived, which was also when the panel discussion began. As a Ninth Circuit obsessive, I found the back-and-forth to be a fascinating, behind-the-scenes look at the workings of the court. The panelists—including Judge Gottlieb, Jeremy's boss—were surprisingly candid and entertaining.

"Audrey, I enjoyed meeting you," Judge Polanski said at the end of dinner. "I look forward to seeing you back in Pasadena."

"Judge Polanski, the pleasure was all mine," I said, smiling as sweetly as I could.

"Feel free to stop by and say hello," he said. "As you may have heard, I don't get out much."

"I know where to find you, Judge," I said, sounding vaguely flirtatious. "I'm sure our paths will cross in the future. And I'd like to meet your clerks sometime too."

"I'm going to hold you to that. I have a feeling this won't be our last interaction."

And with a wink and a smile, the great Frank Polanski vanished into the night.

8

The law clerk orientation ended on Thursday night, and I returned to Pasadena on Friday morning. I would have wanted to spend the rest of the weekend in San Francisco, taking in the city and seeing friends, but I had too much work—especially since we had lost several days to the orientation, counting travel time. Our bench memos were due that Monday, the start of a review week, when we would sit down with the judge and orally review with her the different cases to be argued in court the week after that, during the calendar week—my first calendar with the judge.

I worked on both Saturday and Sunday. As usual, Amit and James toiled alongside me, and Larry was nowhere to be found. I worked until midnight on Saturday night, returned to chambers at eight on Sunday morning, and worked until seven that night, which is when I finished writing and editing my last bench memo and binding up my last bench book. (Some judges had made the move to electronic bench books, loading all the case documents on their iPads, but Judge Stinson hadn't made the jump yet.)

Sunday night had turned into my "free" night, when I allowed myself to see the world beyond chambers. It worked well as an evening for socializing, as long as I avoided excessive alcohol.

I had plans to meet up for dinner with Harvetta at El Cholo. This was our first significant interaction since meeting at the pool; we'd seen each other around the apartment complex from time to time, but not all that often, mainly due to how little time I spent at home.

"So tell me about yourself," I said, taking a sip from my margarita. "You're definitely not the average law clerk."

The moment the words left my mouth, I realized they could be misinterpreted.

"Excuse me?" asked Harvetta, arching her right eyebrow and holding a guacamole-laden chip in midair. "What do you mean by *that?*"

"I'm sorry—what I was trying to say was . . ."

"You know what? You're right. As a black woman, I'm definitely *not* the average law clerk. Did you meet any black women at your fancy-ass Ninth Circuit clerk orientation?"

"One, I think? From Nevada?"

"And any black men?"

"Not that I can recall . . ."

"So with more than 100 clerks, one is a sister, and no brothers," she said, shaking her head and loading up another chip with an obscene amount of guac. "Damn, even worse than I thought."

"How about in Justice Lin's chambers?"

"Fifty percent black chicks! Just me and my co-clerk, who's a white guy. But a lot of the staff attorneys up in San Francisco are minorities or women. Here in state court, we got more diversity going on than you guys in federal court, where everything is lily white."

"Sorry, I didn't mean to get us on a tangent about law clerk diversity. Where are you from? Where did you grow up?"

Harvetta paused to take a hearty swig from her margarita.

"I'm a California girl, born and bred. Grew up in Sacramento. Raised by my mom. Parents never married. Mama and I were poor as shit. Dad had money, but he never sent any our way."

"What did your dad do? Was he a lawyer?"

"Hell no! But he *had* lawyers, lots of lawyers, over the years. He was a drug dealer—the biggest in Sacramento, until the feds busted his ass and shipped him away for 25 years."

"Sorry to hear that. Was he in prison while you were growing up?"

"Naw, he got busted only a few years back. He had a fucking bad-ass defense lawyer who got him off a bunch of times before the feds finally got him."

"How do you feel about him?"

"Selfish asshole. Treated my mom and me like shit. I don't talk to him. He gave me nothing—except for this," she said, tapping her temple.

I looked at her quizzically. I would have asked her to explain, but I was in the middle of chewing, savoring a small chip with a dollop of guacamole.

"My brains," Harvetta said. "He was a deadbeat dad and a no-good motherfucker, but smart as shit—savvy, shrewd, strategic. That's how he was able to rise to the top of the Sacramento drug scene. And stay there. And avoid getting busted. At his peak he was grossing more than a million a year. I got my brains from my dad. That shit is genetic."

"And what brought you to law school? Do you want to become a defense lawyer?"

"Fuck no! A lot of those defense attorneys are scum. Like their clients. Like my dad. I want to be a prosecutor. And put people like my dad in prison. That's why I went to law school."

"You aren't opposed to the war on drugs?"

"Nope. I've seen up close the damage drugs can do to communities, families. My mom was an addict, that's how she met my dad. I am tough on crime. I am pretty conservative, actually, on a lot of issues."

"A conservative African American woman. You are unusual, Harvetta Chambers."

"You can say a lot of shit about me, but I ain't boring!"

"If you're conservative, why are you clerking for a liberal like Justice Lin?"

"Usually judges like clerks who think like them—yes men and ass kissers. Not Lin. He wanted to find someone crazy smart who disagrees with him on a lot of issues. Someone able to challenge him, to find holes in his arguments, to make his opinions stronger. Someone like *moi*."

Harvetta laughed triumphantly, and I couldn't help joining her infectious laughter.

"And how did you decide on McGeorge for law school?"

"I loved McGeorge, but how I got there—well, McGeorge was the only law school I knew about. It was where my dad's defense lawyer went, and he was a great lawyer. And I didn't know of other options. The pre-law advisors at CSU Sacramento aren't worth shit."

"What do you mean?"

Harvetta sat up in her chair and cleared her throat.

"They failed to advise me," she said, shifting into her newscaster voice, "that an African American woman with a 4.0 undergraduate GPA and a score of 175 on the LSAT could win admission to practically any law school in the country."

My jaw dropped. Did Harvetta have better numbers than I did?

"Those stats are incredible, Harvetta. You could have gone anywhere."

"Like I said, I got my father's smarts. And it all worked out in the end. McGeorge gave me a full ride, all three years. I got to stay in Sacramento and take care of Mama. I kicked ass in law school—graduated with the highest GPA in McGeorge's history. And now I'm here, so it's all good."

"Did you apply for clerkships with any federal judges?"

"Federal clerkships, that shit goes down in third year of law school, with that hiring plan. But for me that was when Mama was dying. Between taking care of Mama, keeping up my grades, and running the law review, I didn't have time to deal with that crap."

"I'm sorry to hear about your mother."

"Thanks. But yeah, well, she fucked herself up good with all the shit she did—she coulda died even earlier. Mama passed in January. Before she died, I was gonna go back to Latham & Watkins to make mad bank so I could help her out. After she died, I said fuck it—I love the law, and I wanna clerk. By then it was too late to apply to most judges. But one of my profs connected me with Sherwin Lin, who got on to the California Supreme Court after his Ninth Circuit thing blew up, and who was looking for clerks. He interviewed the Harvetta"—here she paused to point her two thumbs at her ample bosom—"and the rest is history."

Her gestures made me think of hands on a steering wheel.

"So you grew up in California," I said. "Does that mean you know how to drive?"

"What the fuck kinda question is that? Who *doesn't* know how to drive?"

I smiled sheepishly.

"What? Girl, you don't know how to drive? Guess they don't teach that at Harvard and Yale!"

Harvetta cackled. I laughed too.

"I'm from New York, where a lot of us don't know how to drive because mass transit is so good," I explained. "But now that I'm out here, I'm stuck either walking or taking a cab. I like Pervez, the cab driver I always call, but it gets expensive. So I'm thinking of learning to drive. Can you teach me?"

"I sure can," Harvetta said. "I'm a pretty awesome driver, actually. But can I ask you for a favor?"

"Sure, go ahead."

"I'm applying for some stuff for after my clerkship with Lin. Could you take a look at my résumé?"

"I'd be happy to. So you're not going back to Latham & Watkins?"

"Oh, I might, I loved being a summer associate there," said Harvetta, polishing off the last of the chips and guac. "But I want to explore all my options."

"That makes sense. A lot of law firms are interested in recruiting people out of clerkships."

"I'm actually more interested in . . . other government stuff. But maybe I'll talk to some firms too. It's like my daddy used to say: always know your value on the street."

9

Shortly after 1 o'clock on Monday afternoon, Brenda stuck her head into my office.

"Audrey," she said, "the judge is ready to review your Monday cases with you."

I thanked Brenda, grabbed a yellow legal pad and a pen, and walked across chambers toward the judge's private office. This was Monday afternoon of "review week," the week before the week of oral arguments. On the Monday of review week, the judge would sit down with each of the clerks, one-on-one, and discuss with us the cases for the Monday of calendar week. On the Tuesday of review week, she would review with us the cases for the Tuesday of calendar week, and so forth and so on.

As I approached the open doorway, I felt the same nervous energy I felt when I entered her office for my clerkship interview or the first Monday morning meeting. I would be spending significant one-on-one time with Judge Stinson. Although I had been on the job for several weeks, the judge preferred to interact with us through written memos, so I had had fairly limited face-to-face interaction with her on issues of substantive law. This was another opportunity to impress her—or to reveal myself as inadequate and ill-prepared.

I knocked softly on the doorframe with my right hand.

"Judge, Brenda said you were ready to review my Monday cases with me?"

Judge Stinson looked up from the brief she was reading and marked where she stopped with a red post-it flag.

"Yes, please come in," she said, gesturing for me to sit down next to her. She was seated at the head of the marble-topped conference table and directed me toward the seat to her right.

The judge had the bench books for my Monday cases in a neat stack in front of her. As soon as I sat down, we began going through them, case by case. Each review began with me providing a short summary of the facts, identifying the key legal issues, and summarizing the recommendations in my bench memo. The judge would then ask me a few questions about each case, some to confirm her own recollections and some to probe or clarify particular issues. Nothing she asked managed to stump me; her questions were simple, straightforward, and driven by the contents of the briefs and the bench memos. Part of me was relieved by my ability to field all her questions with ease; part of me was slightly disappointed that she didn't ask more challenging questions or have more unusual or interesting takes on the cases. But then I thought to myself: Judge Stinson wouldn't enjoy such an excellent reputation, and wouldn't be mentioned as a possible Supreme Court nominee, if she were anything short of brilliant. And being a judge, unlike being a law professor, isn't about having an "unusual" or "interesting" view of the law; it's about getting the law right and applying it faithfully to the facts.

At the end of the session, we reached *Hamadani*, the case I had struggled with the most.

"Ahmed Hamadani petitions for review of a decision of the Board of Immigration Appeals, which affirmed an immigration judge's denial of his application for asylum," I recited. "Hamadani is a Pakistani journalist who came to the United States on a journalism fellowship and now seeks political asylum here. He claims that his advocacy of greater autonomy for his home province of Baluchistan would cause him to be persecuted if he is deported to Pakistan."

"And what is your recommendation in this case?"

"This is a difficult case. Hamadani cites extensive evidence showing that Baluchistan freedom advocates have been imprisoned, tortured, and even killed. One of his former bosses, the managing editor of the newspaper Hamadani worked at, was arrested on questionable charges. A writer whose articles Hamadani edited at the paper was shot in broad daylight."

"But it's not certain that the murder was politically motivated," Judge Stinson said. "It may have been due to a squabble over a business deal gone bad. Am I remembering that correctly?"

"Yes, Judge. But these are just a few examples of the persecution faced by Baluchistan nationalists like Hamadani."

"As I also recall, the immigration judge—the fact-finder in this case, entitled to deference—also found inconsistencies in Hamadani's written asylum application and oral testimony?"

"True. But Hamadani does offer explanations for the alleged inconsistencies. In the end, based largely on the inconsistencies, I recommend affirming the BIA's denial of asylum. But I'm not certain about that conclusion. This case could go either way."

"You made the correct call. I do not view this case as particularly difficult."

"You don't?"

"There are so many immigrants out there who just want to stay in the United States because, quite honestly, life is better here. They don't want to go back to whatever hellhole they came from—and I don't blame them. But we can't just go around giving out political asylum like Halloween candy. Here's my rule of thumb for immigration cases: when in doubt, the immigrant loses."

The judge chuckled. I froze. Was I supposed to laugh? My general rule was to laugh at judicial jokes, but immigration cases involved people's lives, families, and futures. Was laughter appropriate?

"I should clarify that," said the judge, perhaps detecting my discomfort. "As you know from your research, the legal standard for asylum is demanding. The burden of establishing entitlement to asylum lies with the petitioner, not the government. If 'substantial evidence' supports the decision of the Board of Immigration Appeals, we must affirm—and 'substantial evidence' is a low bar, lower than a preponderance of the evidence, far lower than beyond a reasonable doubt. So that's why I believe, to take a complex area of law and reduce it to something simple, that a 'tie' goes to the government."

"That makes sense to me, Judge," I said, nodding. Her clarification comforted me.

"Being a judge—and, by extension, being a clerk—can be difficult. Ahmed Hamadani sounds like a good man who is doing good work. He is very sympathetic. I have great sympathy for him. I'm the daughter of an immigrant—my father came here from China, smuggled here illegally. I'm very sympathetic to immigrants."

Here she paused, leaned in, and placed her right hand on my left wrist.

"But we can't decide cases based on sympathy, Audrey. We must decide them based on the law."

"Absolutely, Judge Stinson."

"And as a summary and analysis of the governing law, your bench memo was impressive—thorough, careful, and fair. You and Amit are doing superb work so far. Please tell him that I'm ready to review his cases with him."

I left Judge Stinson's office in an excited state. The review session had gone well, and the judge found my bench memo to be "impressive." Excellent.

Less excellent: the competition posed by Amit for the favor of Judge Stinson. I'd have to figure out what to do about that.

10

Walking into work on Monday morning of calendar week, I saw a familiar vehicle parked in front of the courthouse: a minivan painted red, white, and blue. It was the taxicab of Pervez, who was sitting in the driver's seat and talking on his cell phone. I waved and made eye contact with him; I then started to walk away, not wanting to interrupt his call, but he gestured to me to wait.

After he finished his call, I approached on the passenger side, and he lowered the window.

"Hi Pervez," I said. "What brings you here?"

"Hi Audrey. I just dropped off my cousin. He has a case here today!"

I said to myself: proceed with caution. We had been warned repeatedly at the law clerk orientation not to talk too much about our work with outsiders or to reveal information about our cases (except for information that was already a matter of public record).

"What's the case about?" I asked.

"Immigration. They want to deport him. "

Hamadani—of course. My friend Pervez, whom I thought of as just "Pervez," was Pervez Hamadani, as his driver identification card on the dashboard reminded me. His cousin was Ahmed Hamadani, the journalist from Baluchistan. What were the odds?

"We do get many immigration cases here," I said, trying to engage in conversation without saying anything substantial.

"My cousin has serious enemies back in Pakistan. Friends and colleagues of his have been killed. You don't think they would deport him, do you?"

"That's up to the three judges hearing his case. I'm just a clerk."

"You don't think the judges are biased against immigrants?"

"No," I said, "these are federal judges, the best legal minds in the country. I'm sure they'll decide his case based on the law."

"I hope they are fair," Pervez said. "If my cousin gets sent back to Pakistan, he's a dead man."

As I headed into the courthouse, I reflected on what Judge Stinson had told me last week when we reviewed *Hamadani*: judging is not easy work. I believed that ruling against Pervez's cousin was the right decision under the law, but I now felt more uneasy about the possible practical consequences. I would need to get over such feelings if I wanted to be a successful law clerk; as the judge had told me, we don't decide cases based on sympathy.

After a quick stop in chambers to drop off my bag and grab a legal pad and pen, I headed down to the courtroom for the oral arguments. They took place in what everyone called the "Spanish Room," a little cave of a courtroom that got its name from an abundance of dark carved wood and elaborate cast-iron ceiling grilles, both done in Spanish colonial style.

The courtroom, small and low-ceilinged by courtroom standards, did not have a jury box or any other space in the well of court for law clerks, so we had to sit in the gallery with the public, mostly lawyers whose cases had not been called yet. The gallery was packed when I arrived—Amit must have arrived early, since he had a prime spot in the first row—so I headed for a middle pew where Jeremy and James were sitting. Jeremy was speaking just a little too loudly for the room, which was suffused with a prehearing hush, and telling James a story that for some reason required Jeremy to put his hand on James's knee.

Jeremy looked up when I arrived and removed his hand from James's knee.

"Hello, Miss Audrey, nice of you to join us," Jeremy said, looking at his vintage gold Rolex.

"It's only 9:25. Court doesn't start for five minutes."

"Tell that to Amit," James said. "I think he got here before nine."

A few minutes later, the grandfather clock near the entrance to the courtroom hit 9:30. The courtroom deputy cried out, "All rise! The judges of the United States Court of Appeals for the Ninth Circuit."

I felt a chill go through me as I stood along with everyone else for the entrance of the three judges. It felt like the start of Mass. Important things were about to happen. After the judges filed in, the courtroom deputy banged a gavel and declared, "The United States Court of Appeals for the Ninth Circuit is now in session."

"Good morning," said Judge Gottlieb, Jeremy's boss, as he sat down in the center of the bench. "Please be seated."

Everyone in the gallery sat down. After waiting for the room to quiet, Judge Gottlieb spoke again, in a deep, growling voice—fitting given his status as the Ninth Circuit's liberal lion, I thought.

"We will now hear argument in case number 11-72333, Hamadani versus the Attorney General."

A young, trim lawyer approached the podium. We could see him only from behind; he held himself with confidence. Remaining at counsel table was a dark-haired man I guessed to be Ahmed Hamadani.

"Mr. Soloway," said Judge Gottlieb, "you may proceed."

Hamadani's lawyer uttered barely a few sentences—his introduction of himself to the court, his reservation of time for rebuttal—before Judge Stinson interrupted him. People new to the world of appellate advocacy might have found this rude, but I knew from both my reading and from my moot court experience that this was standard.

"Counselor," she said, "didn't the Board of Immigration Appeals find numerous inconsistencies in your client's application for asylum?"

"No, Your Honor," he said with impressive calm, "I would not call them 'numerous.' And they are not, upon closer inspection, true inconsistencies. The board identified a few purported inconsistencies, but all can be explained. First, there was confusion over the identity of a journalist who was murdered in March 2009 and that journalist's relationship to my client. The board concluded . . ."

As he proceeded to clarify the problems that the BIA had identified in Hamadani's asylum application, Jeremy leaned over to me and whispered, "This guy's good."

Judge Arthur Hollingsworth, an elderly conservative judge from Oklahoma who was sitting on the panel as a visiting judge, interjected: "These points you are now making, were these raised in your brief?"

"Yes, Your Honor. They appear under the second point of our argument section, starting at page 18."

"Counselor, you raised all these arguments in your excellent brief," Judge Gottlieb said. "The board did a poor job of making a record in this case. Why should we accord any deference to the BIA given its sloppiness?"

"With all due respect to the board," Lionel Soloway said, "we do not believe it is entitled to great deference. But even giving the board deference, its adverse credibility finding must be overturned for lack of support."

Loyola Larry entered the courtroom through the door near the front of the gallery, attracting stares from practically everyone except Soloway, who was focused on his argument. Larry ambled toward the back of the room, not at all self-conscious about his tardy entrance.

As Soloway continued to score points, deftly fielding hostile questions from Judges Stinson and Hollingsworth while graciously accepting softballs from Judge Gottlieb, Jeremy bounced his leg up and down and smiled. Meanwhile, I stared down at the deep blue carpet, filled with growing anxiety.

Had I made the wrong recommendation in my bench memo? I had tried my best, and I had acknowledged the case was close and difficult. If my recommendation was wrong, I hoped that the judges would ignore it.

I was glad to be "only" a clerk and not a judge. I believed what I had told Pervez that morning: the judges would make the right decision.

II

"Good morning, everyone," Judge Stinson said, starting up the Monday morning meeting after the calendar week. "Are we ready to get back to work?"

Even though the clerkship year essentially revolved around the eight or so oral argument calendars—preparing for the calendar, hearing the cases during the calendar, and writing up the opinions after the calendar—the calendar week itself was actually pleasant. We had done so much work in advance that there wasn't that much to do during the argument week itself. In the morning, we'd watch oral argument, and in the afternoon, we'd draft memorandum dispositions—straightforward rulings, generally just a few pages, written for the specific parties and not binding precedent. We got to leave chambers before seven in the evening. But now that week was over.

After the usual discussion of our weekends, we plunged into the docket and the status of our cases. When we got to *Hamadani*, the judge paused the discussion.

"Audrey, congratulations," she said. "The analysis of your bench memo carried the day. We got the vote of Judge Hollingsworth. Judge Gottlieb will dissent. Also, in case you missed it, the *Los Angeles Times* had an article yesterday about it. Looks like your first case is quite the drama."

"I did see the article, Judge. It was very sympathetic toward Hamadani."

"Excessively so, in my view. But that's the media for you. They have a very unsophisticated understanding of the law. They think that whatever they *want* to happen, as a matter of personal opinion, just *has to be* the law. Hello, *Los Angeles Times*, that's not quite how this all works!"

We all laughed.

"Now, we don't let the media influence our decision making, which would be improper," the judge continued. "But the public is watching this case, and Judge Gottlieb will write a strong dissent, so we need to write our opinion with great care."

"Absolutely, Judge."

"Of course, *all* of our opinions are written with great care, right?"

We chuckled dutifully—law clerks as judicial laugh track.

Following review of the existing cases, we turned to discussion of the new cases that had just arrived in chambers.

"There is one case that you should not assign amongst yourselves as usual," the judge said. "I will personally decide who will work with me on *Geidner*."

"What's that case about?" Larry asked.

The judge sighed; Amit rolled his eyes. Larry didn't know about *Geidner* because he didn't come into work the prior weekend (or any weekend), which is when Amit and James and I had talked about it.

"*Geidner* is an appeal from the ruling of a district court here in Los Angeles that struck down Proposition 8, California's ballot proposition banning same-sex marriage," said Judge Stinson, sounding like a first-year law student who got called upon in class. "Judge Amanda Nathanson held that the ban violated both the Due Process and Equal Protection Clauses of the 14th Amendment. Now the proponents of the ban are appealing, although the official defendants—the governor and the attorney general—are not."

"Okay, I get it," Larry said. "The gay marriage stuff."

"Yes, exactly—the gay marriage 'stuff,'" Judge Stinson said, with barely concealed pique. "This case concerns a politically charged issue and presents many . . . complexities."

We all knew—well, everyone except Larry knew—what the judge was alluding to. Gay marriage was a hot-button issue, and the 2012 presidential election was just a few weeks away, making for a volatile political climate. The opinion polls suggested the election would be very close, and gay marriage could possibly affect the voting, at least in certain swing states.

"This case must be handled with delicacy and finesse," the judge said. "How it is handled could affect my . . . future prospects. I would not mind if this case could be, shall we say, placed on the back burner for a time."

We all knew what this meant too. If the Republican nominee, businessman Craig LaFount, won the presidential election, the judge could be a Supreme Court nominee—provided that her work on a controversial case didn't derail things. A case like *Geidner* was dangerous. If the judge handled it in too liberal a way, she could upset conservatives, including some of the people who might have a say in selecting the next SCOTUS nominee in a Republican administration. If the judge handled it in too conservative a way, she could alienate some Democrats—who controlled the Senate, and who would probably still control the Senate after the election. So the judge just wanted *Geidner* to go away until after the election. If something significant happened in the case before the election, then *Geidner* specifically, or gay marriage more generally, could become a campaign issue—with unpredictable consequences.

"This is a very important and interesting case, certainly one of the most important to come across my desk during my time on this Court. And it involves sensitive issues that some of you might be uncomfortable handling, perhaps because of strong personal views one way or the other. So let me ask: are all of you willing to work with me on this case if chosen?"

I nodded vigorously—working closely with the judge on a headline-making case like this represented a huge opportunity to get into her good graces—and then looked around the table to see who else was volunteering. James and Larry and Amit were also nodding, but Amit looked uncomfortable as he did so. Did he have some deep objection to gay marriage, perhaps on religious grounds? Did he want the assignment so badly that he couldn't bear the thought of *not* getting it?

"Very well," the judge said. "Here is a homework assignment for everyone. Take a look at the briefs and record in *Geidner*, and come to next Monday's meeting with a recommendation for how I should handle it. The clerk with the best recommendation will be the one to work with me on this case."

I spent the next few days trying to come up with a masterful idea for what to do in *Geidner*, but nothing occurred to me. And because of how the judge had structured her request for advice as a contest of sorts between the clerks, I didn't discuss it with Amit or James (or Larry, obviously). But I could tell that the case was on everyone's mind.

On Saturday afternoon, I took a break from work for my driving lesson with Harvetta. After a poolside lunch of homemade sandwiches (neither of us wanted to spend for brunch), Harvetta drove us out to the parking lot of the Pasadena High School in her ancient gray Honda Civic. The vast asphalt expanse, baking beneath the California sun, was deserted.

The driving lesson did not go well—at all. I had great difficulty with the concept of brakes, both the regular brakes, which I applied too forcefully, and the parking brake, which I kept forgetting to disengage. After I made her poor car lurch for the tenth time, Harvetta reached over, turned off the ignition, and touched my forearm.

"Audrey, is everything okay? You seemed a little out of it at lunch. Now you seem super-stressed. And I'm not sure it's just from the driving."

"You're right," I said. "I'm stressed about some work stuff, that's all. Sometimes I just can't believe how much responsibility we have as clerks. We're barely out of law school and we're working on these major cases that affect people's lives."

"Yeah. I'm working on a death penalty case right now. And you guys have that appeal in the gay marriage case coming up."

It was like Harvetta read my mind. The fact that there was an appeal going to the Ninth Circuit was public, but the fact that Judge Stinson was on the panel was not, so I had to be careful. But I was curious to hear her views.

"Oh, yes, the *Geidner* case. Any thoughts on that?"

"Well, it's kinda fucked up—fucked-up weird, not fucked-up bad. There's a tricky jurisdictional issue there. Because the governor and attorney general ain't appealing, do the proponents of the ballot initiative have the standing to defend Prop 8?"

"The law in this area is less than clear."

"It's as clear as a puddle of shit, is what it is."

"One theme running through the cases is that state law can sometimes be relevant to the question of federal jurisdiction," I said. "State law doesn't control the issue—federal jurisdiction is still fundamentally a question of federal law—but state law can have bearing."

"So in this case," Harvetta said, "does the anti-gay-marriage group that sponsored the proposition have a role under California law in defending what it sponsored?"

"Exactly. We sometimes deal with issues of California law at the Ninth Circuit—for example, when we get a case under diversity jurisdiction, or when a state-law issue is included in a case presenting federal claims—but we aren't the experts on California law."

"You guys leave that shit to us. The California Supreme Court has the final word on California law."

"If only there was a way for us to get your views on what California law would say about this situation . . ."

Harvetta paused.

"There is," she said. "The Ninth Circuit can send the case to us, to the California Supreme Court, by 'certifying' the standing question. I'm actually working on another case right now that involves a certified question from the Ninth Circuit. It doesn't happen *that* often, but there's an established procedure for it—just look it up."

"That sounds perfect," I said evenly, trying to contain my excitement. "Given how everyone is watching the case, the Ninth Circuit needs to cross the t's and dot the i's. Sending the standing issue to the California Supreme Court is the safest thing to do."

"Exactly. If we find standing, great, then the Ninth can go ahead and rule on the merits. If no standing, then you guys can save yourselves the time and hassle—and dodge a bullet."

"Harvetta Chambers, you are a genius."

"I know," she said, grinning from ear to ear. "Now take off the goddamn parking brake and *drive*."

The first half hour of the Monday morning meeting passed as quickly as an afternoon at the DMV. We didn't care about how everyone's weekends went, or the status of the draft opinions, or the matters on the en banc list. We were all waiting for one topic: *Geidner.*

Judge Stinson seemed to enjoy torturing us. After we finished reviewing all of the regular cases, which is when we should have turned to *Geidner,* she treated us to a random story about a ridiculous assignment that her youngest daughter received at school. I noticed Amit gnawing on the binding at the top of his legal pad—gross.

Finally, the moment of truth.

"I'm sure you'd love to hear more about the absurdity of elementary education today," the judge said. "But I know you're all eager to share with me your brilliant ideas for how to handle the *Geidner* case. Larry, let's start with you."

"Well, uh, Judge, as you were saying last week, this case is a, um, challenge to California's ban on gay marriage, and . . ."

"Larry, stop stalling. Do you have any clue about what I should do in this case?"

"No, Judge, sorry," he said, as casually as if he knocked a pen out of her hand.

"James, what about you?"

"Well, Judge, what jumped out at me is the jurisdictional issue," he said. "The appeal is being brought by the sponsors of the ballot proposition; the governor and the attorney general are not appealing. That strikes me as unusual and potentially significant. But I just noticed this as a potential issue for focus—I don't have a particular course of action in mind."

"I do," interrupted Amit. "Because the official defendants are not appealing the trial court's ruling, which they apparently agree with, this court should dismiss for lack of appellate jurisdiction."

"But that would leave in place the district court's ruling," the judge said, "effectively legalizing gay marriage throughout California, wouldn't it?"

"Yes, but I think that's the result required by law."

Judge Stinson furrowed her brow. She wasn't thrilled by Amit's proposal—perhaps because social conservatives, whose support she would need if she wanted to be nominated to the Supreme Court by a Republican president, wouldn't approve.

"Federal judges shouldn't overturn the popular will lightly," I said, unable to resist the chance to show up Amit. "The Ninth Circuit is already viewed as an activist court."

"I agree," the judge said. "At the same time, I am concerned about this jurisdictional issue and whether the proposition's sponsors have standing."

"The standing question is complex, but I don't believe the court currently has enough information to decide it," I said. "If you look at the Supreme Court's rulings in this area, such as *Arizonans for Official English*, you'll see dicta suggesting that whether proponents of a ballot initiative have the legal standing to defend it in court depends in part on state law. In other words, have the proponents been granted that role here under California law?"

I had everyone's attention, especially Judge Stinson's.

"So," I concluded, "here the Ninth Circuit should certify a question to the California Supreme Court: under the California constitution or other state law, do the proponents of an initiative have enough of an interest in the initiative's validity to defend that initiative in court when the relevant public officials decline to do so? Once the California court answers the question, then the Ninth Circuit will have enough information to rule on the standing issue as a matter of federal law. It won't have to speculate about California state law. Certifying is the safest course of action."

Silence. But I could hear the applause in my head.

"Excellent advice," the judge said. "In addition to the advantages you identify, certifying the question to the California Supreme Court shows a healthy respect for federalism. And it will send this case away from us until after the—until, well, we enter a . . . calmer period. Very shrewd."

"Thank you, Judge."

I glanced over at Amit. With his mouth wrapped firmly around the corner of his legal pad, he looked like a dog.

"Audrey," Judge Stinson said, "you will work with me on *Geidner*."

12

"Oh James," I moaned, rolling my head back and staring up at the ceiling. "I haven't been this hungover since that first Monday morning meeting. Why did you let me have so much of that toxic beverage?"

It was early November, the morning after Election Day. I was sitting in one of the two guest chairs in my co-clerk's office. One of the perks of clerking, at least for Judge Stinson, was a private office with enough space for visitor chairs—something not enjoyed by our classmates now toiling at New York law firms as junior associates, who had to share offices.

"I didn't know it was so strong," he said, leaning far back in his tilting chair. "It was hella sweet."

"Hella? Is that some California thing?"

"Yeah. It's an intensifier, synonymous with 'very' or 'incredibly.'"

"You can take the boy out of Berkeley, but you can't take the Berkeley out of the boy."

"Well, you should have known better than to drink the 'Right-Wing Kool-Aid' at an Election Night party hosted by a liberal like Jeremy. You're lucky it wasn't poisoned. I'm a moderate, but I stuck to the 'Progressive Punch'—I knew it was fine because Jeremy was guzzling it the whole night. Especially after the last network called it for LaFount."

"I feel so ill," I said. "I need this day to end as quickly as possible."

Suddenly James tilted forward, sat up straight in his chair, and cast his eyes toward the door.

"Heads up, Coyne," he said.

I turned around, following his eyes, and beheld a startling sight: Judge Stinson, wearing a bright red suit with a festively ruched collar, standing in the doorway of James's office.

"Good morning, James! Hello, Audrey!"

We both greeted the judge as effusively as we could. But what was she doing in this part of the office? She rarely came over to the clerks' side of the chambers.

"I have an announcement: we're having a chambers lunch. I'm taking you all to the Parkway Grill. We have a 12:30 reservation and we'll leave at 12:15. See you soon!"

After the judge left, I leaned in toward James, placed my elbows on his desk, and put my aching head in my hands.

"Ugh, not the best day for lunch with the judge," I said. "And we haven't had a chambers lunch in weeks. What do you think is going on?"

"I think the judge is thrilled about a Republican in the White House, that's what I think."

"Do you really think she's that political?"

"We'll find out soon enough."

It didn't take long. As soon as we were seated in the clubby confines of the Parkway Grill, the judge ordered an expensive bottle of cabernet sauvignon from Cakebread Cellars, one of her favorite California vineyards ("Jack Cakebread is an old friend"). As soon as it was poured, she raised her glass.

"A toast," Judge Stinson said. "To our new leadership in Washington!"

James and I exchanged awkward glances and hesitated for a second. But as Amit and Larry moved to clink glasses with the judge, James and I joined in.

"Judge," Amit asked, "what do you think the change in administration will mean for the Ninth Circuit?"

"Maybe I'm being too optimistic, but it could be transformative. Based on the people on his campaign's legal advisory team, I'm expecting President LaFount to be severely conservative when it comes to judicial appointments."

"But is LaFount himself that conservative?" James asked. "During the Republican primary, he got criticized by the other candidates for not being conservative enough."

"True," the judge said, "but you have to understand that conservatives, especially social conservatives, play a disproportionate role in the judicial nomination process for the Republican Party. They pay more attention to the courts than other groups within the party—so even if the party itself is becoming more moderate, the conservatives still control the picking of judges."

"Would you say that's true at the Supreme Court level too?" I asked.

Judge Stinson grew even more animated. I watched the wine slosh around in her glass as she waved it while she spoke.

"Absolutely," she said. "But it gets more complicated and delicate at the Supreme Court level. The president has to pick someone who will excite the conservative base but still win confirmation in a divided Senate—no easy task."

Lunch stretched out over two leisurely hours, with the chatty Judge Stinson regaling us with tales of Hollywood gossip gleaned from her husband. Upon returning to chambers, I did not have a productive afternoon; that one glass of wine made my head heavy. But it didn't matter. The judge left work right at 5:30, and Brenda and Larry followed soon after. At around 6, I went into James's office and closed the door.

"Can I ask you a question?" I said.

"Sure," said James, leaning back slightly and putting his hands behind his head. Even though it was the end of the day, his blue shirt still looked impossibly crisp.

"Were you a little disturbed by the judge's mood at lunch today?"

"How so? She was in a great mood."

"Exactly. She's a judge, not a politician. She's supposed to be impartial. Her glee over LaFount's victory made me a bit . . . uncomfortable."

"Look, the LaFount win is *huge* for her. She now has a real shot at the Supreme Court. You'd be thrilled if you were in her shoes."

"I could never afford her shoes. They cost more than my rent!"

James chuckled.

"You know what I mean," he said. "If LaFount had lost, she'd have another four years to wait before a possible nomination. And now that she's around fifty, she's at a critical age. If she doesn't get nominated in the next five or six years, she'll probably never get it."

"I get that she's happy. But she could keep it to herself. Or be more understated about it."

"Well, we *are* her clerks. Professionally we're just extensions of the judge. If she can't share things with us, who can she share them with?"

"I see your point. I guess I just have an old-fashioned view of judges. Did you know that Justice Harlan wouldn't vote in elections—even though ballots are secret, and even though judges are allowed to vote—because he viewed a judge participating in politics, even in such a small way, as inappropriate?"

"Audrey, our boss is no Justice Harlan."

13

A few days later, my office phone rang.

"Audrey, come to my office. *Now.*"

"Right away, Judge."

I grabbed a pen and yellow legal pad and hurried over to the judge's side of chambers. As soon as I entered her office, she started barking at me.

"What am I supposed to with this?" she said, waving a thick stack of papers in the air as I approached and sat down next to her at the conference table. "I don't even know where to begin."

I had seen the judge get peeved before, but I had never seen her angry—until now. I looked down at the table, to avoid looking her in the face, and the veins in the creamy marble slab swam before my eyes. I took a quiet breath before speaking.

"I'm sorry, Judge," I said with a calm I did not feel. "Can you explain what seems to be the problem?"

"This," she said, shaking the sheaf again, inches away from my face. "*This* is what you consider acceptable work product? This is what you would have me issue under my own name, as an opinion of the United States Court of Appeals for the Ninth Circuit?"

She dropped it on the conference table disdainfully. My draft opinion in *Hamadani*.

"I'm sorry my draft in *Hamadani* did not meet your expectations, Judge. What can I do to fix it?"

"I don't even know where to begin. For starters, you seem to have a problem with forgetting to italicize the periods included in 'Id.' citations. They must be italicized. They taught you that at Yale, didn't they?"

"Yes, Judge. But sometimes it's hard to tell the difference . . ."

"No buts. No excuses. Everything coming out of this chambers from now on must be *perfect*."

"Absolutely, Judge, I will fix all of those."

"People are watching this case. It has been written up in the papers. Judge Gottlieb will write a strong dissent. There is no room for error here."

I picked up the opinion and started turning the pages. To my surprise, they had hardly any markings on them, other than some circled, nonitalicized periods.

"I don't see many line edits here, Judge. Could you give me some general thoughts on how to strengthen the opinion?"

"Audrey, how long have you been in chambers now? How many opinions have you read over the years? You're a graduate of a top law school. I hired you because you're supposed to be one of the brightest young legal minds in the country. I'm not going to sit here and tell you how to do your job."

"Yes, Judge."

"Look at me."

I looked up from the opinion, blinking hard to keep myself together, and made eye contact with the judge.

"Do you want to clerk for the Supreme Court?"

"More than anything."

"When I recommend one of my law clerks to the Supreme Court, I am putting my credibility on the line. I am making a representation and a warranty. I am telling the justices: this is a clerk who is self-sufficient. This is a clerk who knows how to do the job. This is a clerk you don't need to train. This is a clerk who will hit the ground running."

I nodded and nodded, eyes still on the judge. She knew how to get my attention. This was the first time since I started the clerkship that she mentioned her coveted Supreme Court recommendation.

"So go back to your office," she said, "and take this opinion, and just . . . make . . . it . . . better. I want a new draft by tomorrow morning."

"Yes, Judge. I'm sorry, Judge. Thank you, Judge."

I grabbed the opinion, hurried back to my office, and closed the door. I sat down in my chair, back to the door, and closed my eyes. I did not want to cry. Feeling the beginnings of a sob in my throat, I took three big gulps from the bottled water on my desk, then let out a deep breath.

After collecting myself as best I could, I wandered over to James's office, closed the door, and collapsed into a chair. He looked up from the brief he was reading.

"Are you okay?" he asked. "You look upset."

"I am upset. The judge hates me."

"Of course the judge doesn't hate you. You're her favorite clerk. Well, you and Amit, depending on the day and the mood she's in."

"If she doesn't hate me, then why did she just call my draft opinion in *Hamadani* a piece of crap?"

"I doubt she said that."

"Not in so many words. But she told me it wasn't up to snuff. And didn't tell me how to make it better!"

"That's just how she is. She's a 'big picture' person."

"I guess I still have this idea of a judge as devoted to the writer's craft. Someone like Justice Oliver Wendell Holmes, writing his opinions out in longhand while standing at his lectern."

"Very few judges write their own opinions nowadays. You know that. And our boss isn't the kind of judge who gets down into the weeds."

"I wish she were like Judge Gottlieb. He doesn't write his own opinions, but he edits heavily, for both substance and style. He goes over his comments with Jeremy line by line, paragraph by paragraph, explaining each change and making sure the wording of everything is just perfect. Judge Gottlieb pays attention to detail—in a good way. Not like yelling at me for not italicizing the periods in 'Id.' citations!"

James started laughing.

"What's so funny?"

"Because I had a similar absurd experience. The other day she yelled at me for putting a space between 'n.' and the note number in a footnote citation."

"What's going on with her?"

"Come on, Audrey—you know exactly what's going on. Ever since LaFount won the election, the judge sees herself as a possible Supreme Court nominee. And she's right; she has to be on any shortlist. But that means she's going to be super-uptight and super-perfectionist from now on. She sees herself as under heightened scrutiny."

"So she flips out over Bluebooking mistakes? I don't think she'll lose the nomination over nonitalicized periods."

"Of course not," James said. "But since she doesn't dig into the substance of the opinions we draft for her, she uses small Bluebooking errors as the way to police our work."

"Are we doomed to this until she gets—or doesn't get—a Supreme Court nomination?"

"I'm afraid so. Let's hope that she gets it. I'd hate to see what she'll be like if someone else gets the nod."

14

I stared at the screen blankly. This was bad. Very bad.

Whenever an email related to one of my cases arrived in the chambers inbox—I could tell if it was one of my cases from the subject line—I'd get nervous. What was about to happen? Was a judge who had agreed to join an opinion of ours about to announce a change of heart? Was an opinion that I drafted about to come in for harsh criticism from a colleague of Judge Stinson?

Most of the time, my anxiety turned out to be unwarranted; this time, though, my worries were justified. In response to our draft majority opinion in *Hamadani*—which featured properly italicized periods, as well as strengthened legal analysis—Judge Gottlieb had circulated a powerful, blistering dissent. The dissent was so powerful, in fact, that I worried that we might lose the vote of Judge Hollingsworth for our majority.

I stared at the screen, reading the dissent yet again, and wondered how to respond. In terms of what was supposed to happen next, I would edit the majority opinion to respond to the dissent, get Judge Stinson's sign-off on the edits, and circulate the revised opinion to the other two judges. But I was at a loss for how to revise the majority opinion to respond to Judge Gottlieb's persuasive argumentation.

This dissent was great. Did Jeremy draft it? I picked up my office phone.

"Why, hello there, Audrey! I've been expecting your call."

"And why is that?"

"I trust you've just read my handiwork in *Hamadani*?"

"So that *is* your case. Based on all the attitude in the dissent, I suspected that you might have a hand in it."

"Yup. What do you think?"

"It's good."

"It's 'good'? That's all? You're hurting my feelings."

"Okay, it's very good. But it sounds like you don't need me to tell you that."

"Maybe not. But I still like to hear you admit it."

"Well, this isn't over," I said. "You'll be hearing from us."

I wondered if Jeremy could see through my false bravado. After I got off the phone with him, I printed out a copy of the dissent and read it over while wielding a red felt-tip pen, a weapon that I hoped would give me courage. I underlined forcefully, scribbled furiously, and filled the margins with checks and question marks.

But this exercise in engaged reading did not produce the hoped-for insight into the fatal flaw of the dissent's reasoning. Nor did my careful review of all the cases cited in both the majority and the dissent.

Having made absolutely no progress in trying to unravel the dissent, I concluded I had no choice: I had to go see the judge. She'd know what to do. Even if she didn't usually go for hand-holding—she told us early on that she wanted us to be independent thinkers—this was an exceptional case. I had never been this stumped by anything during the clerkship.

I headed over to Judge Stinson's side of the chambers, something I generally didn't do unless summoned, and approached the doorway to her office. The door was open just a crack, in a way that seemed to say "I have an 'open door' policy, but I really don't want to be bothered." When I started clerking, Judge Stinson would usually leave her door wide open, but lately—since November or so—the judge was often on the phone, with the door fully or mostly shut.

I opened the door just a little, enough to stick my head in, and knocked softly on the doorframe. The judge, seated behind her brown barge of a desk, looked up from the brief she was reading.

"Judge, sorry to bother you. Could I ask you about something?"

I thought I detected a flash of irritation cross her face, but if so, she concealed it quickly.

"Certainly," she said.

I sat down opposite the judge in one of the guest chairs, which felt so small in front of her imposing desk. This wasn't like when I interviewed for my clerkship, when I sat on the sofa and she in a club chair, or when we reviewed cases together, when we both sat at the conference table. I could feel the power differential between us.

"Judge, have you had the chance to read Judge Gottlieb's dissent in *Hamadani* yet?"

"I saw that he circulated it, and I skimmed it. But I haven't looked at it in detail yet."

"It's strong. Very strong."

"Of course it is," she said, swatting an imaginary fly with her small pale hand. "I warned you about that when you submitted your weak first draft to me. But I thought your revision—which you turned around very quickly, I must say—was significantly improved. I would not have allowed it to leave chambers if I did not think it was solid."

"Well, I feel that even with the improvements, our draft opinion doesn't hold up well against the dissent. I'm not sure if we have good arguments to respond to Judge Gottlieb's points, especially his analysis of prior Ninth Circuit cases about what constitutes persecution. I wonder if, maybe, the outcome of the case should be, perhaps, revisited . . ."

"Are you suggesting that I *change my vote* in this case?"

I paused and took a breath. My mouth felt as dry as the pages of the Federal Reporter.

"I'm sorry, Judge. Of course I'll revise the majority opinion. But could you perhaps—after you've had the chance to read the dissent, of course—give me some, well, additional guidance in terms of how you'd like the opinion to be revised?"

Silence. The judge stared at me, lips turned inward to form a grim, angry line. It was as if I had asked something patently offensive, like when she and her husband last had sex.

"Audrey," said Judge Stinson, leaning across the massive mahogany desk, "I am a federal judge. I do not concern myself with trivialities."

I was about to protest that the legal arguments for and against political asylum are not "trivialities," but thought better of it—which was just as well, because the judge wasn't finished.

"If you can't think of the arguments to sustain my position, which was also the position of the third judge on the panel, Judge Hollingsworth, then I suggest you consult with Amit. He has excellent analytical skills."

15

I was not a fan of Intelligentsia Coffee. The café itself, a loft-like space with one wall of exposed brick and another painted an electric blue, exuded an industrial, hipster coolness. I preferred my coffee shops to be cozier—and less expensive. Intelligentsia charged four dollars for a small cup of overly bitter coffee. Granted, it was individually prepared, by an elaborately tattooed barista, on a long counter made of Douglas fir, but I could have done without the pageantry. I would happily have met up at Starbucks. Jeremy, however, wouldn't hear of it; as a coffee snob, he viewed Intelligentsia as the only acceptable coffee place in all of Pasadena.

Despite living (or perhaps because he lived?) just a few blocks away, in a luxury apartment building in downtown Pasadena, Jeremy was running late. I sipped my milky and sweet coffee, sitting at a high-top by the wall, and read *New York Times* articles on my phone.

A family with a daughter with Down syndrome entered the café and walked past my table toward the counter. I watched them as they lingered over the pastry selection (which I had passed on, due to cost and calories).

Even though the daughter was just a teenager, she reminded me of my older sister, Elizabeth. My sister suffered from Prader-Willi syndrome, a rare genetic disorder that caused her to have cognitive disabilities and behavioral problems. My parents tried to keep Elizabeth at home with them for as long as they could, but after an incident in which my sister came at my mother with a knife, they had no choice but to put her in a center for disabled adults. They felt great guilt over doing so and tried to see her every week, either going to Staten Island to visit Elizabeth in her group home or bringing her to Woodside to spend the weekend with them.

My parents loved my sister but never expected anything from her. The extra expectations landed on me. Growing up, I alternated between competing with Elizabeth for my parents' attention and trying not to give them additional stress—both paths leading to overachievement. But sometimes I felt like little more than the sum of my accomplishments, my GPA and my SAT and my speech and debate trophies. And sometimes I envied Elizabeth for the unconditional love my parents gave her, how she could just be herself and win their attention and affection.

I missed my parents. I didn't have time for a phone call, but I texted a quick hello to my mother, as I often did. She texted right back. As I guessed, my parents were on their way to Staten Island to visit Elizabeth. I imagined them boarding the ferry, swaddled in their puffy winter coats, and thought about how I was enjoying the weather here in southern California. I didn't feel quite at home here and planned to return to the East Coast after my clerkship, but it was a nice change of pace for a year—part of the adventure of clerking, the freedom to try out a different part of the country. When my mother asked how I was doing, I couldn't resist texting back to brag, as Californians so often do, that it was 70 degrees and sunny on this December day.

The clink of a saucer on the table caused me to look up. Jeremy had arrived, bearing a latte with a beautiful heart made out of milk foam on the top. I texted my mom to tell her I had to go and greeted Jeremy. We chatted about random matters for a while—how sore he was from a new class he was taking at his gym, how my driving lessons with Harvetta were progressing—but I could tell we were both thinking about the same thing.

"So," he said, sipping judiciously from his latte, "when are we going to be seeing a revised majority opinion in *Hamadani*?"

"I'm putting the finishing touches on my masterpiece this weekend. You should be getting the revised majority opinion sometime next week."

"You're not changing your vote? Our powerful dissent didn't persuade you?"

"It's not *my* vote, it's Judge Stinson's. I'm just the law clerk. The Senate didn't confirm me to anything. I don't have a signed commission from the president hanging in my office."

Jeremy seemed annoyed.

"Okay, fine," he said, "but if you were the judge, how would you vote?"

I shifted uncomfortably. I raised my coffee cup to my lips but found to my dismay that it was empty.

"It doesn't matter what I think," I said. "I'm just a clerk. One of four clerks to a judge. One of three judges on a panel. My personal views are irrelevant."

"You're just a cog in the machine, then?"

"You're painting this as much more black and white than it really is," I said. "This is a hard case, and I don't know how I would vote if I were a judge. But reasonable minds can disagree, and there are strong arguments on both sides. Our position—Judge Stinson's position—is not frivolous. In fact, as of now, it's the position with two votes."

"Because Hollingsworth is a right-wing political hack. Just like your boss, who just wants her Supreme Court appointment."

My face grew warm. And it wasn't from the coffee.

"Excuse me?" I said. "What did you just say about Judge Stinson?"

"You heard me. I hate to break it to you, Audrey, but your boss is a fucking hack. She claims to just want to 'follow the law,' but when the law leads her to a result she doesn't like, she just cooks up some bullshit for not applying it. And to think it's my boss who gets criticized for 'judicial activism.'"

Criticizing someone's judge was like criticizing her mother. I can complain about my mother to a friend, but if *you* complain about my mother, I will defend her to the end. My judge, right or wrong.

"That's completely unfair," I said. "You're doing just what you accuse

Judge Gottlieb's foes of doing: calling a judge you happen to disagree with a 'judicial activist.' And maybe you and your boss are envious of Judge Stinson's Supreme Court prospects under the incoming presidential administration."

"We've been clerking for several months now. We've seen the opinions the judges write. We've seen how they vote on whether to rehear different cases en banc. Stinson is a conservative extremist. She never votes in favor of the immigrant, the criminal defendant, or organized labor. She always votes in favor of the government in immigration and criminal cases. She has never met a big corporation she didn't like."

"The opposite could be said of Judge Gottlieb. He always comes up with some tortured reasoning for voting in favor of the little guy."

"At least when he votes for the little guy, it's because he wants to do justice. It's not because of his own ambition."

"Life isn't like the movies. The little guy isn't always right. And that's why your boss is constantly getting reversed by the Supreme Court."

"No, my boss gets reversed because a majority of the justices are hacks too. Stinson will fit right in if she gets nominated."

"There's only so much the Supreme Court can do to control your crazy boss. It's like a game of Whac-A-Mole—they can only slap down so many of his opinions."

Jeremy paused to sip his coffee. He seemed to have calmed down a bit, but I was still agitated.

"Here's some homework for you," he said. "When you go into chambers today, go on Westlaw or Lexis and look up all the immigration cases that Stinson has heard since joining the Ninth Circuit. See how often she has voted in favor of the immigrant. I bet you'll be surprised."

"And I bet I won't," I said. "Whatever the number is, you'll say it's too low and I'll say it's fine. It's a stacked deck."

"Okay, fine, don't look it up. I was just trying to introduce some data into our argument."

"I don't have time for any 'homework.' I have an opinion—a *majority* opinion—to revise. I'll see you later."

Still upset at Jeremy, I strode out of the coffee shop. It was only once I was standing outside on Colorado Boulevard that I remembered: I was supposed to have gotten a ride from Jeremy to the courthouse. It was about a 20-minute walk away—not a big deal in New York, but not a distance one would walk in California.

A mile wasn't too far to journey for my pride. As I walked from downtown to residential Pasadena, I passed one stunning home after another. An elegant Craftsman with an inviting front veranda. A rambling Mediterranean surrounded by almost overgrown gardens. A dignified Georgian with a lawn as large as a lake. The styles of the houses were so varied, yet standing side by the side, they looked perfectly harmonious. No clashing McMansions, at least not in this part of town.

I thought about the people living in these multimillion-dollar homes. This being southern California in the 21st century, they probably came from varied ethnic backgrounds. And despite L.A.'s reputation as an industry town, they probably came from varied professions as well. Neurosurgeons. Investment bankers. Celebrities—again, this being southern California—and the people who love them, including studio executives, producers, agents, and managers. Plus lawyers, of course, from different precincts of the profession, everyone from M&A partners at O'Melveny & Myers to swashbuckling plaintiffs' lawyers.

What did they all share in common? Wealth. Where did wealth come from? Success. Where did success come from? Ambition.

Where would the world be without ambition? It's the force that drives us to create, to achieve, and to realize our full potential. Life-saving or life-changing inventions, Fortune 500 companies, and great works of art and literature owe their existence to ambition. My mother left the Philippines and my father's ancestors left Ireland because of ambition—maybe not the grandest ambition, but ambition nonetheless. America is a nation built by ambition.

Ambition is an acceptable and even appealing attribute for children. If a little girl says she wants to be an astronaut or president—or both, as I did when I was eight years old—that's endearing. But at a certain point in a person's life, ambition goes from being desirable to discouraged. To describe someone as "ambitious" becomes an insult rather than a compliment. Ambition turns into a dirty word.

During my elementary school years—when I was an awkward-looking girl, half-Filipino and half-Irish, not at home in either community, with immigrant parents who didn't have much money, plus a disabled sister—I often felt like I didn't belong. I took that feeling of not belonging and sublimated it into ambition. My classmates might mock me for having a Tupperware of rice in my lunchbox or a "retard" sister, but I could outscore them on every test.

Things got better as I got older. At Stuyvesant High School in Manhattan, academic achievement was prized, perhaps because we were all nerds, and ambition was perfectly acceptable. Maybe it was due to how many of us were the children of Asian and Eastern European immigrants who had been carried from their impoverished home countries to New York City by ambition. At Harvard College, ambition was once again welcomed—perhaps because Harvard is the kind of school that attracts the openly overachieving, even more so than other elite schools.

Things changed when I arrived at Yale Law School. Even though my class at YLS contained aspiring senators and Supreme Court justices, an institutional ethos prevailed in favor of masking ambition. It manifested itself in the bare-bones grading system, in the inflated membership of the *Yale Law Journal* (about a third of the class belonged), in the classroom discussions (excessive and aggressive participation was frowned upon), and in the way students interacted with professors (careerist sycophancy had to be cast as genuine intellectual curiosity). Maybe that's why Jeremy and I got along so well: we were less willing or able to hide our ambition than many of our classmates, and we viewed such concealment as an exercise in futility.

So perhaps that's why I felt so upset and betrayed by Jeremy's comments about my judge. He seemed to be slipping into the anti-ambition camp that we had both scorned during law school—and, worse yet, his criticisms of Judge Stinson were sexist. An ambitious woman, when she acts forcefully in pursuit of her ambition, gets derided as a "shrew," or a "bitch," or a "political hack," which is what Jeremy called my boss. Meanwhile, a similarly ambitious man gets praised for his "drive" or "determination," or for having "the courage of his convictions" if he acts in a partisan fashion. That was what Jeremy was saying about his own boss, Judge Gottlieb, who was by any objective measure more of a "political hack" than Judge Stinson: Judge Gottlieb was motivated by his desire "to do justice," while Justice Stinson was motivated by her desire to sit on the high court. The double standard angered me.

Being ambitious women: what Judge Stinson and I shared in common. Maybe that's why Judge Stinson and I bonded during the clerkship interview, and why she saw so much of herself in me. I remembered her words to me back then, an observation and a promise and a burden, all at the same time: "There is always somewhere else to go. Always."

Judge Stinson was right: I had somewhere else to go. And my path was clear: impress Judge Stinson, secure her recommendation for a Supreme Court clerkship, obtain a Supreme Court clerkship, and live happily ever after.

When I arrived in chambers, Amit was already there. James was not around because he had a family reunion out of town, and Larry was not around because it was Saturday. I said a quick hello to Amit and then turned on my computer and started to work. After finishing up a quick memorandum disposition rejecting a federal habeas petition as time-barred, I began my primary task for the weekend, revising the *Hamadani* majority opinion.

After Judge Stinson scolded me for bothering her with "trivialities," I set aside the draft opinion and turned to other matters. I decided to let the issues and ideas bounce around in my subconscious for a few days. I consider myself to be reasonably smart, and I like to think—hopefully not wrongly—that I have a fine legal mind. But I'm not a particularly *fast* thinker. I'm able to solve many difficult legal problems, but it sometimes takes me a while to figure them out. I sometimes need to let a matter marinate in my mind before the solution presents itself.

This occasional slight delay in my processing—I wouldn't call myself slow, just not super-fast—has caused problems for me before. In high school, I took second rather than first place at the national debate championship because a killer rebuttal argument didn't occur to me until after the round was over. In college, I graduated magna rather than summa cum laude after I flubbed an answer during my oral examination that, yet again, occurred to me once the exam was done. Missing out on such honors was a high-class problem, but it embodied for me a larger dilemma: always being an also-ran, never being a winner. Not quite making it to number one, always falling just shy. My chance to cure all of these past failings: winning a Supreme Court clerkship.

Now, feeling energized, wanting to wow Judge Stinson and to prove Jeremy wrong, I started rereading the cases related to *Hamadani* with renewed vigor. Because of how my mind works, when I first read a case, I don't always grasp its full implications immediately. Sometimes a second or third reading will reveal nuances to me that I did not see before.

And that's exactly what happened to me that weekend. Reading one of the Ninth Circuit's major immigration precedents for what felt like the tenth time, I managed to find, buried in a footnote, a somewhat obscure and underutilized line of cases that could possibly be read to support our position, in somewhat indirect fashion.

I grabbed all the cases cited in the footnote from Westlaw; printed them, which is what I did when I needed to read something very closely; and pored over them, highlighting and underlining and annotating as I went. My close review confirmed my initial instinct: there *was* something there, even if it would take some selective quotation and massaging of language in order to work. I wasn't sure the reasoning was entirely persuasive, and I suspected that Jeremy and Judge Gottlieb could come back with a powerful rebuttal. But if Judge Stinson wanted to adhere to her position and not change her vote in *Hamadani*, this argument offered the best hope for doing so.

I opened up the draft opinion on my computer and started the process of responding to the dissent. As I tightened up the opinion and swatted away the points of the dissent, one by one, I found my newly discovered argument more and more persuasive. It was a perfectly colorable contention—and even if it wouldn't persuade Judge Gottlieb, it might be enough to keep Judge Hollingsworth on board.

Immersed in my work, I didn't notice the passage of time. Nor did I notice when Amit entered my office, until he cleared his throat rather loudly. I looked up.

"Hey Coyne," he said. "You seem to be working rather diligently on something."

"Yeah, revising the majority opinion in *Hamadani*."

"You love those immigration cases, don't you?"

I thought I detected a sneer in his tone—but maybe I was imagining it because it was Amit.

"I know you find immigration cases boring," I said. "But this isn't your run-of-the-mill asylum case. It got covered in the *L.A. Times*. The immigrant is a prominent journalist. And Judge Gottlieb has written a fierce dissent. I could see the case getting reheard en banc."

"Okay, I get it, it's a big deal," Amit said, backing up and raising his palms in the air. "What I came over to ask was—do you want to grab dinner? It's past seven already."

To be honest, I didn't want to dine with Amit; my preferred chambers meal companion was James. But since James wasn't around and I was starving, I agreed. And I was curious: Amit didn't often extend meal invitations, so maybe he had an agenda in suggesting this dinner meeting.

Since there were no restaurants near the courthouse and neither of us drove, we hopped on Seamless.com and ordered delivery from a Thai place. Forty-five minutes later, we were sitting down at the library conference room table with our meals—green curry tofu with brown rice for me, pad thai for Amit.

"So," said Amit, twirling his noodles around a white plastic fork, "have you noticed anything different about the judge lately?"

I wasn't sure how much I could trust Amit, so I responded guardedly.

"I think she seems . . . a little stressed out."

"A *little* stressed out? She's a nervous wreck these days. And a total bitch."

I was taken aback by Amit's assessment (and language).

"What do you mean by that?" I asked.

"Lately she has been snapping at me for the stupidest things—minor Bluebooking errors, little glitches in formatting, things like that. And she gets really angry about them. It's like it's that time of the month for her. Except it lasts the whole month!"

"I don't think that's fair. She's a demanding boss with high expectations. We have to rise to meet those expectations."

"She was fine when we first got here—demanding, but reasonable. Now she's unreasonable and ridiculous and temperamental. The other day she yelled at me for not following a 'see also' citation with a parenthetical—like, really yelled at me, totally flipped out. She was a complete bitch about it."

"Look, there's no need to be sexist. She's a tough boss who happens to be a woman. You don't have to call her a bitch."

"This isn't about gender. If a man acted like this, I'd call him a prick. This has nothing do with her being a woman and everything to do with her being a possible Supreme Court nominee."

"That's James's theory too, that she's on edge because she might be a SCOTUS nominee. I suppose it's possible."

"You *suppose* it's possible? It's definite. The change in her since the election has been dramatic. At least in how she treats me. Maybe you haven't seen this side of her because you're her favorite law clerk."

My heart jumped into my throat, almost dislodging a broccoli spear.

"What are you talking about?" I asked. "*You* are her favorite law clerk, by far!"

"Are you kidding me? Whenever she scolds me for something, she always compares me to you. The last time I screwed something up, she said, 'Amit, you could learn a thing or two from Audrey. She is an excellent law clerk who never disappoints me.'"

I put down my plastic fork and started laughing.

"She used the same line with me! When I asked her for more guidance on revising *Hamadani*, she dismissed me by saying that if I had no ideas, 'Go consult with Amit, he has excellent analytical skills.' I can't believe she's pitting us against each other in this way."

"I can," Amit said. "She's a former law firm partner who's now a federal judge. She understands office politics. She knows how to use praise and criticism strategically. And she probably figured that we wouldn't compare notes, since you and James tend to hang together while Larry and I tend to hang together."

"That makes sense. I can see why she has come as far as she has. She's impressive."

"But is she truly that impressive?" asked Amit. "Sure, she's a prestigious judge to clerk for. Yes, she's a feeder judge to the Supreme Court. And she might sit on the Supreme Court herself someday. But how involved is she in the details of your cases? How much does she edit the opinions you draft?"

"Not that heavily. Sometimes I get back mem dispos without a single edit. On published opinions, sometimes she has just a handful of edits, most of them just little wording changes—nothing substantive."

"That's my experience too. My friends who are clerking for other judges have their work edited much more heavily. Sometimes I feel like Stinson is just in it for the prestige—because she likes being addressed as 'judge,' having letters addressed to her as 'The Honorable,' and getting sucked up to by lawyers and law students."

"I think you're going a little far. What about when she's on the bench? People are impressed by how engaged she is during oral argument."

"Okay, but when you watch her during argument in one of your cases, how many of her questions are ones that you prepared and put into the bench book for her?"

"Hmm . . . Many of them."

"For me, practically all of them. She rarely comes up with questions of her own. It's like she's playing a judge on TV: she's good at delivering her lines, and she looks good while doing it, but she doesn't go off script."

I finished up the last bite of tofu. My conversation with Amit was enlightening—and I liked him more now, too—but I had to get back to *Hamadani*.

"Well, part of me is glad to hear that she used the 'excellent law clerk' line on both us," I said. "It means that she thinks we're both doing solid work, even if we make mistakes sometimes."

"True," Amit said. "And she still has the power to make or break our careers, to send us to the Supreme Court—or not. I'm going to keep working my ass off for her."

"Speaking of which, we should get back to work," I said, placing my used dinnerware inside the plastic delivery bag and tying it up tightly. "Thanks for suggesting this; it was interesting to compare notes on our boss. And she's still our boss, no matter what we think of her."

"Yup. Even if the empress has no clothes, she's still the empress."

16

I worked late into the night on both Saturday and Sunday to finish revising the *Hamadani* opinion so I could have it on Judge Stinson's desk before that Monday's meeting. But the meeting was canceled because the judge had to take a last-minute trip out of town for some reason that Brenda declined to specify. Based on the printouts of the judge's travel itinerary that Brenda left on her desk, which we looked at one evening after Brenda had left chambers, we learned that the judge had gone to Washington, D.C. She worked remotely while on the East Coast and signed off on my changes to *Hamadani*, which we circulated to Judge Gottlieb and Judge Hollingsworth in the middle of the week. I wondered what Jeremy thought of my revisions, but we hadn't been in touch since our argument at the coffee shop. I wondered if my changes would be sufficient to keep Judge Hollingsworth on board.

It didn't take long for me to find out. The following Monday, shortly before the chambers meeting, an email appeared in my inbox. I could see only the sender, "Judge Hollingsworth," and the subject line, "*Hamadani*." It was surely his vote. Would he remain with us, or was the majority opinion I had slaved over for so long about to become a dissent? Or would he remain with the majority but condition his vote on certain edits? That would be less than ideal—having put so much effort into the opinion, I felt proprietary toward it—but at this point I was willing to do pretty much anything to hang on to his vote.

Whoops. The trembling of my fingers caused me to open the wrong email. While I appreciated the courthouse librarian alerting us to the arrival of a new bankruptcy treatise, I wasn't very interested right now.

I opened the email from Judge Hollingsworth: "I continue to concur in Judge Stinson's very fine opinion."

"Yes!" I said aloud, making a fist and pounding it against the desk. "Yes, yes, yes!"

"Excited about the new bankruptcy treatise, Coyne?"

James stood in the doorway, smiling, and clean-shaven for Monday morning. I felt the blood rush to my face.

"Sorry, I must have sounded like a total dork. I'm just happy that Judge Hollingsworth signed on to the revised *Hamadani* opinion. And called it 'very fine' too."

"Oh, I didn't see that; guess it must have just come in. Congrats!"

"Thanks. I've been worried about that case. Now we can issue it before the holidays. It's a big relief."

"And it's a big case. I wouldn't be surprised if one of Judge Gottlieb's buddies calls for en banc rehearing."

I groaned. James was right. This could just be the beginning.

"Sorry," he said, "I didn't mean to upset you. That's great news. And the judge will be pleased too. It's nice when positive news comes in right before the meeting—it will put the judge in a good mood."

James was right. Judge Stinson was cheerful and chipper, perhaps because of *Hamadani* or perhaps because Christmas was less than three weeks away. I remembered how great a boss she could be when in a good mood.

After we completed the standard discussion of cases, the judge offered some concluding remarks.

"As we near the end of this calendar year, I'd like to thank all of you for your hard work over these past few months," she said. "You have truly been a pleasure to work with, and what you have produced has been just outstanding."

We all smiled. But the judge wasn't done yet.

"Amit, the opinion you drafted in the *Intellectual Ventures* explains the complex antitrust issues with tremendous clarity. James, the dissent you prepared in *Rivera* is a model of persuasive writing. Audrey, congratulations on *Hamadani*—I don't know if we would have kept Judge Hollingsworth's vote if not for your brilliant revisions. Let's get that opinion finalized and published before he changes his mind!"

Everyone laughed—and I beamed. A federal appellate judge just called my work "brilliant." If only Jeremy could see me right now.

"And Larry," the judge continued, "your writing continues to get better and better. The critical work you do on the immigration and habeas memorandum dispositions helps free everyone up to focus on the published opinions."

Larry grinned, seemingly unaware of the backhanded nature of the compliment.

"Now, as you've no doubt noticed, we are coming up on the holidays. So I wanted to say a little bit about the chambers schedule."

"Judge," Larry blurted out, "I should have mentioned earlier, but I'm going to be gone the week of Christmas."

The judge frowned slightly.

"I realize we haven't talked much about vacation policy," she said. "You've all been working so hard that I don't think anyone has taken much vacation. But I generally appreciate at least a month's notice before vacation."

"Judge, my parents and I are going to Aspen. We go every year at this time."

The judge sighed.

"Yes, that's right," she said. "Your father mentioned that to me a few weeks ago. That's fine. Amit and Audrey and James, will you all be around?"

The question put us on the spot. We had actually been discussing, amongst ourselves, whether we'd be getting any vacation around Christmas. Brenda suggested to us that in past years the judge had given clerks some time off around the holidays. But now that the judge raised the matter, nobody had anything to say.

Finally, Amit—of course—broke the silence. I wondered if Amit ever tired of always being the one to say yes. I wondered what that kind of relentless sycophancy did to someone on the inside.

"I'm planning to be around, Judge," he said. James and I quickly joined him in saying we would be present as well. I would have welcomed a few days off, just to catch up on sleep, but it was no great loss; I couldn't afford to fly back to the East Coast (or anywhere else, for that matter). No trip to Aspen for me.

"Excellent. I'm going to be in Hawaii for a few weeks with Robert and the kids, but I will be working remotely. We have a great deal of work to do, and it must be done as carefully as possible. This is not the time for mistakes."

We all nodded dutifully.

"Of course, things will slow down over the holidays because some of my less industrious colleagues will close their chambers. So I have some additional projects for you to handle during this time. You can divide this up amongst yourselves as you see fit, but I'd like the following on my desk when I return in the new year."

Amit and James and I picked up our pens and shifted into note-taking mode.

"I'd like to get a retrospective of my time on the bench," Judge Stinson said. "First, I'd like a look at my time as a trial-court judge. What were my most notable decisions when I was on the district court? How many cases did I decide? How often was I affirmed by the Ninth Circuit, and how often was I reversed?"

Oy. This was going to require a significant amount of work.

"Second, turning to my time here on the Ninth Circuit, what have been the most important opinions I've written? Perhaps pick out ten and write a summary of each—and find my most notable 'liberal' and 'conservative' opinions, too. And quantitatively, how many majority opinions have I written, and how many dissents? How many cases total have I been involved in deciding, whether in the majority or in the dissent?

"Finally, I'd like a close look at my track record in the Supreme

Court—which I believe is quite good, but I would like the statistics. How many Ninth Circuit decisions where I was on the three-judge panel have gone up to the Supreme Court? How many have been affirmed, and how many have been reversed? And don't forget my history of writing 'dissentals,' or dissenting from a denial of rehearing en banc, when the Supreme Court then agrees to hear the case and reverses. They also show how I get vindicated by the Supreme Court when my colleagues here on the Ninth Circuit go down their wayward path."

The last part of the assignment made everything quite clear: Judge Stinson had her designs on becoming Justice Stinson, and she wanted us to gather all the information needed to make her case to the new administration.

"Thank you, everyone. This will be our last chambers meeting of the year, since I'll already be in Hawaii next week. I wish you all very happy holidays."

Christmas fell on a Tuesday, so Christmas Eve fell on a Monday night. James spent the holiday with his family up in the Bay Area, and Amit spent it with an aunt who lived in the Valley. Jeremy and I still weren't talking, but I knew from Facebook—at least he hadn't unfriended me—that he was back in Chicago for the holidays.

So I spent Christmas Eve with Harvetta. We both had nowhere else to go. Harvetta's mother had passed away, and her father was in prison. I couldn't afford to fly back to New York, especially given how ridiculously steep the holiday season airfares were—which pained me, since I missed my parents and Elizabeth so much.

But Harvetta and I made the most of it. We went to Walmart and bought a miniature artificial tree, just under two feet high, which we decorated with a single strand of white lights and a few candy canes. We roasted a small chicken in the tiny oven of Harvetta's apartment. And we exchanged gifts.

Harvetta opened my gift first—and seemed to like it, as I suspected she would.

"Damn girl. This is the shit!"

Probably not a typical reaction to receiving a copy of Evan Lee's *Judicial Restraint in America: How the Ageless Wisdom of the Federal Courts Was Invented*, but Harvetta was not a typical person.

"And I got you a little somethin' somethin'," she said, handing me a small square package. It felt light; I had no idea what it might be. I removed the red wrapping paper, opened the white cardboard box, and fished the object out from under layers of white tissue.

A snow globe. With the U.S. Supreme Court building inside. I shook it, and white flakes rained down on the white marble palace.

"I know how much you wanna clerk there," she said, "so I thought I'd give you some inspiration."

"Oh, Harvetta," I said, choking back a sob, "it's beautiful."

I meant what I said. My present might have cost more, but hers was more thoughtful. And I also felt bad not knowing as much about her career aspirations as she knew about mine. When I helped her with her résumé in exchange for her driving lessons, she just said she was looking at "government stuff"—which I guessed to be openings at local district attorneys' offices, given her interest in working as a prosecutor. Clerking for the Supreme Court was probably not on her radar screen.

"I'm glad you like it," she said. "Took me forever to find that shit on eBay!"

We laughed and hugged.

"And I got another gift for you too," Harvetta added, a twinkle in her eye. "But you gotta wait until the new year to open it."

As the judge predicted, things were slow over the holidays. We would send out draft opinions to other chambers and get nothing back but silence. Judge Stinson probably should have closed up chambers between Christmas and New Year's, but instead she seemed to revel in how we were working while so many others were not. She would call into chambers at random times, supposedly to ask questions about individual cases, but it felt like she was really just checking in to make sure we were all there (except for Larry, whose Facebook feed showed him enjoying "champagne powder"—whatever that was—out in Aspen). Because of the time difference between Hawaii and California, the judge could keep us in chambers well into the evening simply by calling us right before she had dinner.

Stuck in chambers but with less work to do than usual, I found myself reading legal blogs—SCOTUSblog, devoted to the Supreme Court; How Appealing, focused on appellate litigation; and a number of blogs run by law professors, such as the Volokh Conspiracy and Balkinization. I also started reading a relatively new and strange blog, mentioned to me by Amit, called Beneath Their Robes. The site, launched in November, offered "news, gossip, and colorful commentary about the federal judiciary." It had a pink and green color scheme and a cheeky, irreverent tone. The author called herself "Article III Groupie"—a reference to Article III of the United States Constitution, the provision establishing the federal courts—and she described herself as an overworked associate at a large law firm with an unhealthy obsession with federal judges. She fixated in particular on the Supreme Court and its clerks, whom she called "The Elect"—a group that she came close to joining, after clerking for a feeder judge and interviewing (unsuccessfully) with some of the justices. She viewed SCOTUS clerks much as I viewed them: superhumanly bright, halfway between man and god.

One post on Beneath Their Robes, looking ahead to the start of President LaFount's term in January, tackled the subject of Supreme Court vacancies—specifically, which justice might be next to leave the Court. The speculation centered on the liberal Justice Hannah Greenberg, well into her eighties and fighting her third battle with cancer. Even though Justice Greenberg would clearly prefer to step down under a Democratic administration, it seemed doubtful she could remain on the Court for another four years. Some suggested she might even have to step down at the end of the Court's current term. Another possible retirement was the second-oldest member of the Court, Justice Aidan Keegan, who was pushing 80 and not in the greatest overall health—overweight and a smoker. But since he didn't have any specific illness and seemed as feisty as ever during oral argument and frequent public appearances, Justice Keegan was viewed as more of a long shot for leaving.

Reading the post reminded me: I still had to finish my homework regarding Judge Stinson's dossier on herself. Amit snagged the task of examining the judge's record in the Supreme Court, which was the most interesting part of the project, and James volunteered to look at the judge's record when she was a trial-court judge, which was the least interesting. That left me with the judge's Ninth Circuit tenure to review.

Finding the judge's most conservative opinions wasn't hard, since she took public pride in them, mentioning them frequently during speaking engagements and media interviews. The challenge came from choosing the highlights: in her relatively short (by federal judge standards) time on the Ninth Circuit, Judge Stinson had already issued major rulings that advanced religious freedom, cut back on excessive protections for the rights of criminal defendants, upheld reasonable regulations on abortion, and protected corporations from overzealous plaintiffs' lawyers. Making the case for her SCOTUS candidacy to conservatives wouldn't be hard—and her status as an Asian American woman, and an attractive one at that, wouldn't hurt.

Locating prominent liberal rulings by Judge Stinson, which she presumably wanted to show she wasn't a right-wing extremist, presented greater difficulty. She had joined a number of decisions supporting "the little guy"—a criminal defendant against the government, a plaintiff against a multinational company—but many of these rulings were unpublished or written by another judge. I did find one published opinion by Judge Stinson herself that reversed a criminal conviction, which I included in the collection of her "liberal" opinions, but it involved a textbook case of prosecutorial misconduct that even the most law-and-order judge could not condone. On the civil side, I found an opinion written by the judge in a high-profile lawsuit against a major pharmaceutical company, in which she upheld a jury's $200 million damages award. It wasn't exactly "liberal"—jury verdicts are entitled to significant deference when reviewed on appeal, and the smart and careful district judge had made no legally erroneous rulings—but it would have to do.

Then it came to me: what about the immigration context? Immigration was a hot-button issue for both the right and the left, with conservatives railing against "illegals" and liberals defending "undocumented immigrants." Surely I could find some notable opinions from Judge Stinson in her immigration jurisprudence.

I quickly found a good "conservative" opinion to showcase, a published opinion by Judge Stinson rejecting the asylum claim of an immigrant from Mexico. The facts of the case were not particularly interesting—his claim of political persecution seemed dodgy at best, and internal inconsistencies marred his asylum application—but the language in the opinion jumped out at me. Judge Stinson included the requisite expressions of sympathy for the immigrant, who came from a poor family in a part of Mexico torn apart by the drug wars, but went on to discuss how recognizing dubious asylum claims would be unfair to the many law-abiding immigrants who wait patiently, sometimes for years, so they can come to the United States through proper channels.

Then I turned to searching on Westlaw for a "liberal" immigration decision by the judge. I expected to find a ruling in which Judge Stinson, herself the daughter of an immigrant, deployed some fine rhetoric about the United States as a refuge for the persecuted.

Hmm. That didn't seem right. I tinkered with my search terms and tried again.

How odd. Could I be missing something? I didn't think so—I view myself as a legal research queen, or at least a duchess—but just in case, I switched to a different database and ran all my queries again.

Strange. Could Westlaw be missing something? I hopped over to Lexis and tried my searches in multiple databases. Zilch.

I couldn't believe it. In all her time on the Ninth Circuit, Judge Stinson had never ruled in favor of an immigrant, despite hearing literally hundreds of immigration cases. In the few cases where the panel majority voted for the immigrant, the judge dissented. Sometimes she would offer strong reasoning for her dissent, often getting the better of the majority. But in the toughest cases, the ones where the immigrants had seemingly ironclad cases in favor of asylum, she would still dissent from the ruling in favor of the immigrant. In these cases, she provided no real reasoning to support her vote, just a single-sentence mantra: "Based on the exceedingly demanding standard applicable to claims of political asylum, set forth by the Supreme Court in *INS v. Elias-Zacarias*, 502 U.S. 478 (1992), I respectfully dissent."

Staring at the stark reality on the computer screen before me, I remembered the "homework" assignment that Jeremy had given me when we met up at Intelligentsia Coffee: to look up Judge Stinson's past rulings in immigration cases. I was surprised. And concerned. Was Jeremy right? Was my boss—one of the most well-regarded federal judges in the country, a possible nominee to the United States Supreme Court—nothing more than a political hack?

I wasn't prepared to go that far, but I did feel I owed it to Jeremy to admit when I was wrong. I picked up my iPhone and texted him impulsively, before I had the chance to get second thoughts: "Hey. About that 'homework' assignment you gave me . . . Call me when you get the chance?"

17

January brought with it many things. A new year. A new leader in Washington, President Craig LaFount. A renewal of my communications with Jeremy—we still didn't agree on everything, but at least we were talking again, after I acknowledged he had a point about my boss's immigration jurisprudence. And Judge Stinson, back in chambers, sporting an impressive tan. And that wasn't all, as I learned at our first Monday morning meeting after the break.

"Welcome back," the judge said. "I hope everyone had lovely holidays. Speaking for myself, I highly recommend the Four Seasons Hualalai as a place to spend Christmas and New Year's."

We all laughed at the judge's joke: the notion that any of us, except for Larry, could possibly afford to stay at the Four Seasons during the most desirable (and expensive) week of the year.

"Before we go through all the cases, I'd like to mention two things. First, I'd like to thank you for working so diligently over the past two weeks. I realize that I've been working you much harder than most of my colleagues work their clerks, especially during the holiday season. And I gave you that extra project as well, the comprehensive review of my jurisprudence. I'm not at liberty to explain it fully at this time, but please know that I am aware of, and deeply appreciate, all of your hard work."

I got the warm pleasing feeling I used to get from scoring a 100 on a spelling quiz in second grade. I loved the approval of authority figures—and the judge knew just how and when to dole it out. All the long nights in chambers in late December and early January suddenly felt worth it.

"Second: what do we make of the California Supreme Court's ruling in the *Geidner* case?" asked Judge Stinson.

Whoa—*Geidner* was back? I had been so immersed in working on a complex trademark opinion that I hadn't even realized the California high court had issued its ruling on standing—which I hadn't even had the chance to read. Luckily, Loyola Larry played the stooge so I didn't have to.

"Is that the gay marriage case that got kicked to the California Supreme Court?" he asked.

"Yes," said the judge with a patient smile. "The case that we certified to the Supreme Court of California so that they could decide whether the proponents of Prop 8 have the legal standing to defend the initiative in court."

Suddenly it dawned on me: this was Harvetta's other holiday "gift" for me, the one that I'd have to "wait until the new year" to open. As a clerk to Justice Sherwin Lin of the California Supreme Court, she would have known that the court was about to issue its opinion. But was this really a gift? I wasn't so sure.

And neither was Larry: "Wasn't this the case that you wanted to go away, Judge?"

"When the case first came to the Ninth Circuit, the timing of its arrival struck me as . . . less than ideal," she said. "And I had my doubts as to whether the Ninth Circuit, as a federal court, should be resolving what is arguably a matter of state law. But Audrey's excellent idea of certifying the standing question to the California high court bought us just enough time for the calculus to have changed. And we now have the political cover—er, shall we say guidance—of the California courts. So it now seems to me that the case presents . . . possible opportunities."

The judge directed me to work with Brenda and the other judges' chambers on setting up a date for the oral argument in *Geidner*. That would be a major event. It might even get televised, as the Ninth Circuit did from time to time for certain high-profile arguments.

After the meeting ended, I went into James's office for our usual gossip session. I wanted to check my intuitions about some of the judge's comments against James's. I thought that I had a slightly sharper legal mind and better writing skills than James, having read some of his bench memos and draft opinions over the course of the clerkship so far, but I felt that he had stronger interpersonal skills and a superior ability to read people and situations.

"So," I said, closing his office door and sitting down in one of his visitor chairs, "the judge's super-secret extra project—that has to be about her SCOTUS candidacy, right?"

"Definitely," James said. "And remember her random trip to D.C. in December, the one that caused us to miss a Monday meeting? My guess is that she was meeting with the LaFount transition team. I was reading in the *Washington Post* that LaFount is moving very efficiently on possible appointments, even though he hasn't been inaugurated yet. And even though there's no vacancy on the Court right now, he probably wants to be ready to move at a moment's notice, especially given how elderly and ill Justice Greenberg is."

"That makes sense. But what about the judge's reference to 'possible opportunities' coming out of *Geidner*? Isn't a controversial issue like gay marriage just nothing but trouble?"

"Here's my read. Social conservatives aren't big fans of LaFount; they didn't turn out for him in the general election, and he barely won. He probably wants to figure out how he can win their trust and support—both for governing and for the next election—without alienating moderates. One way of doing that is through judicial nominations, especially Supreme Court nominations, which social conservatives follow closely."

"And so what does that have to do with *Geidner* coming back to the Ninth Circuit? And with Judge Stinson having to deal with gay marriage? How is that a 'possible opportunity' for her?"

"It's an opportunity for the judge to raise her profile, among social conservatives especially, and to advance her Supreme Court candidacy.

I'm assuming, of course, that she reaches the merits of the case and rules against a constitutional right to gay marriage. That would allow Stinson to cast herself as a principled conservative on the ultra-liberal Ninth Circuit."

"Ah . . ."

"Of course, she—or should I say *you*—would have to write the opinion very carefully. It would have to go against gay marriage as a constitutional matter, not a policy matter, and say that an important issue like this should be decided by the people, not unelected judges. That would be how to win over social conservatives without pissing off supporters of gay marriage too much. If you can pull that off, the judge will owe you—big-time."

Exactly, I thought to myself. That's the kind of feat that would get Judge Stinson to recommend me without reservation for a Supreme Court clerkship. Or maybe land me a clerkship with the newly appointed Justice Stinson. Some newly appointed justices take their most favorite law clerks with them from the court of appeals to SCOTUS.

"Sorry we haven't had the chance to chat much lately," I said to James. "I've just been toiling away on this trademark opinion. How was your trip back to San Francisco over Christmas?"

James looked down at his desk blotter for a second.

"I've had better holidays," he said. "My girlfriend and I finally broke up. We had been heading in that direction over the past few months, but over the break we made it official."

Ah, so James *was* straight. And now single. Jeremy might have been right about Judge Stinson's track record in immigration cases, but I was right about the far more important matter of James being straight. Not all well-dressed, well-groomed, well-mannered men are gay.

"Long-distance relationships can be hard," I said to James. "I'm sorry to hear about your breakup."

But was I?

18

Later in January, a few days before Craig LaFount's inauguration, an interesting post appeared on Beneath Their Robes.

President LaFount at Bat: Could It Be the Ninth's Inning?
By Article III Groupie

The Ninth Circuit is hard to beat—when it comes to getting reversed by the Supreme Court. Thanks in large part to outspoken liberals like Judge Sheldon Gottlieb and Judge Marta Solís Deleuze, the infamously left-wing appeals court is constantly getting benchslapped by SCOTUS. And many of the Supreme Court's reversals of the Ninth are summary reversals by a unanimous Court, joined even by such stalwart liberals as Justice Hannah Greenberg.

So this news might come as a surprise for some: as President LaFount prepares to take office, word on the street is that his two top picks for the next opening on the Supreme Court both hail from the Ninth Circuit: Judge M. Frank Polanski and Judge Christina Wong Stinson.

Of course, Judge Polanski and Judge Stinson are not the types of judges who give the Ninth Circuit a bad name. Both are Republican appointees who frequently find themselves dissenting from their colleagues on the left—and ultimately getting vindicated by the Supreme Court.

Even though the Ninth Circuit is the nation's largest appeals court in terms of the number of judges, the Ninth hasn't produced a justice in de-

cades. So the Ninth may be overdue for having one of its members join the high court.

As between Judge Polanski and Judge Stinson, who has the edge? It's hard to say. Polanski has more judicial experience; he was appointed to the Ninth Circuit by President Reagan, while Stinson was appointed by President George W. Bush. Thanks to his longevity on the bench, he also enjoys the advantage of the "Polanski Mafia," his network of powerful former clerks who are sprinkled throughout the upper echelons of Republican legal and political circles. These ex-Polanski clerks, scattered throughout the White House counsel's office, the Justice Department, and Capitol Hill, are fiercely loyal to their former boss and will no doubt push his SCOTUS candidacy.

But Stinson has her strengths as well. She is a few years younger than Polanski, which is a plus in an age when youth is sought not just in Hollywood actresses but in Supreme Court nominees, and she is an Asian American woman, also a definite advantage. If nominated to SCOTUS, Christina Wong Stinson would be the first-ever justice of Asian ancestry—an appointment that would surely play well in the Asian American community, a growing sector of the U.S. population and electorate. And if the next justice to depart the Court is Justice Greenberg, as many suspect, President LaFount will feel intense pressure to replace her with another woman.

But let's not count vacancies before they're hatched. Much will turn on who leaves the Court next, under what circumstances, and when. Stay tuned, chickadees!

Toodles,
Article III Groupie

The Beneath Their Robes post got picked up by Tom Goldstein of SCOTUSblog and Howard Bashman of How Appealing, two leading bloggers about the Supreme Court who were closely followed by the mainstream media. Goldstein and Bashman's write-ups in turn got picked up in the

Los Angeles Times, which ran an article entitled "California Judges Are High Court Contenders." Judge Stinson printed out the *L.A. Times* piece and circulated it at the next Monday meeting.

"Of course, I can't comment on speculation," she said, as we passed the article around the table (although we had all read it already). "But it's certainly nice to be mentioned."

"So it looks like it all started with the blogs—specifically, this Beneath Their Robes story," Amit said.

"I noticed that," the judge said. "I'm familiar with How Appealing and SCOTUSblog, but not with Beneath Their Robes. What do we know about it?"

"It's a new site, all about federal judges, but from a personality-focused rather than jurisprudential perspective," I said. "It's entertaining, sometimes irreverent, quite insidery. The author, who calls herself 'Article III Groupie,' is a woman working as an associate at a law firm who is obsessed with federal judges. And Supreme Court clerks—she clerked for a feeder judge and interviewed with some of the justices, but never got a SCOTUS clerkship herself."

"She sounds like she could be you in a few years," Judge Stinson said. "Except, of course, *you* still have a chance at clerking for the Court."

An awkward silence ensued for a few seconds, which James broke.

"I'm not sure that Article III Groupie is who she says she is," he said. "My guess is that this persona is just an attempt to conceal her true identity."

"I disagree," Amit said. "The bio makes sense in light of the content of the blog. She has the knowledge you'd expect of someone who clerked for a federal judge. The obsession with Supreme Court clerks seems genuine too. And it would be logical for someone who clerked recently to now be working at a law firm."

"Regardless of who she is, I'm grateful for being mentioned in such a positive light," Judge Stinson said. "Let's keep an eye on Beneath Their Robes going forward."

19

As expected, an ally of Judge Gottlieb called for rehearing en banc in *Hamadani*. Judge Marta Solís Deleuze, Judge Stinson's archenemy on the Ninth Circuit, disagreed with the decision and wanted the case to be reconsidered by a larger panel of 11 judges—an en banc court, consisting of Chief Judge Runyan and ten randomly selected judges. Judge Deleuze issued a "call memo" in support of her request for reconsideration.

And it was no ordinary call memo. It was a muscular document, full of vigorous prose, explaining why Judge Stinson's opinion in *Hamadani* was wrong on the facts, wrong on the law, and inconsistent with Ninth Circuit precedent—in short, an embarrassment to the court. The powerful intellect of Judge Deleuze was on full display.

I read through the *Hamadani* call memo three times, each time making me more dizzy than the last. Was I overreacting? Since I had put so much effort into *Hamadani*, Judge Deleuze's harsh criticism felt personal to me. I called up Jeremy for a second opinion.

"Have you read Judge Deleuze's call memo?" I asked.

"Of course! Everyone's talking about it."

"It's a good memo, right?"

"Yeah, and Alinea is a good restaurant."

"Come again?" My familiarity with the world of fine dining was limited to the places Cravath had taken me to as a summer associate.

"It's not just a good memo," Jeremy said. "It's an *amazing* memo. An *intergalactic* memo."

"Ha, well, let's not get carried away. Of course you like it. It's very liberal."

"I'd say this even if I disagreed with its conclusions. Audrey, seriously, it's a fucking great memo. Powerful. Persuasive. The best thing I've seen so far this year."

"Really?"

"Yeah, really. I told you Deleuze was brilliant. I told you about my clerkship interview with her, right? She digested my 30-page writing sample in a matter of minutes, then started asking me incredibly incisive questions about it—better than the ones my faculty adviser posed to me. The woman's a genius."

"I have to run. I need to figure out how to respond."

"Respond? Why bother? You and Stinson are toast."

I thanked Jeremy for his candor and hung up. I needed to go talk to Judge Stinson. But I didn't want to get scolded again for bothering her with "trivialities." I decided to approach the judge casually and not in a way suggesting I wanted advice on how to respond to the call memo.

The door to the judge's office was halfway shut. I knocked, softly, and she called out for me to enter.

"Hello, Audrey," she said cheerily from behind her desk. "Please sit down."

I seated myself in one of her visitor's chairs. The judge was wearing a lilac suit—a little flashy, but perfectly tailored—and still had her tan from Hawaii.

"Judge, have you seen Judge Deleuze's call memo in *Hamadani*?"

"Ah, yes, that just came in. It's no surprise. Given the strength of Judge Gottlieb's dissent, I expected one of his allies to call for rehearing en banc. And Judge Solís Deleuze—she's the daughter of immigrants herself, from Mexico, I believe—has a soft spot for immigration petition-ers. She's never met an asylum claim that she didn't like!"

I chuckled and nodded.

"Judge, have you had a chance to look at the memo?"

"Yes. It's a well-done memo. Judge Deleuze and I are not the closest of friends—let's just say she's no Miss Congeniality—but I don't deny her brilliance."

"Are you . . . concerned that we'll lose the en banc vote? Not because we aren't right—we are, of course—but this is the Ninth Circuit, after all, which historically has been very sympathetic to asylum claims. I'll certainly do the best I can in drafting a response to the call memo that explains why we're right on the law . . ."

"We will soon enter the en banc voting process—emphasis on the word 'voting.' It's not about law; it's about politics. And it's about the numbers. What was Justice Brennan's famous saying about votes at the Supreme Court?"

"Something like, 'Five votes can do anything around here.'"

"The same holds true with Ninth Circuit en banc voting. There are 29 active judges, and you need a majority vote from them to go en banc—so with 15 votes, you can do anything around here. What was the last immigration case that went en banc?"

"I believe that would be *Bitong*, Judge."

"That was a close vote. Let me pull up the tally."

The judge swiveled around in her chair to her computer, found the *Bitong* tally, printed it out on her desktop printer, and handed it to me.

"Take a look. *Bitong* got exactly 15 votes. The *Hamadani* vote should be similar. So we just need to take one or two 'yes' votes and move them to the 'no' or abstention columns. Based on what you know of their overall jurisprudence and their views on immigration cases in particular, who of the 'yes' votes from *Bitong* do you see as most persuadable on *Hamadani*?"

I scanned the list. Even though I wasn't even at the halfway mark for the one-year clerkship, I already felt I knew these judges and their views reasonably well. I zeroed in on two: Judge Dennis O'Sullivan, a highly regarded Republican appointee with chambers in Portland, and Judge Robyn Hagan, a conservative Democratic appointee down in San Diego.

"I would say . . . Judge O'Sullivan and Judge Hagan."

"Excellent. Those are names I can work with."

Judge Stinson picked up the phone. "Brenda, get me Judge O'Sullivan on the phone, please."

I started to stand up, to give Judge Stinson privacy for the call, but she gestured for me to remain seated.

"Dennis, how *are* you? It's Christina Stinson . . . Excellent, thank you. How were your holidays? Did you and Melinda go skiing at Sunriver again? . . . Yes, Robert and I and the kids were in Hawaii, as usual . . . It *is* exciting about President LaFount, isn't it? Perhaps he can shift this court a little more in our direction over the next few years . . . So, on that note—as you may have seen, Marta has called for an en banc in *Hamadani*, one of my immigration cases. And last week, she called for an en banc in *Grimaldi*, one of your habeas cases. I honestly can't fathom it, since your opinion in *Grimaldi* is just superb . . . Well, thank you, that's very kind of you to say. *Hamadani* is a tough case, as is *Grimaldi*, but I don't think either merits rehearing en banc—at this point, I say let's leave it to the folks upstairs . . . Excellent. I'm glad we see eye to eye on this. I have to run now, but I look forward to seeing you at the en banc hearing in San Francisco in a few weeks. Regards to Melinda!"

Judge Stinson put down the phone, smiled, and picked up the phone again.

"Brenda, please connect with me with Judge Hagan . . . Robyn, how *are* you? It's Christina Stinson . . . Yes, just lovely—Robert and I took the kids to Hawaii again. And were you and Jonathan in Cabo? . . . Wonderful. Now, I know it's only January, but I just wanted to call to remind you to 'save the date' for our Oscars party, if you'd be free then . . . Yes, just like last year—we do it on the Friday night before because so many of Robert's clients have to, you know, actually *go* to the Oscars! . . . Great, so glad you can make it—I know it's a bit of a schlep for you to come up here from San Diego, but you're of course welcome to stay overnight in our guest house if you like. Oh, one other thing—as you may have just seen, Marta has called for an en banc in *Hamadani* . . . Yes, that's the case, it was covered in the *L.A. Times*, although I think the article got some things wrong . . . It's a difficult case, yes, but I think if you look closely at the opinion, you'll see that it's not worth revisiting en banc—it's just a difficult case that reasonable minds can disagree about . . . Yes, I think that would be a sound approach—abstention. I certainly know I abstain from voting in favor of en banc unless I'm 100 percent certain the panel got it very, very wrong . . . Lovely. Well, I look forward to seeing you and Jon at our party in a few weeks!"

Judge Stinson hung up the phone and flashed a big grin at me.

"I'm certain your response to Judge Deleuze's call memo will be excellent, but rest assured that *Hamadani* is not going en banc. We should put our best effort into the legal arguments, but allow me to paraphrase Carl von Clausewitz: law is just politics by other means."

I laughed at the judge's witticism—but when she met my laughter with a serious look, I quickly stopped.

"Sorry, Judge, I just thought that was a great description of how things work. And you did such an amazing job of talking to Judge O'Sullivan and Judge Hagan."

"Thank you for noticing. Some people naively think that being a good appellate judge is all about legal analysis, but that's so far from the truth. Yes, you need a decent legal mind, but that's necessary rather than sufficient. You need to be a good manager, so you can make the most of your chambers staff. You need to be a shrewd politician, so you can deal with your colleagues. For me, coming up through the ranks at Gibson Dunn, and then overseeing associates and staff while I was a partner, was excellent preparation for being a judge. Now I'm essentially running a small law firm—this chambers. This is why those of us who came to the bench from high positions in private practice or government are such better judges than the former law professors, whose 'management' experience consists of supervising a research assistant or two."

I nodded enthusiastically. I always enjoyed when Judge Stinson would take the time to offer career advice or share her insights into her work as a judge.

"Speaking of politics," she said, "let's discuss *Geidner* for a moment."

Uh-oh. I hadn't had the chance to dig into the case since it came back from the California Supreme Court.

"I'm sorry, Judge, I've been so busy with other cases that I haven't had the chance to focus on *Geidner*. I haven't delved into the record or read all the cases yet . . ."

"Oh, don't worry, let me just give you some guidance for when you turn to writing the bench memo. By the way, you should order the full record, the complete original case file, from the district court. It will make things much easier for you as you work on the case. And in a case of this importance, we need to make sure that everything is perfect."

"Yes," I said, jotting down a reminder to myself to order the record.

"In terms of my guidance: your bench memorandum should recommend reversing the district court and upholding the ban on gay marriage as constitutional."

I reflexively started to write this down but stopped mid-sentence. Judge Stinson had never before told me, in advance of my writing a bench memo, what my recommendation in a case should be. To the contrary, she seemed interested in getting her clerks' honest take on each matter. What was I missing?

"But Judge," I said, "I haven't had the chance to review the case yet. I mean, it does sound like Judge Nathanson might have gone a bit far, in terms of striking down a ballot proposition supported by millions of Californians. But perhaps I should take a look at the record and do some research into the case law, and then maybe we can discuss . . ."

"Audrey, you are normally highly perceptive, but I fear you are not understanding me here. Your bench memo *will* recommend reversing Judge Nathanson and upholding Proposition 8. And I will review it personally before you circulate it to the other judges on the panel."

I paused, unsure of what to say next. Being told what to write in a bench memo had me feeling uncomfortable.

"Well, I always try to give you and the other judges my most carefully researched work product and my most candid recommendation in each case. And so I do want to be sure to present all sides of the argument when sending out a bench memo that goes out under my name."

Here Judge Stinson paused, picking up a pen and touching its tip to her perfectly glossy lips.

"You have a point. I do not know whether you intended to do so, but you have raised an important issue."

"I have?"

"I do not want the *Geidner* bench memorandum to be received like an ordinary bench memo, sent out by a law clerk in the ordinary course of business, under the law clerk's own name and representing only the law clerk's view. I would like the two other judges on the panel to know that it reflects *my* view of *Geidner*—that I have reviewed the memo and that I agree with its conclusion."

"So how should we proceed?"

"Here is what we'll do. When the *Geidner* bench memo goes out, send it out from the 'Judge Stinson' chambers account, not your personal account. In the memo itself, the 'From' line should read 'Chambers of Judge Stinson' instead of your name. But your other bench memos for this calendar should go out from your personal email account and under your own name. That way there will be no mistaking that this bench memo bears my personal seal of approval."

"Thank you, Judge. I will let you know when my draft memo is ready for your review."

As I left Judge Stinson's office, I felt a sense of relief. I liked Judge Stinson's solution. Having the memo come from the "Chambers of Judge Stinson" rather than "Audrey Coyne" would make clear to everyone that I was merely following orders from my boss.

And that was totally acceptable, given that the judge-clerk relationship is no ordinary boss-subordinate relationship. Even though law clerks are generally intelligent and well educated, we have less of an independent professional identity than even middle managers at a large corporation. Our incorporation into our bosses' professional identities is more complete; we might be able to (gently and gingerly) disagree with our judges privately, in chambers, but to the outside world, we get subsumed under our bosses. Opinions get issued by the judge, not by the clerk who drafted them, even if the judge wrote just a handful of the sentences contained therein (often the case with Judge Stinson, a very light editor—especially when she didn't care much about the subject matter at hand). Clerks are like research assistants to a professor—but at least research assistants get thanked in a footnote or the acknowledgments, while clerks don't get any credit, disappearing into the background so that our boss can get all the glory.

So while the notion of writing a bench memo with a particular conclusion in mind troubled me somewhat, I thought to myself: Judge Stinson is my judge—a federal appeals court judge, nominated by the president, confirmed by the Senate, and boasting years of experience in both practice and on the bench. I'm just a law clerk, less than a year out of law school, who passed the bar exam just a few months ago. Who am I to question her?

20

Superhotties of the Federal Judiciary: Judge Christina Wong Stinson
By Article III Groupie

"Va-va-voom!" Is that the sound of Judge Stinson's red Jaguar? Actually, no—it was what a BTR reader wrote when enthusiastically nominating Judge Stinson in our contest to find the most pulchritudinous federal judges in all the land. This half-Asian hottie combines "fantastic bone structure" with a "rocking body," showcased quite nicely by her "elegant and expensive ensembles." She can easily afford the fabulous fashions of Armani and Chanel: her husband, super-agent Robert Stinson, is one of Hollywood's wealthiest and most well-connected power brokers. He also has strong ties to the Republican Party—which could help Judge Stinson's Supreme Court candidacy, discussed previously in these pages. If confirmed to SCOTUS, this luscious litigatrix would be the first Asian American justice—and the hottest member of the high court.

But does some of that hotness come from the fiery breath of this dragon lady? Word on the street is that Judge Stinson can be something of a judicial diva: temperamental, manipulative, and less than delightful to work for. Sometimes she fires law clerks mid-year, an almost unheard of practice. But even if she's hard on her clerks, she's definitely easy on the eyes!

Will this "lovely lotus blossom" flower into a Supreme Court justice? That's not as clear as her alabaster skin, but here's one thing that's certain: given her beauty, supporters of cameras in the courtroom at One First

Street would love to see President LaFount go the Wong way.

Xoxo,
Article III Groupie

After Judge Stinson told us to keep an eye on Beneath Their Robes in the wake of its mention of her as a possible Supreme Court nominee, I set up a Google alert to inform me of new BTR posts. So I read this post nominating the judge in the blog's judicial "hotties" contest shortly after its publication—as did Judge Stinson, apparently, who summoned me to her office within minutes of the story going up.

When I entered her office, the judge was standing rather than seated, holding a printout of the BTR story. The fact that she had bothered to print out the story struck me as amusing, and I was almost going to joke about it—but it was good that I didn't.

"Have you seen this?" she asked me, tossing the printout across her desk. I picked it up—remaining standing, because the judge was still standing—and nodded.

"Yes Judge," I said sheepishly, not sure of the direction the discussion would take. "I received a Google alert when it went up . . . Congratulations?"

"Congratulations? On being a 'lovely lotus blossom' with a 'rocking body'? This story is sexist and racist, offensive and trivializing. How will I be taken seriously as a possible Supreme Court nominee with this kind of coverage?"

She had a point—which I could appreciate, as an ambitious Asian American woman myself. The world would always find ways to put us in our place, even taking an asset like physical attractiveness and turning it around on us. If we were too assertive, we were dragon ladies; if we were too submissive, we were geisha girls.

"You're absolutely right," I said. "It is quite offensive. But who would take it seriously? The language is so over the top; it's clearly intended as humor, even if misguided humor."

"But the comments about my appearance aren't the end of it," she said, picking up the printout to read from it. "What about the claims that I'm a 'dragon lady' and a 'judicial diva,' and that I'm 'temperamental, manipulative, and less than delightful to work for'? This is damaging to my reputation. It makes me out to be—please excuse the vulgarity—a bitch, for lack of a better word."

There was, of course, some truth to these assessments. But I wasn't about to say so.

"It's just a blog, an anonymous gossip blog," I said. "It's not worth worrying about. It's so far beneath you."

"The problem is that it has what some might view as indicia of re-liability—inside information. The fact that I drive a red Jaguar. That I wear Armani and Chanel. That I'm married to Robert. Where could this be coming from? It's not . . . you?"

"Of course not, Judge! I would never say such things about you!"

"I didn't think so—which is why I summoned you upon reading this. You don't think any of your co-clerks are behind these attacks on me, do you?"

Amit: too much of a suck-up, too ambitious, too risk-averse. James: too nice. Larry: too indifferent, too clueless.

"No, Judge. The story doesn't give information about sources—it just cites 'word on the street'—but I wouldn't be surprised if it came from some of your prior clerks. Perhaps a clerk you didn't get along with, a clerk who turned in subpar work that you disapproved of, a clerk with an ax to grind."

I recalled my orientation with Janet Lee when I first arrived in chambers, including her cryptic comments about how I'd find clerking for Judge Stinson to be "very interesting." I didn't know Janet well enough to have a sense of whether she could have contacted Article III Groupie with dirt on the judge, but I could certainly imagine that there could be disgruntled ex-Stinson clerks out there. She could be a difficult boss sometimes, as all of us had witnessed at one point or another. This didn't mean she wasn't a good judge or a good boss overall; it was simply that she, like so many successful and powerful people, had periods when she might be under stress and more challenging to deal with than usual.

"Audrey, I want to learn more about this Article III Groupie character, but I don't want to contact her myself. I'd like you to reach out to her and see what you can find out about her sources for these negative rumors. And even if it's just a gossip blog, it's clearly one that people are reading. So see what you can do to remedy my reputation."

"Certainly, Judge. I'll email Article III Groupie and open up the channels of communication."

"Oh, but one thing to note: don't mention that you're reaching out to her at my direction. I don't want my fingerprints on this. This should be coming from you as a concerned clerk who feels that her boss has been unfairly maligned."

"Absolutely. I'll convey that I'm acting on my own—which is true. I *do* feel that you've been unfairly attacked, Judge, and I'm happy to do what I can to remedy that."

"Thank you, Audrey. That means a great deal to me."

Before I realized what was happening, Judge Stinson approached me and gave me a hug. I returned the embrace, awkwardly. It was exciting to be so appreciated by my boss, but it still felt . . . weird. You'd get a hug from your second-grade teacher when you left school for summer vacation, not from a prominent and well-respected judge and possible Supreme Court justice.

I was about to return to my office, but the judge motioned for me to sit down in one of the visitor's chairs in front of her desk. She then seated herself in the other visitor's chair, so we were sitting side by side, knees touching. She leaned in.

"Look, I'm not a fool," she said softly. "I know that I can be . . . difficult."

"Judge, I don't think you're at all . . ."

"No, you don't need to come to my defense. I know that I can be— what was the blog's term?—a 'judicial diva' sometimes. I can be difficult, demanding, moody, and manipulative. I like to think that I'm not like that all the time, or even most of the time, but I know I'm like that at least some of the time."

I sat still, looking into the judge's dark brown eyes (which were quite lovely). She clearly did not want to be interrupted.

"But before people criticize me, they should think about where I'm coming from. They should walk a mile in my Manolos—and trust me, these heels are brutally high!"

I laughed, as the judge continued.

"As you may have already experienced in law school, and as you will learn during the rest of your legal career, it's not easy being a woman in our male-dominated profession. And it was even worse when I was coming up through the ranks, when there were many fewer women law students and lawyers compared to today. When I was on the law review at Berkeley, I was one of ten women—on a 50-person masthead."

"It's not that much better today," I said. "In my class, there were 15 women out of 50 editors."

"That gender imbalance will follow you throughout the profession, Audrey. My starting associate class at Gibson Dunn was about a quarter women. It got worse over time, as my female colleagues relinquished their ambition, trading in law firm life for cushy in-house gigs or 9-to-5 nonprofit jobs or, of course, motherhood. And I could have done that too, left the law to become a stay-at-home mother—Robert was already making *tons* of money by that point—but that's not how I'm wired. I run toward challenges, not away from them."

"So how many other women were in your partnership class at Gibson?"

"Other women? Ha! I was the only woman who made partner in my year; there were no women in the partner class before me, and no women in the partner class after. There was only one other woman even up for partnership in my year; she didn't make it, and I knew she wouldn't make it. She was an M&A lawyer, perfectly smart, but not tough enough. If you wanted to make partner as a woman back in those days, especially in litigation, you had to be a real hard-ass—meaner and more aggressive than the men. Because otherwise you'd just get leered at and run over. You should have seen me at depositions; I'd go in there and be a raging bitch. Because if I wasn't, the men in the room would ask me to get them coffee. Or gawk at my—how did that blog put it?— my 'rocking body.'"

I felt such deep admiration for Judge Stinson at that moment. And a new understanding for why she could sometimes be, well, difficult.

"So people need to understand where I'm coming from before they judge. To get where I am today, I had to spend years being tough, strident, and manipulative. That kind of behavior is ingrained in me. It's not something that I can just unlearn—and, to be honest, I'm not sure that I'd want to unlearn it. It's part of who I am, for better or worse."

"So what advice would you give to young, ambitious women today?"

"To be a successful professional woman, you need to be a little monstrous."

Later that afternoon, I sent my email to the author of the Beneath Their Robes blog.

Dear Article III Groupie,

Greetings. My name is Audrey Coyne, and I am a current law clerk to Judge Christina Wong Stinson of the Ninth Circuit. I am writing in response to your recent story that nominated Judge Stinson as a "Superhottie of the Federal Judiciary."

I have had the privilege of clerking for Judge Stinson for several months, and I can emphatically state that she is a pleasure to work for. She is thoughtful, kind, and generous with her praise and her advice. I consider her not just a boss, but a mentor and a friend.

Your story cites "word on the street" for the negative rumors about Judge Stinson. I would like the opportunity to refute these rumors with more specificity. Would you be able to share additional information about your sources so that I can respond to or provide greater context for these allegations? If there is any information I can provide to you to assist in your reporting about Judge Stinson, please don't hesitate to ask.

Your post concludes by raising the possibility that Judge Stinson might someday be nominated to the Supreme Court. I can only hope that this aspect of your reporting is correct, because Judge Stinson would make a superb justice. She is an outstanding judge with an unmatched commitment to the rule of law—a value not universally embraced at the Ninth Circuit, but one that would be welcomed at the Supreme Court.

Sincerely,
Audrey Coyne

Within an hour, I received a response from Article III Groupie:

Hi Audrey. Thanks for your message. I'm afraid I can't say more about my sources, who must remain anonymous to prevent retaliation, but I stand by my earlier reporting. I can assure you that my sources know just as much about Judge Stinson as you do.

While I have you here, let me ask you a few questions about Judge Stinson. You describe her as an "outstanding" judge. What's the basis of your opinion? Is it based on her intellect and her wisdom, as reflected in the quality of her opinions? If so, does she write them herself, or does she edit the work of her clerks? If she edits her clerks' work, how heavily does she edit? In other words, how engaged is she in the day-to-day work of judging? How involved does she get in the intricacies of legal analysis, writing, and editing—the central elements of judicial craft?

I eagerly await your responses to my queries. They will be helpful for purposes of my forthcoming profile of Judge Stinson and whether she truly would be, as you put it, a "superb" addition to the Supreme Court.

Xoxo,
A3G

So much for my foray into public relations. Article III Groupie hadn't just called my bluff; she had seen my bet and raised me. If I were to answer her questions, the answers would not be flattering to the judge—and A3G seemed to know this, with her gloating final paragraph, threatened exposé, and breezy sign-off. I feared that my attempt to rehabilitate Judge Stinson's reputation had actually made things worse.

What to do? I wished I had someone to discuss this with, but I really didn't; it was clearly something that Judge Stinson wanted kept between the two of us. In fact, I felt honored that she picked me out of all the clerks to handle this highly sensitive matter. I was arguably the natural choice as the only female clerk—the "hotties" post raised gender issues, and perhaps the judge felt that I, as a woman, would have a better chance of establishing a rapport with a female blogger—but I still viewed it as a vote of confidence.

After spending half an hour staring at the bare walls of my windowless office—since we were there for just a year, clerks generally didn't bother decorating—I decided I needed to talk to the judge and update her on the latest developments. I feared that she'd blow up at me for failing to make the problem go away, but I didn't have much of an alternative. If I continued to try and handle this on my own, only to see it get worse and worse, I'd be in much deeper trouble than if I had kept her in the loop the whole time. (Yes, I watched ABC Afterschool Specials as a child.)

I printed out my email exchange with A3G and went in to see Judge Stinson. I tried to manage her expectations as soon as I crossed the threshold into her office: "Judge, I'm afraid I have some bad news."

I handed the printout to the judge and seated myself in one of the visitor's chairs as I watched her read. Anger flashed across her face for a moment, before she started shaking her head in a "no" motion—while smiling.

"For someone who writes a blog about the federal judiciary, this Article III Groupie has a very naive view of the judicial role," Judge Stinson said. "She seems to think we still live in the age of Justice Jackson, with judges laboring for hours on the language in each opinion, like Michelangelo painting the Sistine Chapel. I decide hundreds of cases each year. Do you think I have the time to write each one of those opinions myself?"

"I don't think that would be possible, at least here on the Ninth Circuit. Maybe on the Supreme Court, which hears under a hundred cases a year."

"But even the justices don't write their own opinions! Judges today aren't writers, but managers. I am the CEO of this chambers: I use my expert judgment and accumulated wisdom to make the big, important decisions. As the president who appointed me famously said, 'I am the decider.' The president, as commander in chief of the armed forces, decides whom we fight and when, but we don't expect him to drive a tank. Similarly, I decide how a case should come out—like *Geidner*, say—and my team executes. The president didn't appoint me to this job so that I could dither over whether to cite this case or that one for the summary judgment standard. Legal analysis is for little people."

I laughed, then caught myself. Was I one of the "little people"?

"Sorry, don't get me wrong. Legal analysis is very important. But I'm comfortable leaving it in the hands of my very capable law clerks."

"Whom you've hired and trained, of course."

"Exactly—and whom I continue to oversee, even if I don't micromanage. Some judges take pride in drowning their clerks' drafts in red ink, but that's not my approach. I don't believe in editing for the sake of editing; it's a waste of time and resources. If a clerk gives me a good draft opinion that reaches the right result for the right reasons, I'm not going to take the thing apart and put it back together again just for kicks, or to gratify my own ego by putting the opinion more in my own voice."

"I have a friend clerking for Judge Gottlieb right now, and that's what he does—he edits his clerks so heavily that he basically rewrites their work."

"That's just judicial self-indulgence. Some judges enjoy getting down in the weeds, arguing with their clerks over the meaning of some patch of dicta in a Supreme Court case, or how to word a particular case parenthetical in a footnote. These judges are actually insecure—they feel they have something to prove, they want to show they've still got it when it comes to legal analysis.

"I'm sorry, but that is ridiculous," the judge continued, putting the printout down on her desk and pressing her hand to her collarbone. "Does anyone think that *I* couldn't do detail-oriented legal analysis if I had to? I served on the *California Law Review*, graduated near the top of my class at Boalt Hall, clerked for a federal judge, and made partner at one of the country's top law firms. Trust me—I can do legal analysis if I want to."

I wanted to give the judge a round of applause; her indignation was nothing short of magnificent. But this still left us with the problem of Beneath Their Robes.

"So Judge," I said after a respectful pause, "what should we do about Article III Groupie?"

"It's simple: since she's not willing to play ball, we have to neutralize her. For now, write back to her and say that you can't answer her specific questions without violating your duty of confidentiality as a law clerk. Then find out who she is in real life, and destroy her."

This raised so many questions. How was I supposed to unmask Article III Groupie? And how was I supposed to "destroy her"? I was a law clerk, not a hit man. Law clerk orientation focused on things like Westlaw research and standards of review, not blogger assassination.

"But Judge," I said, "A3G writes under a pseudonym. I don't know very much about blogging or technology. How can I obtain her real-life identity?"

"You're a smart girl—figure it out. But fast. Take her out before she takes me out."

21

"Wake up, Coyne!"

I startled and sat up. It took me a few seconds to get my bearings. I had fallen asleep at my desk, resting my forehead against my forearms. James stood in my office doorway, holding a giant sheaf of papers held together with a black binder clip.

"What time is it?" I asked.

"It's 8 o'clock on Thursday morning. Hey . . . isn't that the same outfit you were wearing yesterday?"

I looked down at myself. Yes, I was wearing the same navy suit I had worn to the office on Wednesday—although it didn't look quite so crisp on day two.

"Crap! I need to run home and shower and come back. I was here all night working on the *Geidner* bench memo, which the judge wants by tomorrow afternoon so she can read it over the weekend."

"Well, congratulations," James said, tossing the sheaf of papers onto my desk. "It looks like you finished. It was hogging the printer—I had to refill the paper tray."

"Thanks," I said, picking up the memo and flipping through it. "Sixty-two pages—my longest bench memo yet. But it's rough. I wanted to finish it by this morning so I could work on revising it today and tomorrow. I need what I give to Judge Stinson to be my best work product."

"How did it feel writing a bench memo where the conclusion was given to you in advance?"

"It wasn't that bad, actually. It felt like a law school assignment or moot court case where you're just given a side and have to work with it. There are decent arguments on both sides."

I stood up from my desk to get going—and felt slightly dizzy. I was more exhausted than I realized. Even after my morning coffee, I still wouldn't be in the best shape.

"Hey," I said, "can I ask you a favor? I could use another pair of eyes on this bench memo, since it's so important and I'm so zonked. Would you mind reading it over and giving me an edit?"

"No problem," said James, taking the memo as I handed it to him. "Happy to. This is going to be the biggest case we have in chambers the whole year. I'll start reading right now and we can talk this afternoon."

"Thanks a ton. I remember you had some good thoughts on the careful line the judge has to walk here in light of her . . . aspirations. I owe you."

I hustled home to shower and change so that I could be back in chambers before the judge, who usually arrived between nine and ten. When I got back to my apartment, I discovered that my only clean outfit was my least favorite one, a cream-colored pantsuit that I had picked out with my mother before law school. I had been working such long hours over the past few days that I had completely neglected the practicalities of life. The suit was a little wrinkled; I hung it in the bathroom while I showered to try and steam out the creases.

Fortunately, most of the wrinkles came out, and fortunately, I made it back into chambers before Judge Stinson. I still didn't feel that great, but at least I looked presentable, and I made it through the morning with the aid of three cups of coffee.

The clerks had our usual lunch in the chambers library, but Amit and Larry finished and excused themselves fairly quickly; they were both busy with their own bench memos. James and I remained to talk over *Geidner.*

"So," said James, putting my magnum opus on the conference table, "I read your memo."

Why was I so nervous? Don't react defensively, I told myself. You asked James to read the memo because you want it to be as strong as possible. Don't let your ego get in the way.

"Thanks again—and thanks for turning it around so fast. I realize it must have been quite the slog."

"Actually, it was fun to read. I caught a few typos, probably just from you being so tired, and I think the summary of Judge Nathanson's ruling can be tightened. But honestly, as you'll see when you look at my mark-up, there's very little I'd change here. You did a great job."

"Really?" The insecure little girl in me could hardly believe the praise.

"Really. Like your point about how conventional equal protection analysis can't be mechanically applied to 'the right to get married' because this case is all about the definition of marriage itself—in other words, what we talk about when we talk about marriage, and whether the 'marriage' right extends to same-sex couples. Or your point about how our society is currently engaged in a profound and spirited discussion over the meaning of marriage, and how the courts owe both sides the right to democratic debate—that the winners deserve an honest victory, and the losers a fair defeat. You're a very strong writer, Audrey."

"Wow," I said, my voice wavering a bit, "that's . . . so nice of you to say."

"It's the truth. I'm very objective when I put on my editor's hat; just ask the student note writers I terrified back when I was at Berkeley. I've given you my honest opinion, not at all colored by . . . any feelings I might have."

Before I knew what I was doing, my hand was on top of his, James was leaning toward me, I was leaning toward him, and we were kissing. But I broke the kiss quickly—and not just because we were in the chambers library.

"I'm sorry," I said. "I don't know where that came from. Lack of sleep is getting to me."

A wounded look flickered over James's face.

"So . . . was that just a one-time thing?" he asked. "Have I misread things between us?"

"No, it's not that—not that at all. Because . . . I also think there's something here. I just think we should revisit this when we are—or when I am, at least—in a better frame of mind. And not in the chambers library."

"Okay. I'm glad to hear that. Because—and I have to say, this surprised me a bit—you kiss as well as you write."

22

After revising my *Geidner* bench memo with the help of James's excellent edits, I submitted it to Judge Stinson on Friday at the end of the day (so she could take it with her to Malibu over the weekend). After catching up on sleep on Friday night, I headed into chambers on Saturday morning to resume my other mission: finding and destroying Article III Groupie.

As I surfed through my usual favorite law-nerd blogs—SCOTUSblog, the Volokh Conspiracy, Balkinization, PrawfsBlawg, Concurring Opinions, Simple Justice—I found a fresh post from How Appealing that was perfectly on point:

"I have reason to believe that the author of Beneath Their Robes is an employee of the federal government."

Posted at 01:22 PM EST by Howard Bashman

How could Bashman have figured this out about Article III Groupie? All I had was the website address, http://beneaththeirrobes.com/, and an anonymous email address, ArticleIIIGroupie@gmail.com. Bashman didn't have A3G's name, but he knew more about her than I did. And it seemed that, contrary to the claim in her bio that she was an associate at a large law firm, she actually worked for the federal government. This made me wonder: What else about her bio might be manufactured? Could it actually be a ruse?

This was one research project that Westlaw or Lexis couldn't help me with, so I turned to the almighty Google. My reading informed me that the key to solving this puzzle was the IP address, the four-number identifier associated with a particular computer on a network. Numbers scared me a little—an affliction common among lawyers—but thankfully no math was necessary. I just needed to find out Article III Groupie's IP address and see what it matched.

Thanks again to Google, this wasn't hard. I found my last email exchange with A3G—which had ended when I told her I couldn't answer her specific questions about Judge Stinson due to judge-clerk confidentiality—and followed the steps set forth online for opening up email headers. A3G's IP address: 206.18.146.144. I then fed this into a website for looking up the organization associated with a given IP address. The organization associated with 206.18.146.144? The U.S. courts. So not only was A3G probably a federal government employee, as Howard Bashman noted, but she worked for the courts—possibly as a judge or secretary, but most likely as a law clerk.

I thought back to the preceding class of Stinson clerks—Janet Lee, Michael Nomellini, and their two co-clerks. Had any of them left Judge Stinson to go do second clerkships for different judges? Nope—they were all at private law firms now.

Then I thought about my co-clerks and whether one of them could be behind Beneath Their Robes. It definitely wasn't Loyola Larry; he couldn't pull off something like BTR. I also couldn't see it being James—he was too level-headed to revel in the kind of gossip seen on the site.

What about Amit? I had previously dismissed him as too much of a sycophant and too risk-averse. But I didn't know him that well—and I always suspected he was hiding a secret or two. He was the most high-strung among us; could that disposition have driven him to a reckless outlet for the stress of the clerkship?

I thought back to when the site started and how I first learned about it. It launched back in November, after the election—around the time that Judge Stinson become more difficult and Amit started to get frustrated with her, as he confessed to me over our Thai dinner. As for how I learned about the site, it was also from Amit, who mentioned it to the rest of us over one of our lunches in the library. He dropped in the mention casually, but as I replayed the scene in my head, I could absolutely imagine it as an effort to draw our attention to his handiwork.

It soon dawned on me: I didn't need to speculate. I actually had, in my work email account, emails from Amit.Gupta@ca9.uscourts.gov. All I needed to do was open one up and compare the IP address to A3G's address.

My right hand trembled slightly as I guided the mouse through the motions. I found a random message from Amit, when he circulated to the rest of us a list of grammar tips (which I already knew), and opened it. Then I displayed the full original message to open up the headers.

206.18.146.144. Bang. AG, as in Amit Gupta, was A3G. How apropos.

And how advantageous to me. After pondering the matter for a few minutes, I developed my game plan, then exited my office to execute. Standing in the hallway, I surveyed the chambers to see who else might be around. Larry wasn't in (of course), nor was James (who would work on weekends but not until the afternoon, after his long run).

But Amit was in: his door was slightly ajar, his office lights were on, and I could hear typing coming from inside. Perfect. After picking up some pages from the office printer, I knocked on Amit's door and entered, without even waiting for him to answer. He hastily closed a browser window on his computer—clearly I had caught him off guard. Perhaps he had just seen the How Appealing post?

"Good morning, Amit. Reading anything interesting?"

I seated myself in one of his visitor chairs and made myself comfortable.

"Um, no, just came into chambers to do some work for the coming week, you know . . ."

"What else other than work might bring you into chambers on a Saturday?"

He seemed jumpy. I almost felt sorry for him—almost.

"Other than work? I don't know that many people here in town, so I probably spend more time here than I have to."

"And not all of that time is spent on bench memos and opinions, is it?"

"Well, I surf the web and read the news online like everyone else . . ."

"And do you read . . . blogs?"

"Doesn't everyone? The judge expects us to be on top of the blogs."

"But I don't think she expects us to be, well, *writing* one of the blogs."

Amit cast his eyes downward and bit his lower lip. This was too easy.

"What are you talking about?" he asked.

"Amit, I know you are Article III Groupie."

He started laughing—and he was actually not half-bad. I would have to present my proof. I stood up, so that I could look down upon him sitting at his desk, and placed my printout in front of him.

"Take a look at these pages," I said. "The first is an email message from you, Amit Gupta. The second is an email message from your alter ego, Article III Groupie. I've opened the headers to display the IP addresses on both messages, and I've circled each IP address. As you can see, they're identical—just as you and A3G are one and the same."

"I don't know what you're talking about. I don't know this business about IP addresses."

"Exactly—which is how you got busted. I'm guessing that right before I came in you were educating yourself about IP addresses, perhaps after reading the How Appealing post revealing that you work for the federal government. Maybe that's the browser window you closed right before I came in?"

He was speechless. Time to go in for the kill.

"What were you thinking?" I said. "You attacked our boss, a distinguished federal judge. You utilized your work computer for this, a gross misuse of government resources. You wrote about goings-on in chambers, a violation of your duties of loyalty and confidentiality as a law clerk."

I towered over Amit in triumph. He buried his head in his forearms, which were resting on his desk blotter, and whimpered like a dog.

"I'm going to have to report this to Judge Stinson on Monday," I continued. "That won't go over very well. I hear she sometimes fires law clerks—I think I read that on, oh yes, Beneath Their Robes. And in this case, firing would be fully deserved."

"What do you want?" he moaned, his voice muffled by his forearms and his possible sobs. "Tell me what you want. Just promise me you won't tell the judge."

"My demands are quite modest. I have no desire to destroy your promising legal career, and I wish you great success when you return to New York to work at Sullivan & Cromwell. But yes, I do have some requests. First, I have to protect the judge. You need to shut the blog down immediately and never blog again."

"Consider it done. I've learned my lesson."

"Second, you need to withdraw all your pending applications for Supreme Court clerkships. And tell Judge Stinson you're no longer interested in clerking for the Court."

Amit looked up. His eyes were red; he *had* been crying.

"No," he said, with surprising firmness. "I won't do that. I can't do that. It's my dream to clerk for the Supreme Court."

"It's my dream too. But your dream just turned into a nightmare. You should have thought more carefully about your future before you decided to start your stupid blog and trash our boss."

"I didn't trash our boss! I was just blowing off steam. I've been so lonely out here, and it has been so stressful, and I've had no one to talk to about this. My friends are back on the East Coast. My parents don't understand anything about clerking—you can probably relate. The blogging was a kind of therapy for me. I didn't write about any of my cases or anything of substance. It was just harmless, silly gossip. Please, Audrey—don't make me withdraw. That's too much to ask."

"I'm sorry, but I have to protect the justices. Given what you've done to Judge Stinson with Beneath Their Robes, how could you be trusted with the even greater responsibility of clerking for the Supreme Court? You would be a danger to the Court, a time bomb waiting to go off. This is for the good of the Court."

"The only thing I've ever wanted as much was to win the National Spelling Bee—and I did that. I know I have a shot at getting a clerkship with one of the justices."

"I know you do too—which is why you need to bow out."

"You're just doing this so *you* can secure Judge Stinson's recommendation to the justices. But you don't have to force me out like this. We can *both* get Supreme Court clerkships. There's no rule saying that only one clerk in a chambers can get a SCOTUS clerkship. Judge Polanski feeds almost all of his clerks to the Court, year after year."

"Amit, don't play games with me. I'm not one of those pimply teenagers you used to spell circles around in your bees. You know as well as I do that Judge Stinson is no Judge Polanski. She has never had more than one of her clerks at the Supreme Court in a single term."

Amit looked up at me pleadingly. I wasn't wearing heels, but I sure felt like I was, feeling tall and powerful as I loomed over Amit.

"There's a first time for everything?" he offered. "Judge Stinson is getting lots of positive buzz from being mentioned as a possible justice. There's a chance that this could be the year she sends more than one clerk to the Court."

"I can't take that chance. I need to maximize my own odds of landing a SCOTUS clerkship—which means getting you out of the picture."

Amit knew he was defeated, as if he had heard the dreaded ping that sounds when someone gets eliminated from a spelling bee.

"I can't believe this," he said, shaking his head. "You're blackmailing me. This is completely unethical and wrong."

"Not as unethical as what you did. I'm actually doing this for your own good. And for the good of the Court. Anyone who has the poor judgment to do what you did should not be allowed anywhere near the justices' chambers."

"You're an evil bitch."

"I'm going to pretend I didn't hear that. You will go in and talk to Judge Stinson on Monday morning, telling her that you're withdrawing all your Supreme Court clerkship applications. Then, in the afternoon, you will send her an email confirming the conversation. You will bcc me on that email. I want the proof that you followed through on our agreement."

Amit nodded.

"I underestimated you," he said. "I knew you were smart, but I never expected you to be this ruthless."

"I'm just doing what needs to be done. To be a successful professional woman, you need to be a little monstrous."

23

What were all these news trucks doing outside the courthouse? It looked like a crime scene as I walked up South Grand Avenue. It took me a minute to realize that they were here for us—for the Ninth Circuit. This morning the court would be hearing oral argument in *Geidner*.

After a brief stop in chambers, I headed straight down to court. Courtroom 3 was already almost full, even though it was the largest courtroom—the ballroom back when the building was a hotel. The judges' bench was vast, able to fit a dozen chairs instead of the usual three—and this wasn't even the full bench, because a curtain was drawn to hide two additional rows of seating. When the curtain was open, Courtroom 3 looked like a legislative chamber. This courtroom, along with one up in San Francisco, was designed for the possibility of a so-called "super en banc," featuring all active judges of the court—almost 30 in all—hearing a case at the same time. A super-en-banc hearing had never happened in the history of the Ninth Circuit, but it was good to be prepared.

This courtroom, while less attractive than the more intimate Spanish Room, at least had superior seating. The long benches, upholstered in a red-orange fabric, were surprisingly comfortable. I seated myself between James and Jeremy, with James on my left and Jeremy on my right. When James slid over on the bench so that our legs were touching, I didn't move away; the contact increased my nervous excitement.

"This will be a fun argument," Jeremy said. "We know where your boss stands and where Deleuze stands. It all comes down to Hagman."

Judge Richard Hagman, a senior-status judge appointed by the first President Bush, was known for being pro-business in civil cases and tough on defendants in criminal cases. His views on social issues like same-sex marriage were largely unknown.

"Hagman is definitely the swing vote," James said. "Hard to predict on something like this. But Audrey did write a great bench memo."

"Of course she did," Jeremy said. "Good training for when she becomes a foot solider to Justice Keegan in his war against the homosexual agenda!"

"How do you know what my bench memo recommended?" I said. "Maybe I came out in favor of striking down Prop 8."

"Ha," Jeremy said, "that's a good one. But I actually do know what your bench memo—or should I say, the 'Chambers of Judge Stinson' bench memo—recommended. My spies are everywhere."

"And what else did your spies have to say about the memo?" I asked. "Did they say it was a good memo?"

"Actually," said Jeremy, flashing a mischievous grin, "they said it was an *amazing* memo. An *intergalactic* memo."

"Seriously?"

"Not quite," Jeremy said. "But yes, your memo apparently impressed Deleuze and her clerks. Not enough to change Deleuze's mind, of course, but enough to worry her over where Hagman might come out."

"That's nice to hear," I said. "But I wouldn't call it *my* memo. It came from the Stinson chambers. And I had a lot of help on it."

I subtly nudged James with my left leg; he returned the nudge.

"All rise! The judges of the United States Court of Appeals for the Ninth Circuit."

We all stood as the panel members filed in and took their seats. Judge Stinson, the most senior active-status judge on the panel, took the center seat and presided.

The courtroom deputy banged her gavel. "The United States Court of Appeals for the Ninth Circuit is now in session."

"Good morning, ladies and gentlemen," Judge Stinson said—somewhat grandiosely, as if welcoming everyone to an evening at the theater. "Let us proceed with this morning's calendar and the case of *Geidner v. Gallagher*. Mr. Sawyer, you may begin."

"Thank you, Your Honor. May it please the court. My name is Gregory Sawyer, and I represent the appellants. They are the official proponents of Proposition 8, which amends the California constitution to provide that only marriage between a man and a woman is valid or recognized in the state . . ."

"Mr. Sawyer," Judge Stinson said, "before you proceed to the merits, let's discuss jurisdiction—something of an obsession of mine. Does this court have jurisdiction? Do your clients have standing to prosecute this appeal, since the governor and attorney general actually agree with the district court's ruling and did not appeal?"

"Judge Stinson, your status as a stickler for jurisdiction is well known to all who practice before this court."

"Indeed," said the judge. "Call me a juristickler!"

The courtroom laughed at Judge Stinson's well-delivered quip.

"Fortunately, Your Honors wisely certified a question to the California Supreme Court . . ."

"Thank you for recognizing our wisdom, Mr. Sawyer!"

More laughter. The judge knew how to work a crowd.

". . . concerning whether my clients under California law have enough of an interest in Proposition 8's validity to defend its constitutionality in court, including in an appeal. The California court answered that question in the affirmative."

This seemed to satisfy the panel. The judges posed a few more questions to Sawyer about jurisdiction, but with all the enthusiasm of toll takers. And the jurisdictional issue was, in a sense, like a tollbooth—something that had to be passed through before picking up speed. Which is what the argument did upon reaching the main issue: the constitutionality of Proposition 8 and its ban on same-sex marriage.

"And now, with the court's permission, I'd like to turn to the merits. The people of California, as well as the people of many other states, are currently engaged in a profound public debate over the meaning and purpose of marriage. The importance of this debate cannot be overemphasized, given the significance of the institution of marriage—an ancient and venerable institution, one that the Supreme Court has described as 'fundamental to the very existence and survival of the human race.' After a full, fair, and extensive public discussion, the people of California enacted Proposition 8, resolving—at least for now—the definition of marriage under California law. And this is what the democratic process is all about, the ability of we the people to decide for ourselves . . ."

"Mr. Sawyer," interrupted Judge Deleuze, "could we the people of California ban interracial marriage through a ballot proposition?"

"No, Your Honor."

"And why not?"

"Because that was previously decided by We the People, capital 'W' and capital 'P'—in the United States Constitution. The Supreme Court has declared state bans on interracial marriage to be inconsistent with the 14th Amendment . . ."

"How is this different? How is Proposition 8 not a flagrant violation of both equal protection and due process?"

"Well, from an equal-protection standpoint, there is simply no rational basis for denying a mixed-race couple the right to marry. There is simply no . . ."

"The rational basis test is the weakest level of scrutiny," Judge Deleuze said. "Throughout the history of our nation, gay and lesbian Americans have been subjected to the most awful and invidious forms of discrimination. Why shouldn't a law denying the right to marry to gay and lesbian couples be subject to heightened scrutiny? Hasn't this court already held that sexual orientation–based laws are subject to heightened scrutiny?"

Greg Sawyer, despite being a seasoned appellate advocate, seemed rattled. Even though Judge Deleuze's questions were not unexpected (and meant largely for the ears of Judge Hagman as swing judge), she asked them with chilling intensity and obvious hostility.

"Well, Your Honor, the precedent you're referring to, the *Witt* case, I believe, is, you see, somewhat . . ."

"Actually," interjected Judge Hagman, quietly and thoughtfully, "I wonder whether the conventional equal protection framework works all that well here, given the nature of the 'right' involved. Can we really say that 'the right to marry' is being denied to a particular group when, in essence, this case is all about the *meaning* of the right itself? Isn't it the position of your clients, Mr. Sawyer, that the right to marry does not include—and has never included, at least in the history of our nation—the right to marry someone of the same gender?"

"Exactly, Judge Hagman. That is exactly our position, Your Honor."

James elbowed me and smiled; the point just made by Judge Hagman came straight from my bench memo. Judge Deleuze scowled, furiously shuffling through a mountain of papers in front of her, while Judge Stinson smiled with her eyes.

"Even if we were to hold that rational basis applies," Judge Deleuze said, "how was there any rational basis for Proposition 8? The extensive record in this case amply demonstrates that this enactment arose out of pure animus—out of nothing more than prejudice against gays and lesbians."

"I would respectfully disagree, Your Honor. There is a rational basis to support the California electorate's decision to reaffirm the traditional definition of marriage. Sexual relationships between men and women—unlike sexual relationships between men and men, or women and women—naturally produce children. As a result, society has a vital and special interest in those relationships, which bring the possibility of unplanned and unwanted pregnancy."

This argument did not go over well with Judge Deleuze. She swiveled her chair so that its back faced Greg Sawyer—an astonishingly rude gesture for the genteel world of appellate advocacy.

"I don't think I disagree with you on that, Mr. Sawyer," Judge Hagman said. "But maybe there's a more basic point here. We can go back and forth over pregnancy and procreation, and over which environments are best for raising children, and over how long we've had the traditional definition of marriage and why. But at the end of the day, is this a debate for the federal courts, or for California? Traditionally, marriage has been the province of the states, not the federal government. And if this is a debate for California, isn't it a debate for the *people* of California? Don't we as judges owe both sides the right to that debate, without interference, so both sides will feel that they got a fair shake?"

Another argument paraphrased from my bench memo—James elbowed me again, and I pressed my leg harder against his in response. I was trying not to smile, but it wasn't easy. We wouldn't know until Judge Hagman cast his vote, but it seemed quite likely that I had made a difference. I just hoped it was in a good way.

24

The next morning, I immersed myself in the statutory intricacies of SORNA, the Sex Offender Registration and Notification Act. It was a big comedown from the excitement of oral argument in *Geidner*, but it accurately reflected the rhythms of life inside the federal courts. Major matters of constitutional law jostled up against cases whose subject matters were boring, distasteful, or both—like SORNA.

I was in the middle of familiarizing myself with the "travel" element of SORNA when my office phone rang. Grateful for the interruption, and seeing from the display that it was Judge Stinson calling from her cell phone, I picked up before the second ring.

"Audrey, please meet me outside in front of the courthouse."

"I'll be right down, Judge."

What could this be about? And why was I the only clerk being summoned? I grabbed a legal pad and pen—going to see the judge without these items would be like showing up to a drug deal unarmed—and rushed downstairs.

When I stepped outside, the judge was sitting inside her red Jaguar coupe, parked at the curb with the engine running. I approached, still puzzled, as she lowered the passenger-side window.

"Hop in," she called out.

"Good morning, Judge," I said, getting into the front passenger side and buckling my seat belt.

"We're taking a little field trip today, Audrey. We're going shopping!"

"Great!"

I hoped my feigned enthusiasm convinced Judge Stinson. The propriety of a midday shopping trip didn't bother me, since it was being led by my boss, but the news filled me more with anxiety than excitement. First, I didn't like relating to familiar people in unfamiliar settings, and a shopping trip with Judge Stinson qualified. Second, I had no money to spend—my modest law clerk salary covered my living expenses and student loan payments, but not much beyond that—and I suspected that we weren't going to Loehmann's.

"We have some things to celebrate," the judge said, putting the car into drive. "And we have some things to discuss. And I have some things to pick up at Giorgio Armani in Beverly Hills. So I thought this would be a good way of hitting multiple birds with a single stone."

"Sounds good."

"And you deserve a break. I know how hard you've been working over the past few weeks, on *Geidner* and all your other cases. You promised me during your clerkship interview that you would work hard for me, and you have kept your promise. I might not always comment on how hard you work—honestly, I take it as a given that my law clerks will work hard—but rest assured that I notice and appreciate it."

"Thank you, Judge. That means a lot to me."

And I meant what I said. This was so much more than a perfect score on a second-grade math quiz or a victory in a high school debate tournament; this was a nationally respected judge praising my work ethic.

The judge glided through a stop sign, then made a wide turn onto South Grand Avenue. I wasn't a good driver, and I could recognize a similar lack of skill in Judge Stinson.

"So the first thing we have to celebrate: Beneath Their Robes has gone dark. Which is a relief, since it sounded like the writer was working on some kind of hatchet job about me."

"Yup, that's right. The site has been taken down completely."

"Now, please don't mistake me; I have nothing to hide, so I wasn't terribly afraid of any so-called exposé. But it might have generated modest controversy. And given certain—shall we say, sensitivities—I don't want any controversies right now."

The judge braked for a red light—sharply—and I lurched forward, before being pulled back by the tightening of the seat belt. Judge Stinson wanted to converse, but I wanted her to focus more on the road.

"Absolutely," I said. "People can seize on the most ridiculous things when trying to oppose someone for high office."

I hadn't mentioned the words "Supreme Court nomination," nor had Judge Stinson, but we understood each other perfectly.

"The demise of Beneath Their Robes—do I have you to thank for that, Audrey?"

The question caught me off guard. My conversation with Amit about it had taken place several weeks ago, followed by all the craziness with *Geidner*, and so I hadn't thought about how to explain the situation to the judge—without outing Amit as Article III Groupie, of course, since that was part of the bargain we had made.

"I don't think so, Judge," I said slowly. "My last email contact with her was telling her that I couldn't answer her specific questions about you because of my duty of confidentiality as a law clerk."

That was technically true. My confrontation of Amit, A3G's alter ego, had taken place in person, not over email.

"So what do you think prompted her decision to take her blog down?"

"Hmm . . . I think she was afraid that her true identity was about to be discovered. Howard Bashman wrote on his How Appealing blog that he suspected the author of Beneath Their Robes was a federal government employee. A few days later, BTR vanished. So I think Bashman was onto something and A3G got scared that she was about to be outed."

Again, technically true—and maybe even more than technically. I wouldn't have figured out that Amit was behind Beneath Their Robes if not for Bashman's comment about A3G working for the federal government. Yes, I was omitting my role in all of this—but I had to, in order to honor my deal with Amit.

"Do you think," said Judge Stinson, craning her neck out to the right as she sloppily switched lanes, "that Beneath Their Robes might return?"

"Absolutely not," I said, this time with more confidence. "I think we've heard the last of Article III Groupie."

"Excellent. That's all I need to know."

We merged onto the 110 going south, where the traffic was moving along nicely—not surprising, given the mid-morning hour. The smoothly moving traffic reduced the judge's sudden braking, which reduced my nausea—a relief to me, since throwing up inside her Jaguar would not enhance the judge's opinion of me. As we drove, we made small talk—catering complications for an upcoming party she was hosting, her daughters' latest successes in violin and soccer playing, and the difficulty of finding a good nanny who was also willing to be paid on the books. Part of me wanted to ask the judge about what she thought of yesterday's *Geidner* argument—and, most importantly, how Judge Hagman had voted at the panel's conference—but I had the sense that Judge Stinson was deliberately avoiding the subject.

In about half an hour, we arrived in Beverly Hills—my first time in the world-famous city, despite having been in Los Angeles for months now. As we drove past the Electric Fountain, which I recognized from the movie *Clueless*, and then along the legendary Rodeo Drive, I openly gawked at the palm-lined streets, intimidatingly glitzy boutiques, and sidewalks so immaculate you could let a baby crawl on them. Judge Stinson mercifully opted for a garage with valet, sparing me the agony of watching her attempt to parallel park, and we started walking down the avenue.

"Welcome to Beverly Hills," said the judge, gesturing toward Rodeo Drive's center divider, planted with a profusion of impossibly iridescent flowers. "Can you smell the floral perfume in the air? This place has spoiled me for the mall."

"I have a feeling I'm not in Woodside anymore," I said, imagining how my mother would react if transplanted from Queens to where I now stood.

"You've come a long way, baby," the judge said. "And so have I. My mother couldn't have afforded a keychain from one of these stores."

We arrived at the Giorgio Armani shop, whose square glass facade, consisting of many smaller glass squares, made it look a little like an Apple store. But once inside, there was no mistaking it for anything other than an ultra-luxurious fashion boutique—especially given the greeting extended to the judge. We were barely inside the store when a tall, athletic woman, boasting a halo of short, perfectly golden hair—a natural blonde, or the best dye job ever—rushed over to us.

"Judge Stinson! So lovely to see you! And is this your sister?"

Shameless flattery—but delivered so earnestly, one couldn't help but admire it. The judge laughed.

"Peggy, this is Audrey, one of my law clerks. Audrey, this is Peggy, who makes sure that I look fabulous underneath my robes."

"It's a pleasure," said Peggy, shaking my hand with a salesperson's enthusiasm. "Are you really a law clerk? You're too gorgeous to be a legal nerd!"

Even though I recognized her effort to butter me up as a potential client—I couldn't afford anything in this store, but she didn't necessarily know that—I still blushed at the praise.

"But I suppose that could be said of Judge Stinson here too," Peggy added. "And I was just reading the other week, she might end up on the Supreme Court?"

The judge politely demurred, but I could see she was pleased that even a layperson like Peggy knew about Judge Stinson possibly becoming Justice Stinson.

"Your Honor," Peggy said, "if you wind up on the Supreme Court, you will be the most stylish justice by far."

"With all due respect to the justices, that's not a high bar," Judge Stinson said. "There's a reason they all wear black muumuus!"

"Well, Judge, you have nothing to worry about—your dresses and suits are ready. Shall we take a look?"

Peggy escorted us back to a large and elegant salon, then left to get the judge's garments. Another salesperson, a petite Asian woman who looked about my age, asked us if we wanted anything to drink. I declined, fearing I'd spill whatever I got, while the judge requested a Pellegrino.

"Here we are," Peggy said, returning with two garments in each hand. "Which would you like to try first, Your Honor?"

"Let's start with the suits and work our way up to the dresses."

First the judge tried on a dark charcoal suit with a skirt that fell below the knee. She looked magnificent—because of course she did.

"It's perfect," Peggy said, as the judge studied herself in front of a three-way mirror. The Asian woman nodded in agreement.

"Audrey, what do you think?" the judge asked.

"The tailoring is impeccable," I said—but not wanting to sound too much like a yes man (or yes woman), I added, "It's more conservative than what you usually wear, in terms of the color and the cut."

Judge Stinson beamed.

"That's exactly what I was hoping to hear," she said. "I want something that communicates 'conservative,' not 'California.'"

Next the judge donned a bright pink suit in wool crepe with long sleeves and a softly rounded neckline.

"Even better than the last suit," Peggy gushed.

"Audrey?"

"You look amazing, Judge. The cut is still conservative, but the color is more aggressive."

"Excellent," she said. "I want the color to pop. I want it to be a victory suit, a suit that says, 'Yes, I'm wearing shocking pink, and you can't stop me!'"

We all laughed. I wondered what occasion the judge was buying the suits for; she already had an extensive collection of Armani, Chanel, and St. John outfits.

After the judge tried on her two dresses—a short turquoise cocktail dress and an elaborate beaded evening gown, both beautiful—the judge turned to me.

"Okay, Audrey, now it's your turn. Let's find you a new suit!"

Yikes. I couldn't afford to buy a suit here. I briefly debated in my head whether I could buy a suit today, to make the judge happy, and then come back and return it over the weekend—but if any alterations were required, that plan wouldn't work. Feeling the beginning of a blush in my cheeks, I leaned in toward the judge and lowered my voice.

"Judge," I whispered, "the suits here are, um, a little beyond my price range . . ."

"Oh goodness, my apologies—I should have clarified beforehand. This suit is my treat."

"But the suits here cost thousands of dollars, Judge. I can't accept such a gift."

"Audrey, you *must* accept—I'm giving you an order, as your judge. I'll explain why later, but it's very important that you accept. Now let's see what they have in your size."

Before I could protest further, the judge had summoned Peggy.

"We need to find Audrey a suit," the judge said. "I'm guessing she's a size two. I was once a size two. Ah, to be young again!"

The judge herself was only a size four, but I refrained from pointing that out—I suspected she still aspired to be a size two, despite being a few decades my senior.

"What kind of suit are you looking for?" Peggy asked.

"An interview suit," said the judge. "Classic and conservative. A 'do no harm' type of suit. Nothing crazy."

"Judge, this is Giorgio Armani. We don't do crazy."

The judge and Peggy chuckled. I wasn't sure why I needed an interview suit, but I wasn't about to argue.

"Audrey, I have just the suit for you," Peggy said. "It just came in, and it will look incredible on you."

Peggy rushed off toward the front of the store, the judge followed, and I trailed behind dutifully.

"Take a look at this," said Peggy. "Isn't it gorgeous?"

It sure was: a classic black suit, with notched lapels, in featherweight Italian wool. It also cost more than $2,000. I felt torn—between desire and embarrassment.

"It's beautiful," I said politely. "But the color black—you don't find it too austere?"

"It can be," Peggy said, "which is why folks often go for navy or dark gray when it comes to interview suits. But I don't think this will be too severe on you. There's something about the cut of the jacket and how it comes in at the waist that makes it almost girlish—still professional, of course, but definitely not the 'I'm going to a funeral' look. Try it on; you'll see!"

The next thing I knew, I was standing in front of a three-way mirror in the most beautiful suit I had ever worn in my life. It felt so right—feminine but professional, playful but elegant, classic but not boring. And definitely not funereal (even though, since I had never been to a funeral, I had no idea what funeral dress might look like).

"I overrule all objections, Audrey," Judge Stinson said, standing behind me and nodding with approval. "It looks sensational."

I couldn't disagree. It was perfect right off the rack. No alterations needed.

"Peggy," said Judge Stinson, pulling out her American Express black card and handing it over with a flourish, "we'll take it."

After effusive farewells from Peggy and her assistant, Judge Stinson and I emerged from the store, shopping bags on both arms. I felt like the Julia Roberts character in *Pretty Woman* after her epic shopping spree.

"So let me tell you about what we have to celebrate," said the judge, as we walked back toward the garage. "First, Judge Hagman will join us in *Geidner* in voting to uphold Proposition 8. Judge Deleuze will dissent."

"That's great news!"

"Second, Judge Hagman told me privately, after conference, that he was very impressed by your bench memo. This didn't come as a surprise, given that several of his questions at oral argument were basically taken straight from the bench memo, but it was very nice to hear. You made a difference here, Audrey."

"Thank you, Judge."

"Finally, I was so impressed by your work on *Geidner* that I called up Justice Keegan and told him that he simply *had* to interview you . . ."

I stumbled on the sidewalk, but fortunately righted myself before falling on my rear. I did stop and put down the shopping bags, as did Judge Stinson.

"Oh wow, Judge, thank you!"

"Audrey, don't act so surprised! You've earned my highest recommendation. You did superb work on *Hamadani*, then you outdid yourself with *Geidner*. I told Justice Keegan about your work on *Geidner*—which impressed him, not surprisingly, given his previously expressed views on constitutional issues relating to same-sex marriage. And after Amit told me he was withdrawing his applications for Supreme Court clerkships—he said he wanted to go straight into private practice and start making money—that removed any doubt in my mind that you're the clerk to push to the Court this year."

"And what did Justice Keegan say?"

"What do you think he said? The Honorable Christina Wong Stinson called to tell him about her best clerk of all time? Of course he wants to interview you!"

The judge reached out to hug me—a surprisingly vigorous hug.

"That's why I wanted to buy you a new interview suit," the judge said. "To thank you for all your amazing work, and to get you ready for your interview with Justice Keegan. It's an investment in your future and mine—my reputation as a judge is enhanced when I send more clerks to the Court. When we get back to chambers, you need to call the justice's assistant, Mary Katherine, and schedule your interview."

"Will do, Judge."

"Also, have Brenda book your plane ticket to D.C. using my frequent flier miles. If you try to buy your ticket now, it would cost a fortune."

"Thank you, Judge. And thank you again for the suit—it's beautiful."

"It's classic and conservative, perfect for you to wear to your interview with Justice Keegan. Thoreau once said to beware of all enterprises that require new clothes, but from that assessment I respectfully dissent."

When we returned to chambers, after stopping for lunch at the Polo Lounge, I was hoping to slip into my office unnoticed so I could hide the Armani bags under my desk. No such luck: I bumped into both Amit and James in the hallway outside our offices.

"Well hello there, 'Pretty Woman,'" James said. "Did Cravath send over a signing bonus?"

"Her name is Audrey, and she's a shopaholic," Amit said.

"I can explain," I said, waving them inside my office. I then told them the whole story of how Judge Stinson conscripted me for shopping duty, concluding with the news about my landing an interview with Justice Keegan.

"Congratulations! That's awesome," James said, with obvious enthusiasm (had we been alone, I bet he would have kissed me). "Good luck. You'll do great. Let me know if you need any help preparing."

"Congrats," Amit said, with considerably less enthusiasm. "It's your last clear chance at a SCOTUS clerkship, so don't blow it."

"What do you mean by that?" I asked—trying to sound nonchalant, but actually concerned.

"Judge Stinson feeds to only two justices on the Court: the two most conservative justices, Keegan and Wilson. Wilson had one slot left for the coming term, but he just filled it."

"Who got it?" I asked.

"Some girl clerking for a state supreme court," Amit said, waving his hand dismissively.

The only state-court clerk I knew was Harvetta. But she had never mentioned to me that she was applying for Supreme Court clerkships.

"Oh, and she graduated from a TTT, too," Amit added.

"What's a TTT?" James asked.

"It stands for 'third-tier toilet,' and it's used to refer to lower-ranked law schools," I explained.

"I thought that the justices hired mostly from the elite law schools," James said.

"Yes, but not Wilson," said Amit. "Even though he graduated from

U. Chicago himself, he has a soft spot for overachieving TTT grads. Last year, for example, his clerks came from Chicago, Harvard, and two low-ranked state schools. He's weird."

"Or different," I said. "That's why so many people admire him. Not many prominent African Americans have the guts to speak out against affirmative action. Not many judges are so critical of stare decisis. Justice Wilson marches to the beat of his own drummer."

"No, he's just weird," Amit said. "Another strange thing he does is hire clerks years in advance. Now that he's filled his last spot for next year, he's done with clerk hiring for the next few terms, because he has that odd practice of hiring years ahead of time and allocating his clerks between the different terms to have a balanced chambers each year—male and female clerks, clerks from top schools and TTT schools. So with Wilson out of the picture, Audrey, your upcoming Keegan interview is really your only shot at a SCOTUS clerkship."

"But people can apply more than once, right?" asked James. "I've heard of people getting Supreme Court clerkships the second or third time around."

"Yes, but Audrey's situation is different," Amit said. "She's interviewing with Keegan, and Keegan doesn't interview people twice. He considers himself a good judge of character, so when he passes over a potential clerk after an interview, he doesn't consider that person again, even if that person reapplies. He's a grumpy old man, pushing 80, and that's just how he rolls."

"How do you know so much about this process?" asked James.

"It's just a subject I follow. And you hear stuff from people, like law school classmates—word on the street."

Amit and I made brief eye contact. His explanation to James was truthful, but incomplete. Back when Amit wrote Beneath Their Robes, he covered law clerk hiring as closely as TMZ covers celebrity DUI accidents.

"And what's the word on the street about what it's like to interview with Justice Keegan?" I asked Amit.

"It's intense. You meet with the justice for half an hour. Then you meet with the clerks, who grill you about substantive legal issues, focusing on constitutional law. It's a brutal four-on-one interrogation that can go on for two to three hours. And they're also trying to assess your positions on issues, to see if you'd be a good fit with the justice's views—as in, are you conservative enough?"

"Yikes," I said. "That sounds intimidating."

"It is," Amit said. "I don't know how well you'll do, to be honest. You have to remain calm under stress. I imagine it being like the final round of the National Spelling Bee."

"Or like the final round of a high school debate tournament, where you often won," said James, coming to my rescue. "Or the final round of moot court in law school."

"It's not all bad news," Amit said. "You have two things in your favor going into the interview."

"I do?"

"First, unlike some of the other justices, Keegan doesn't interview many people. He typically interviews eight to ten people for four spots."

"Effectively a coin flip," I said.

"Sure—a coin flip with ridiculously high stakes, the most prestigious and coveted credential a young lawyer can get, the pathway to law firm partnership, high government office, a tenured professorship, maybe even a seat on the Supreme Court itself someday . . ."

"And what's the second thing in my favor?"

"You're a girl."

"That *helps* her?" asked James. "I didn't realize Justice Keegan was known for his feminist views."

"Actually, the reason he likes female law clerks got him in some trouble with some feminist law professors," Amit said. "Keegan once said in an interview that, all things being equal, he'll pick a female clerk over a male clerk because he sees having a woman in chambers as a 'civilizing' influence. That remark ticked off some feminists, but if it's true, it's good news for you."

"So be on your 'civilized' best behavior, Coyne," James said.

"Look feminine and conservative," Amit said. "Wear a skirt."

"Of course," I said. "I'll even put on panty hose. I'm leaving nothing to chance."

25

That Saturday, I took a break from drafting the *Geidner* opinion to take a driving lesson with Harvetta. I had graduated from the high school parking lot to the quiet side streets near the courthouse.

"How am I doing?" I asked Harvetta, as I drove her Honda slowly down South Grand Avenue.

"Well, you haven't killed anything yet, so that's good."

"I've never killed anything while driving!"

"Other than the brakes on this car. We're not in the parking lot anymore, so be careful."

I drove along for a few more blocks, at a slow and cautious pace.

"You can go a little faster," Harvetta said. "We're about to be passed by that old lady. In a walker."

I pressed my foot to the gas pedal. The car zoomed forward with unexpected force.

"Audrey, you just blew through a stop sign! Pull over."

I brought the car to a stop in front of a graceful white colonial and turned off the engine.

"You seem distracted," Harvetta said, turning to her left to look straight at me. "Even more spacey than usual while driving. What's up?"

Even though we didn't see each other that often, Harvetta had an uncanny ability to read me.

"I have some good news, but it's also making me nervous. I have a clerkship interview with Justice Keegan in two weeks."

"Shit, that's awesome! Congrats, girl!"

She held her right palm up toward me. After a second or two, I realized what she was going for and high-fived her.

"I'm excited but anxious. His clerkship interviews are supposed to be rough, like an intellectual hazing."

"That was how my interview with Justice Wilson and his clerks went," Harvetta said. "They quizzed me on everything from the history of the 14th Amendment to scienter requirements for the securities laws. It was like an intellectual dick-measuring contest. But I survived it, so you can too."

"Wait," I said, feeling a tightness in my chest. "You had a clerkship interview with Justice Wilson?"

"Yup. And I got the job! I hope you get the Keegan clerkship. Then we can clerk and hang out in D.C. together!"

"Hold on—you got a clerkship with Justice Wilson?"

Harvetta nodded. So *she* was the unnamed TTT grad and state-court clerk who snagged the last Wilson clerkship.

"Remember when I asked you to look over my résumé because I was applying for 'government stuff'?" Harvetta asked. "I was applying for SCOTUS clerkships. I got a call from his chambers about a month ago. I had the interview two weeks ago, and I got the offer a few days ago—Justice Wilson's last clerkship slot for the next few years."

"How come you didn't mention this earlier?"

"We haven't seen each other much lately. And I didn't want to jinx it. And, you know, it's just a job—a job I think I'm gonna love, because I love reading and thinking about the law, but just another job."

"A Supreme Court clerkship is *not* 'just another job,' Harvie," I said, trying to regain my composure. "It's immortality. It's acceptance. And it's incredible that you got it!"

Harvetta's eyes narrowed.

"You seem so . . . surprised. What do you mean by 'incredible'?"

Uh-oh. Had my tone revealed my surprise—my shock, even—at Harvetta landing a Supreme Court clerkship? I'd had no idea that SCOTUS clerkships were even on her radar. Had any graduate of McGeorge Law ever clerked for the high court?

"Oh, well, I just didn't know that you had applied," I said, trying to pick my words carefully, despite the distracting tightness in my chest. "It's just, you know, you're not the typical . . . Your background is . . ."

Harvetta frowned.

"You don't need to finish that thought," she said, holding her pointer finger aloft and waving it in angry circles, like a buzzing bee. "I know the shit that you and your co-clerks talk about people like me. 'Oh, she went to a TTT law school.' 'Oh, she's clerking for a fucking state court judge.' Well, here's something you should know: I *love* the law—I live, eat, sleep, and *shit* the law—and I'm pretty fucking awesome at it."

I remembered the first time I met Harvetta, sitting by the pool reading the *Stanford Law Review*.

"And that's what Justice Wilson looks for in his clerks," she continued. "Smart people who love the law. And luckily for me, he knows that smart people who love the law can be found everywhere. He's not like Justice Keegan, who's super-ass old and buys into all that conventional-wisdom bullshit about pedigree and prestige. Justice Wilson wants diamonds in the rough. He knows that not all smart people go to Harvard and Yale. Or clerk for federal rather than state judges."

I nodded vigorously and let Harvetta continue.

"As for my unusual background, that was a plus for him too. Justice Wilson is a black conservative; so am I. Justice Wilson grew up poor, in a single-parent household; so did I. We totally bonded during our interview. And when I interviewed with his clerks, and started schooling *them* on the ratification debates over the Fourth Amendment and the legislative history of the Fair Labor Standards Act, it was a done deal."

"I'm sorry, Harvetta. I didn't mean to offend you . . ."

"You have a lot to learn, girl. And not just about driving."

That afternoon, I went into chambers to resume work on the *Geidner* opinion. After working for several hours, I decided to take a break and called Jeremy—who was, of course, also at work. I wanted to tell Jeremy the news about my interview with Justice Keegan; I knew he'd be pissed if he heard about it through the law-clerk grapevine first. I dialed his internal extension at the courthouse.

"Hey, it's me. Busy?"

"Of course, my dear. It's a Saturday afternoon in the Gottlieb chambers, and there are progressive causes to be championed."

"Can you spare a few minutes from cause championing?"

"I can spare a few—but just a few, because the judge will be editing one of my opinions soon, and I need to sit there as he goes through it."

"Okay, meet me outside in front of the courthouse in five."

I arrived downstairs before Jeremy did, as always, and seated myself on one of the benches in the garden. I could smell the perfume of the white roses and feel the warm sun on my forearms. Despite having spent so much time inside it, the beauty of the Richard H. Chambers Courthouse and its gardens never got old for me. Even though lawyers and judges worked with words, airy and abstract things, we had done a fine job of appropriating societal resources to build magnificent temples of the law for ourselves.

"Hello, Miss Audrey!"

Jeremy and I exchanged a quick hug as he sat down next to me.

"To what do I owe this pleasure?" he asked.

"I have some exciting news to share. I'm interviewing with Justice Keegan in two weeks."

His face lit up like Christmas. I thought to myself: that's how I should have reacted when Harvetta told me about her Wilson clerkship.

"Oh. My. God! Congratulations!"

"Thanks," I said. "I wanted to share the news with you myself, before you heard about it through the law clerk rumor mill."

Jeremy cast his eyes down for a moment, pausing in thought.

"Do you have something to share with me, Jeremy Silverstein?"

"Your mention of the law clerk rumor mill reminded me: I have some info you might want to know."

"What is it?"

"I heard it a few days ago and I've been going back and forth over whether to tell you. If you didn't also have a Keegan interview, maybe I wouldn't tell you, because it would just demoralize you. But since you do have a Keegan interview, it's actually relevant."

"Spit it out!"

"So one of my co-clerks is a Harvard Law grad. He's friends with another HLS grad who clerks here in Pasadena with us. And she's also interviewing with Keegan this coming Friday—for his last clerkship, apparently. Which he wants to give to a woman, if possible."

"So who is it? Stop keeping me in suspense!"

Jeremy put his hand on my knee. This could not be good.

"Lucia Aroldi. The Polanski clerk."

Lucia Aroldi—the frosty, fashion-challenged HLS grad I had seen in Judge Stinson's waiting room on the day of my interview. I had seen her around the courthouse over the past few months—not that often, because Judge Polanski's clerks seldom left chambers—and she was never friendly.

"Lucia Aroldi—crap," I said, feeling slightly light-headed. "Excuse my French, but—crap, crap, crap."

"Yeah, I know, she's a beast. No offense, Miss Audrey, but since she's coming out of the Polanski chambers, Lucia would be the odds-on favorite here. You know that Judge Polanski is the top feeder judge in the country—and that he has sent lots of clerks to Justice Keegan."

"Yes, Jeremy. I am well aware of his track record."

"And you know that Lucia was a Marshall Scholar."

"Yes, Jeremy."

"And you know that she was the first woman to win the Fay Diploma in a decade."

"Yes, Jeremy. She was tacky enough to mention that in her law clerk orientation bio—along with her 'future plans' for 'world conquest.'"

"This is why I didn't want to mention the news to you. I knew you wouldn't take it well."

I stood up from the bench, dislodging Jeremy's hand from my knee, and turned around to face him.

"No, it's fine," I said, starting to pace back and forth. "I'm glad you told me. I should know who I'm up against. Even if I'm David and she's Goliath."

"Well, maybe David versus Goliath isn't a bad comparison," Jeremy said, a half-smile playing across his face. "You might have a better shot of toppling Lucia than you think."

"Really? You think I can somehow beat out the top graduate from Justice Keegan's alma mater for a clerkship with him? He's a Harvard Law grad himself, and he loves to hire Fay Diploma winners. I'm toast."

"On paper, yes, she's a perfect fit with Keegan. But I'm not so sure that she . . . would fit so well in his chambers, in terms of what he's looking for."

"Why wouldn't she? He's looking for a clerk who's brilliant. She's brilliant. He's looking for a woman . . ."

"And so is she, according to my gossipy co-clerk."

"Are you saying—Lucia is gay?"

"That's what people at HLS speculated. She didn't date in law school—too busy studying—but people called her 'Lesbia Aroldi' behind her back. And all the other LGBT clerks here think she's one of us too. I don't mean to propagate stereotypes, but she does look rather butch, doesn't she?"

"That is true," I said, recalling her mannish haircut and masculine swagger.

"So if Keegan is looking for that 'civilizing' female influence in chambers, I'm not sure Lucia fits the bill. And given how old and conservative he is, and how outspoken he is about the 'homosexual agenda,' I don't think he'd love to have a lesbo in chambers either."

"But we're not *sure* about this, right? And even if we were, there's not really anything that I can do about it, is there? I'm not about to go in for my Keegan interview and out her—'Oh, you should hire me because the other woman you're interviewing is a big old lesbian!'"

"Oh no, you wouldn't *dare* out a gay person," Jeremy said. "You and your boss just want to deny us our constitutional right to marry. How's *Geidner* coming along?"

I stuck my tongue out at Jeremy and mock-kicked his shin.

"It was the people of California who voted against gay marriage, when they passed Proposition 8. And the fate of Prop 8 is now in the hands of three federal judges."

"One of whom wants to sacrifice the rights of gay Americans on the altar of her boundless personal ambition. Who wants to uphold Prop 8 in a barn-burning opinion that will raise her profile among social conservatives and advance her candidacy for the Supreme Court."

"You're being unfair. Judge Stinson might not agree with you on gay marriage, but I can assure you—based on months of working with her closely—that she's a good person and a good judge. There's a reason she enjoys such an excellent reputation as a judge. There's a reason she's being considered for the Court."

"Well, I can think of several reasons she's being considered. She's Asian. She's a woman. She's young. And she's a hack."

"And so is your boss—a results-oriented judge who twists the law to advance his political agenda. But you don't see me going around saying that."

"Actually, you just did. And you and Stinson said as much in *Hamadani*, when responding to our dissent and the en banc call."

"So is *that* what this is about? About you being a sore loser over how Judge Stinson and I trounced you and Judge Gottlieb in a high-profile case?"

"No, what it's really about is you being blinded by your own ambition—just like your boss. You can't—or won't—see Stinson's failings as a judge, because she's your ticket to a Supreme Court clerkship. You've hitched your wagon to her star—and you won't unhitch, even if the star turns out to be an ugly-ass asteroid."

"Say what you will about Judge Stinson, but she's gorgeous. Even a gay man like yourself should be able to see that."

"Jeez. Is that what you're reduced to—defending your boss because she's a judicial hottie? Even though she's a lazy judge who, as you've admitted to me before, depends heavily on her clerks and barely edits what you write for her?"

"For someone who has been clerking for several months now, you have a very naïve view of the judicial role. Hardly any judges draft their own opinions—not even justices of the Supreme Court. A modern-day judge is a CEO. She exercises her *judgment* to make the big decisions. The details can and should be left to us, the law clerks."

Jeremy sighed and stood up from the bench.

"Speaking of those details, duty calls—I need to go over my opinion with the judge. I didn't mean to be such a bitch and get into a big argument. Congrats again on Keegan—and good luck."

"Thanks. I'll need it."

26

When Monday rolled around, I found it very difficult to work. My mind kept wandering to my interview with Justice Keegan, scheduled for the Friday after the coming Friday, and to the formidable competition posed by Lucia Aroldi. Part of me was glad that Jeremy had told me about her, but part of me was not; I felt that all I could do was stress about it. It was an itch that I couldn't scratch.

Finally—without any concrete plan, but feeling that I had to do *something*—I emailed Lucia at her Ninth Circuit email address:

Hi Lucia. My name is Audrey Coyne, and I'm also a law clerk for the Ninth Circuit in Pasadena, clerking for Judge Stinson. I've heard through the grapevine that you have a clerkship interview with Justice Keegan coming up. Congratulations!

I'm actually interviewing with the justice as well. Would you be interested in meeting up for lunch sometime this week to chat and compare notes about what we've heard about the process?

Best,
Audrey

I received a response from Lucia within minutes.

Hi. We don't get a lunch break here in the Polanski chambers—or any

break, really—but we have a roughly 90-minute window in the early eve-
ning when we are free (when the judge drives home to Santa Monica, be-
fore he starts sending us emails and calling us from his home). I use this
time to get the coffee that fuels me through two or three in the morning. I
could do coffee tonight if you'd be up for it.

   —L.

We agreed to meet at 6 that evening and drive over to Intelligentsia
for coffee—with Lucia driving, since I had neither a car nor a license
(just a learner's permit). I was a little surprised by Lucia's willingness
to meet me, given the "I'm going to eat you for breakfast" stare she gave
me when we first saw each other, followed by her general unfriendliness
when we'd see each other around the courthouse. But perhaps she had a
newfound respect for me now that she knew I was also interviewing with
Justice Keegan. Or perhaps she, like me, wanted to size up her competition. I thought to myself: be careful, Audrey.

When I arrived at the courthouse parking lot, five minutes before
the hour, Lucia was already there, standing next to her green Subaru
Outback. We shook hands—and her grip, dauntingly strong, lasted a few
seconds too long. I discreetly massaged my right hand with my left to
help it recover.

"So you don't drive?" Lucia asked as we pulled out of the parking lot.

"No," I said, trying to sound matter-of-fact rather than defensive. "It's
a New York thing. We can get pretty much wherever we want with mass
transit."

We settled into a minute of silence. I noticed Lucia was a very good
driver.

"So where are you from?" I asked, breaking the silence—which bothered me, even though it didn't seem to faze Lucia.

"Oregon," she said, without volunteering any further details.

"Where in Oregon? Portland?"

Because Portland was, of course, the only city I knew in Oregon.

"Eugene."

More silence. Was Lucia trying to intimidate, or just plain awkward?

Thankfully the trip to Intelligentsia wasn't long. Lucia parallel parked with ease, and we went inside. We both ordered coffees, except Lucia took hers black, while I added my usual large dosages of milk and sugar.

"Why do you do that to your coffee?" Lucia asked.

"Do what?"

"Add all that milk and sugar."

"Because I like the taste?"

"I drink mine black."

"I can see that," I said, starting to get annoyed.

We both paused to sip our beverages. I silently admonished myself not to let my irritation get the better of me.

"So," I said, as brightly as possible, "are you excited about your interview with Justice Keegan?"

"Not really. He interviews the winner of the Fay Diploma every year. Obviously I'll do my best, and accept the job if he offers it to me, but there are other justices I'd rather clerk for."

She was practically looking down on a clerkship with Justice Keegan, while for me it represented my last hope of SCOTUS clerkship glory. I tried not to get angry.

"When's your interview?" I asked.

"This Friday."

"I guess he likes to do them on Fridays. Mine is the Friday after this Friday. Are you nervous?"

"No. Why should I be?"

"Oh, I wasn't saying that you *should* be nervous; I'm sure you'll do great . . . But, well, I've heard the process is tough—especially the four-on-one grilling by the law clerks, where they ask you about every complex constitutional-law issue under the sun."

"I can handle tough. That's what drew me to Harvard Law School. I got into Yale too, but one of my mentors at Princeton, who graduated from Yale Law himself, warned me that Yale babies its students. I didn't want to be babied—I wanted the intense, brutal, *true* law school experience, straight out of *One L* or *The Paper Chase*. So I turned down Yale and went to Harvard instead. It wasn't as tough as I had hoped—apparently Harvard has softened over the years—but it was still good training."

Gulp. Lucia sounded like a machine.

"And have you done extra research and preparation for the interview?"

"Polanski sends a clerk to Keegan practically every year, so many former Polanski clerks know the process inside out. I've spoken to every one of them, either in person or over the phone, to get the inside scoop on the experience. Then, this past Saturday, I did eight hours of practice interviews. First the judge and my co-clerks interrogated me for four hours. Then four Polanski-Keegan clerks—two who live here in southern California, and two who participated by Skype—raked me over the coals for another four hours. I'm ready."

Double gulp. Lucia sounded like The Terminator of judicial clerkship interviews—while I hadn't done any preparation, and certainly not an entire day of mock interviews. Feeling stressed out by Lucia's superiority, I steered the conversation in another direction.

"Well, it certainly sounds like you've done your homework. It probably hasn't been easy, given how hard Judge Polanski works all of you. How have you liked clerking for him?"

"It's been a good experience. I wanted tough, and it's been tough. We work seven days a week. During the week, we work from 8:30 in the morning until two or three in the morning, or whenever the judge stops emailing us or calling us or faxing us—yes, he still uses a fax machine—from home. On the weekends, it's a little better—sometimes we can get out by seven or eight at night if we're lucky."

"Those sure are long hours."

"I don't mind. The more I work, the more I learn. Polanski drafts most of his own opinions, including all the published opinions, and we do research for him and give him edits. Once he trusts us, he lets us draft a few things, mostly mem dispos or sections of opinions, but he edits those extensively. We go through as many as 30 drafts of an opinion before we're done. I learn so much from him during editing. He has an incredible legal mind—he can recall the tiniest details, like some footnote of dicta in a case from ten years ago, but he can also see the big picture, in terms of how one opinion might affect the development of the law in, say, a completely different area. He's so fair-minded—he calls each case as he sees it, based on the law. Even though he's personally conservative, he'll vote for the liberal outcome when it's what the law calls for. And he's a great writer—so stylish, yet so clear. I don't think I'll ever have a boss as brilliant as Polanski—even if I clerk for SCOTUS."

So this was how to get Lucia to open up: ask her about work. I enjoyed my work as a clerk, and I liked thinking and writing about the law—especially when a case presented interesting issues, like *Hamadani* and *Geidner*—but I didn't love the law as much as Lucia or Harvetta did. And I suspected that my boss, Judge Stinson, didn't love the law as much as Judge Polanski did. For her—and perhaps for me—excelling in the law was less about law for the law's sake and more about the attendant prestige or status or approval.

"Judge Polanski sounds like an amazing boss," I said. "What's he like as a person?"

Lucia paused. I guessed she preferred talking about the professional over the personal.

"As a person, he has his . . . quirks. He is not your typical federal appellate judge. For a judge, he crosses a lot of boundaries. His sense of humor can be . . . irreverent."

"I sat next to him at the law clerk orientation, and he was very entertaining," I said. "He regaled me with tales of his childhood growing up in Poland under Communism. Some judges can be distant, but Judge Polanski was so warm and friendly."

"Of course he was—to you. You're pretty."

The remark caught me off guard. It was a strange thing for her to say.

"That's very nice of you, but I don't consider myself pretty," I said, babbling nervously and trying to control the flush in my cheeks. "I'm half-Filipina and half-Irish, and growing up, I looked rather . . . odd. I wasn't quite Asian, I wasn't quite white, I wasn't welcomed in either community. I got teased a lot. I was overweight. A definite ugly duckling."

"And now you're a swan," Lucia said. "A gorgeous, beautiful swan."

Suddenly it dawned on me: Lucia was attracted to me—very, very attracted to me. That devouring gaze she gave me when we first saw each other wasn't a look of intimidation, but a look of lust. And now she was attempting—clumsily, ham-handedly—to flirt. I guess they didn't teach Seduction 101 at Harvard Law School.

"And so are you," I said—trying to be polite, the way my Filipina mother raised me. "You are very pretty."

"No, I'm not. I know my strengths, and I know my weaknesses. My strengths are that I'm smart, tough, and hardworking. Pretty I am not."

"But you *are* pretty," I insisted. "You have the most lovely eyes."

"Really? You think so?"

"Absolutely. They convey your intelligence, but also reveal a hidden vulnerability."

This was my Irish side talking, the art of blarney I learned from my father. Because Lucia was right: she was not particularly attractive, at least by conventional standards. Her surprisingly large, limpid eyes were her best feature, but not enough to make her pretty.

Lucia lifted her coffee cup to her lips, finished what was left, and smiled with her eyes over the rim. I smiled back.

"This was fun," she said. "I have to get back to work, but can we do this again sometime?"

"Definitely. And soon."

27

Over the next two days, Lucia and I exchanged a flurry of emails and text messages that hovered between friendly and flirty. I played along, somewhat unthinkingly and half-heartedly. I felt so inferior to Lucia in so many ways—no Marshall Scholarship, Fay Diploma, or clerkship with Judge Polanski—that part of me enjoyed interacting with her in a realm where I had the upper hand. She kept on complimenting me, especially on my looks, and while part of it felt creepy, part of it felt good. Ever since my days of childhood insecurity, I've always had a weakness for praise and positive reinforcement—whether in the form of good grades, debate trophies, or text messages from quasi-closeted lesbians.

I got the sense, from how quickly Lucia responded to every message, that she was starved for human contact, smitten with me, or both. She invited me to join her for her early evening coffee run on Tuesday and then again on Wednesday, but I declined both times—the first time because I was busy talking to Judge Stinson about something, and the second time because, well, I felt a little weirded out and wanted some space.

On Thursday afternoon, Lucia emailed me: "Polanski's releasing me early because I'm taking the redeye out tonight for my interview tomorrow with Keegan. Want to wish me luck over a quick drink?" Since I had blown her off on Tuesday and Wednesday, and since Judge Stinson had left chambers early because of one of her daughter's violin recitals, I agreed.

We wound up at Bodega Wine Bar and each ordered a glass of pinot noir. With both of us sober and straight from the office, the conversation started off just as stilted as I expected. Not surprisingly, Lucia was less forward in person than she had been over text message. To help herself prepare for her interview with Justice Keegan the next day—or perhaps to make me feel bad about how underprepared I was for my interview the next week—Lucia made me listen to her recite the holdings of the most important cases of the Supreme Court's last term, along with who wrote the majority opinion and who wrote the dissent, if any. In the digital age—when so many facts are just a few keystrokes away, thanks to Google—rote memorization is less important than it used to be. But I still couldn't help but be dazzled by Lucia's power of recall, which surely played a role in helping her become Harvard Law's top student.

After one glass of red, I was pleasantly buzzed—but with Lucia spouting con law doctrines like the Electric Fountain gushing water, part of me wanted to be outright drunk.

"Let's order a bottle," I suggested. "It's more economical that way."

"I really shouldn't," Lucia said. "I have the interview tomorrow."

"Come on," I said. "One bottle. One bottle!"

"I don't know if that's a good idea."

Feeling slightly tipsy, I grabbed Lucia's right hand with my left and squeezed; she squeezed back, shyly but unmistakably.

"Just one bottle," I insisted. "I'll drink most of it! I can drink—I'm half-Irish, don't you know."

This was something of a lie—not the part about my being half-Irish, but the part about my drinking ability—since I inherited my limited tolerance for alcohol from my Asian side. But before Lucia could protest further, I had obtained the wine list from the bartender and was perusing it eagerly.

One item immediately jumped out at me: the McManis Petite Sirah. The extremely potent California wine that Jeremy and I had gotten majorly drunk on near the start of my clerkship. The wine that sent me into my first Monday morning meeting nursing a serious hangover. Perfect.

Before we knew it, we had a bottle of the McManis and two full glasses in front of us.

"Cheers," I said, raising my glass and looking straight into Lucia's eyes—which were, come to think of it, quite pretty. "To world conquest!"

"I'll drink to that," Lucia said, clinking glasses with me.

We made our way through the bottle, continuing to talk about constitutional law and the Supreme Court's recent big cases. I knew much less than Lucia, but I knew enough to be a decent conversation partner. I consoled myself with the thought that I could do some studying over the weekend; I was always good at cramming.

I noticed that Lucia was drinking more than I was. She seemed nervous—maybe because she had the interview tomorrow, maybe because she was out with me—and seemed to be constantly refilling her glass. I didn't object, since I was already getting fairly drunk myself.

"So," said Lucia—her face wobbling like a bobblehead, the wine strong on her breath—"are you . . . seeing anyone out here? Or elsewhere—maybe a long-distance thing?"

I looked around the bar—partly out of caution, partly for dramatic flair—and leaned toward Lucia confidingly.

"Well, it's a little early, but I think there might be something between my co-clerk and me."

"Which one? The little Indian guy?"

"Oh God, Amit? Absolutely not!"

"Ha, of course not—I think he's gay, actually."

"Really? That never occurred to me. I think he's just asexual. And high-strung."

"I don't know, I've never really talked to him—we Polanski clerks keep to ourselves, in case you haven't noticed—but that guy just sets off my gaydar. And I have good gaydar. Usually. Except when it gets interfered with by . . . projection."

"Projection?"

"You know—psychological projection. Say, you *want* someone to be gay, so they might be interested in you, so you project gayness onto them. So anyway, you were telling me about this thing with your co-clerk."

"My co-clerk James."

"Oh, I know the one you're talking about—the tall, really good-looking one?"

"Yes, I guess you could describe him that way. He broke up with his longtime girlfriend over the holidays. And then recently we were editing a bench memo, and we kissed . . ."

"No, no—*not* good. That's a recipe for big trouble."

"You think?"

"I don't just think—I know. Take it from me. I graduated from Harvard Law School with the highest GPA in five years."

"With all due respect, Ms. Aroldi, your alma mater isn't known for teaching about matters of the heart."

"Actually, Ms. Coyne, the same analytical skills can be applied to romantic concerns. Here are my five reasons why you should not move forward with this co-clerk romance."

"Proceed, counselor," I said, taking another sip of wine. Maybe the alcohol was clouding my brain, but I was strangely intrigued.

"First, a guy that good-looking is going to be a player. That's trouble."

"I know James. We were friends before anything romantic developed. I don't think he's that kind of guy."

"Second, he's your colleague. Everyone knows that workplace romance is a bad idea. There's wisdom to the old saying about not shitting where you eat."

"That's fair," I acknowledged. "Continue."

"Third, you said he just broke up with his longtime girlfriend—over the holidays, quite recently. Any relationship with you would have 'rebound' written all over it."

"I hadn't thought of that," I said, "but you might be right. What's reason number four?"

"Is he your equal?"

"We're clerking for the same judge. That sounds pretty equal to me."

"Nonresponsive. Is he as professionally accomplished as you?"

"He graduated from Berkeley. He was on the law review. And now we're co-clerks."

"Berkeley—isn't that where Judge Stinson went to law school?"

"Yes. What's your point?"

"He's a sentimental hire. She hired him because he graduated from her alma mater. And with all due respect to Berkeley, which is a great law school, it's not Harvard or Yale."

"For your information, not all smart people go to Harvard and Yale. A friend of mine who graduated from McGeorge just landed a clerkship with Justice Wilson."

"Of course she got hired by Wilson," said Lucia, rolling her eyes. "He's the patron saint of TTT schools on the Supreme Court."

"You're such a snob!"

"I'm a little drunk, but in vino veritas. My main point is: even if his credentials are fine with you, how do you know that your credentials are fine with *him*? They've done studies showing that relationships where the woman has more money or power than the man are inherently unstable. Men don't like it when the women they're with outearn them, outshine them, out-anything them."

"I don't think James is like that. He is not the insecure type. I'm far more insecure than he is."

I didn't want to believe her. But part of me wondered whether she might be right.

"He might seem like he's okay with it at first, with you being in the superior position," Lucia said. "Over time, it will get under his skin. It happens to all of them, even the most 'enlightened' ones. This is why I can't deal with men. Or why they can't deal with me. I'm too smart, too aggressive, too intimidating."

Lucia raised her wine glass and downed its contents in an almost violent gulp. She set the empty glass down next to the empty bottle of McManis.

"Here's my final reason you shouldn't date your co-clerk."

Lucia leaned toward me, guided my own wine glass toward the counter, and planted a kiss on my lips. She didn't part her lips, and I didn't part mine—but I leaned into the kiss ever so slightly, almost imperceptibly. I wasn't sure why—was it the wine?—but I did.

"Res ipsa loquitur," she said. Latin legal lingo for "the thing speaks for itself."

"You're a fun one," I said, laughing and touching her knee. "For a Harvard girl."

"I really have to get going," Lucia said, noticeably slurring her words. "I have to go home and pack and get to the airport. But shit, I'm in no condition to be driving."

I motioned to the bartender, who figured out what I needed without my having to say a word—perhaps because Lucia was barely able to hold her head upright—and told me a cab would pull up in five minutes.

"They're getting you a cab. It'll be outside in a minute. I'll handle the check. And give me your car keys. I'll come back tomorrow with James, who does know how to drive, and we can take your car back to the court-house parking lot."

"Thanks, Audrey," Lucia said, stumbling to her feet, then steadying herself by placing her hand on the barstool. "Wish me luck tomorrow!"

"Good luck!"

She dug into her purse, fished out her car keys, and handed them to me.

"Thanks again, Audrey. You're like my only friend out here. Or maybe more than a friend? I hope whatever this is turns out fine. And I hope my interview tomorrow turns out fine."

"Don't worry," I said, stroking Lucia's hand and staring into her eyes again. "Everything will turn out great."

28

I did not feel so great the following morning. Even though Lucia had done most of the drinking, I had still consumed far more wine than I should have. I managed to make it into chambers more or less on time, but with a headache as powerful as last night's Petite Sirah, I was not in peak condition.

"Good morning," said James, materializing in my office doorway. "Whoa—what happened to you?"

"What do you mean, what happened to me?"

"Don't take this the wrong way, but you're not looking so hot."

I glared at him. He stepped inside my office, closed the door behind him, and sat down.

"I mean, you still look hot," he said, flashing that killer smile of his. "Just not as hot as usual. Are you okay?"

"I've had better days. I had a little too much to drink last night. And now I have a hangover—which is the last thing I need right now, given all the work I need to do. I have to finish drafting the *Geidner* opinion, which the judge wants to finalize and circulate early next week. That opinion needs to be perfect, since it's a huge case and Judge Deleuze is just waiting to slice it and dice it in dissent. And I need to prepare for my interview with Justice Keegan, which I can't believe is taking place a week from today. I feel like I'm going out of my mind."

"Relax. Everything is going to be okay."

James looked so calm, and so handsome, and for some reason I just hated him in that moment.

"Relax? Relax? Don't patronize me. Are you working on anything as big as *Geidner* right now? Or do you still have your hands full with that little Indian law case of yours?"

"I happen to find federal Indian law quite interesting."

"And what about my interview with Justice Keegan? It's in one week! Do *you* have an interview for a Supreme Court clerkship?"

"No, I do not. I do not have a SCOTUS clerkship interview. And I'm not working on a blockbuster case like *Geidner*. But there's no reason for you to lord it over me like that."

Was James acting insecure? Resentful of my success?

"Well, I *do* have a SCOTUS clerkship interview coming up," I said. "And I haven't done anything to prepare. Lucia read every single opinion from the last term, as well as all the major opinions of Supreme Court history. And she did a full day of mock interviews with former Keegan clerks too—eight hours!"

"Who's Lucia again?"

"Lucia Aroldi. The Polanski clerk. She's in D.C. today for her interview with Justice Keegan."

Bringing up Lucia reminded me of the kiss. And even with a cloudy mind, I could still feel guilt.

"How do you know this Lucia? I've never said a word to any of the Polanski clerks. They're kind of cliquish. Or maybe they just never get to escape from that prison of a chambers."

"She and I have been . . . hanging out. We went out for drinks last night, actually."

"She went out drinking with you last night? And now she's in Washington interviewing with Keegan?"

"She flew out on the redeye. She didn't have much of a choice—Judge Polanski doesn't like his clerks to miss work."

"Going out drinking, then jumping on a redeye for a Supreme Court clerkship interview the next morning. That doesn't sound like the greatest idea . . . Why are you smiling?"

"I'm smiling?"

"You were. Now you're not. But a second ago you had a big grin on your face."

Was I grinning? If so, why?

"Look, James," I said, "we need to talk."

"Um, isn't that what we're doing right now?"

"No. I mean *talk*. Like really, really talk."

Now he looked less relaxed. He leaned forward in his chair and rested his elbows on his knees.

"Okay. Go ahead. Let's talk."

"Whatever there is—or was?—or is between us, I think we should put that . . . on hold."

James tilted his head to one side, quizzically.

"To be honest," he said, "although I think we acknowledged certain feelings, I don't think we had really started acting on them. So I'm not sure there's anything to put on hold."

"Well, to the extent that there's anything to be put on hold, let's put it on hold."

"That's . . . very lawyerly of you. Okay. Fine."

I paused and put my face in my hands. Why was my head hurting so much? And why was I being so difficult? The anger I felt toward James just a few minutes ago had turned into anger at myself.

"I'm sorry," I said. "I don't mean to be a bitch. I just have a lot on my mind right now."

"I know you do," James said. "And you're not yourself right now. And it's freaking me out a little. I'm blaming this on the stress you're feeling over *Geidner* and the Keegan interview. But when all this is over, let's talk—like, really, really talk."

29

"Back from DC. Dinner?"

Ugh. I had received the text from Lucia hours ago but had not yet responded, instead immersing myself in revisions to my *Geidner* draft. I was torn about seeing her: dying to hear how her interview with Justice Keegan had gone, but not eager to discuss what had happened between us on Thursday night.

But I knew I didn't want to do dinner.

"Really swamped, can't do dinner. But would like to catch up. You here at the courthouse?"

Since we both had company in chambers—Amit was around, and so were Lucia's fellow Polanski clerks (of course)—we agreed to meet in the main courthouse library. It would be deserted on this Sunday afternoon, but it was mostly empty even during the week. In the digital age, legal research had moved online, making physical libraries somewhat obsolete. But I still loved law libraries for their stately quiet and for how they embodied the majesty of the law, contained in endless rows of case reporters. I could see why these beautiful books, in brown and gold and black and red, were now being used to decorate Brooks Brothers stores and high-end hotel bars.

The library of the Richard H. Chambers Courthouse—originally the hotel dining room, back when the courthouse was the Vista Del Arroyo resort—was especially gorgeous. Several large plaster columns supported the high, beamed ceiling, from which hung wrought-iron chandeliers straight out of a medieval castle. At the far end of the room, arched windows admitted plentiful sunlight and offered sweeping views of the Arroyo Seco canyon.

When I arrived, Lucia was already there, sitting underneath the "Chicago Clock"—an 800-pound, wall-mounted clock that had been salvaged by Judge Chambers himself from a demolished courthouse in the Windy City. Seeing her sitting below the massive clock made me think about time—how we use it, how quickly it passes—and how little I had left to prepare for my own interview with Justice Keegan.

As I approached, I wondered how we would greet each other. The answer: awkwardly, with a clumsy half-hug that captured all of the weirdness between us. Sitting down, with the distancing feel of a table separating us, was a relief.

"So," I asked, trying to sound like a curious friend rather than an anxious rival, "how did your interview with Justice Keegan go?"

"Not well."

"I bet everyone comes out of there thinking that. You're just being hard on yourself. How could it have been that bad? You went in so well prepared!"

"And so hungover. First, I showed up late."

Yikes. She showed up late to a Supreme Court clerkship interview.

"Yeah, I know," she said, catching the frown I had tried to suppress. "I've never been late to an interview. But of course I'm late—maybe just five or ten minutes, but still late—to the most important interview of my life."

"It can happen to anyone. How did the interview go once it got started?"

"Not well. I was so hungover, had a huge headache, and couldn't remember anything. I confused *Marbury v. Madison* with *McCulloch v. Maryland*. The justice was giving me a strange look, which was unnerving me, until finally he just interrupted me and said, 'Are you sure you don't mean *Marbury*?'"

"It sounds like just a slip of the tongue . . ."

"Even a 1L at the worst law school in the country knows the difference between *Marbury* and *McCulloch*. Mortifying. But I guess it could have been worse. At least I didn't throw up on him."

I couldn't help laughing. But Lucia wasn't joking.

"I saved the near-vomiting for my interview with the clerks," she continued. "They were ganging up on me, four on one, about substantive due process, and I was flailing, and suddenly I felt this awful welling up from the top of my stomach, and I realized: holy shit, I'm about to puke. I had to excuse myself *in the middle of the interview*—which looked terrible, like I couldn't handle the heat of their questioning—and run to the ladies' room, where I vomited. Audrey, I puked in the bathroom of the Supreme Court of the United States."

"Wow."

"I didn't come back until 15 minutes later. I spent several minutes staring at myself in the bathroom mirror and also sniffing at myself, fearing I had gotten vomit on my suit. When I came back, I knew it was all over. They had hardly any more questions for me. My interview with the clerks lasted for maybe an hour—it's supposed to go on for two or three hours, but it was clear after an hour that I was not Keegan clerk material, so they cut it short. And I was fine with that, because by then I just wanted to get the hell out of there. I tried to explain that I wasn't feeling well that day, and they seemed somewhat sympathetic, but we all knew the truth: it was a debacle."

We sat silently for a few moments. There wasn't much point to my trying to reassure her. She was convinced that it hadn't gone well—and it sounded like she was right. I felt a complex mix of emotions: sadness for her dashed hopes of a Keegan clerkship, guilt over my role in dashing those hopes, excitement for my improved odds of a Supreme Court clerkship, and guilt over that excitement.

"Lucia, I'm sorry."

"It's fine," she said, sighing. "I'll get over it. I just need time."

"No—I mean, I'm really sorry. For any role that I might have played in all of this."

"What do you mean?"

"You were hungover because you went out drinking the night before. With me."

"That was my own choice—and my own fault. It was my idea to go out for drinks in the first place."

"But I shouldn't have encouraged you to drink more. We shouldn't have had that whole bottle of wine."

Lucia gave me that intense stare of hers, the same one she subjected me to when we first saw each other in Judge Stinson's chambers, and placed her hand on top of mine.

"I have no regrets about that wine," she said. "It gave me the courage to share my feelings with you. Which is another reason the Keegan interview was tough for me; my mind was . . . elsewhere. How do you feel about me?"

Guilty. But I didn't say that.

"It's . . . complicated. The other night was . . . intense. I'm still processing it all. I need some time. Can we talk in a week, after I get back from D.C. myself?"

Lucia couldn't hide her disappointment.

"Okay," she said. "I'm holding you to that. We'll talk in a week. Good luck with your Keegan interview."

And she seemed to mean it. Which only made me feel worse.

30

At the conclusion of the Monday morning meeting, Judge Stinson asked me to stay behind after everyone else left—supposedly to discuss the *Geidner* draft opinion, which we were about to circulate, but I suspected she had other matters to discuss as well. It felt a little awkward, but not very awkward; it was clear by now that I was the judge's favorite clerk.

"So, Audrey, how is *Geidner* coming along?"

"Very well, Judge. I should have a draft for you later today."

"Very good. So we should be able to send that out before you leave for Washington. When are you flying out again?"

"Thursday morning."

"Excellent. So that will get you into D.C. by Thursday afternoon. Be sure to get a good night's sleep before the Friday morning interview."

"Absolutely," I said, thinking about how I wouldn't make the same mistakes as Lucia.

"This interview is obviously your highest priority right now. After we send out the *Geidner* opinion—I'll try to turn around your draft quickly—you should shift all your efforts to interview prep. Everything else can wait."

"Yes, Judge."

"Although . . . I don't want to jinx you, but this job is really yours for the taking."

I felt my pulse quicken, but willed my voice to stay calm.

"In what sense, Judge?"

"You may already know this, but you're the final candidate the justice is interviewing. It's between you and a young woman from Harvard Law School named Lucia Aroldi, who's currently clerking for Judge Polanski. I actually interviewed Lucia when she was applying for circuit court clerkships, and she's very bright. Anyway, for whatever reason, apparently she did not meet Justice Keegan's expectations."

For whatever reason? I knew the reason, having brought it into being.

"So I think this clerkship is yours to lose," the judge continued. "If you go in and deliver a half-decent performance, you should get the job. And I know that you'll do far better than that—you'll be splendid."

She stood up from the conference table, as did I, and she hugged me again.

"Judge, can I ask you a question?"

"Certainly."

"Have you ever . . . taken advantage of someone's feelings to get ahead professionally?"

"Do you mean . . . have I taken advantage of my looks to get ahead, taken advantage of someone's attraction to me?"

"Yes. Have you ever done that? And would you say it's . . . ethical?"

"Of course I have," Judge Stinson said, laughing. "And there's nothing wrong with it at all. I actually object to your loaded question, which uses the formulation 'take advantage.' That makes it sound unfair, when it's not. Why not use a word like 'utilize' or 'use'? Have I, on occasion, used my beauty for professional purposes? Of course. And I've also used my brain, my work ethic, my connections, and all my other God-given attributes. What could be wrong with that?"

"Well, if you look at it that way, I guess it doesn't sound that wrong. But some might say—well, if you play on their emotions, aren't you using people?"

"Audrey, should I ship you back to law school?" the judge asked, playfully. "Save your philosophizing for the classroom. This is the real world. This is the legal profession. People use other people all the time; it's called billing by the hour. Clients use their lawyers, lawyers use their clients, and everyone uses everyone else. You need to use everything in your power to get ahead, because rest assured that your rivals are doing the exact same thing."

"And it doesn't make you feel . . . guilty?"

"Not at all. Here's an example. When I was coming up for partner at Gibson, the head of the litigation department—whose support I badly needed—had a thing for me. I'd catch him looking at my legs during meetings, or he'd make inappropriate comments to me when we were alone. What did I do in response? Did I go running to the managing partner to complain? Of course not; I flirted right back. We never *did* anything—he was married, I was already with Robert—but we always had this sexual tension between us, which I did everything I could to stoke rather than dispel. And sure enough, when I made partner, it was with his strong support."

It wasn't exactly like my situation with Lucia—this partner was senior, not a peer, and a man, not a woman—but there were similarities.

"And it was a good thing I made partner, for me and for the firm," she added. "I was the only woman to make partner at the firm in a three-year span, and the only person of color in a four-year stretch."

I nodded and nodded. Judge Stinson was right.

"As women and as minorities," the judge said, "we have a duty to rise as far and as fast as we can. Now, I have nothing against white males—after all, I married one—but the upper echelons of the legal profession are still far too white and far too male. When they were coming up the ranks, white males used every advantage they had, including their status as white males. So we as women should use everything we can—including but not limited to our sexuality—as we climb the ladder. As a wise woman judge who has served on the bench for decades told me at the orientation for new judges, 'There is no more potent weapon in any profession than a woman with a feminine exterior and a will of steel.'"

I smiled. A woman with a feminine exterior and a will of steel. That was me.

"Don't let guilt hit you just because you're so close to achieving your dream," Judge Stinson concluded. "Guilt and self-doubt affect many successful women and people of color. They call it 'impostor syndrome.' We wonder if we deserve to be where we are, if we somehow 'cheated' to get here, if we got unfair boosts along the way. Get rid of the guilt. When you walk into One First Street on Friday for your interview with Justice Keegan, tell yourself this: 'I belong here.'"

31

I had come to appreciate having a windowless office. The austerity of it all cut down on my natural tendency to daydream and live in the future. Without such distractions as views and weather, my office suspended me in time, allowing me to focus on one thing and one thing alone: law.

But on Tuesday afternoon, not even my office could control my thoughts. The day after tomorrow, I would be flying out to Washington, and the day after that, I would be interviewing for a clerkship with the Honorable Aidan Keegan, associate justice of the Supreme Court of the United States.

My office phone rang. I could tell from the display that it was Jeremy.

"Hi Jeremy."

"Hey girl. What are you up to?"

"Nothing. I can't concentrate. I'm pretty useless from a work perspective right now."

"Well, good thing you sent out that *Geidner* draft this morning, I guess."

"How do you know about that?"

"Come on, Ms. Coyne, you've been here long enough to know how everything works. People talk."

"So what else have your spies in the Deleuze chambers told you?"

"You'll be getting the draft dissent in record time. Deleuze is a genius and works fast, and she's been riding her clerks hard on this—they started working on it right after oral arguments, not even waiting for

Stinson's draft majority. Deleuze wants this issue decided as fast as possible, for the sake of all the gay couples it affects."

"Even if her position is going to lose?"

"She'll lose in the three-judge panel. But Deleuze thinks she might win if the case gets reheard en banc. Or if it goes to the Supreme Court. She's super-liberal and super-brilliant, so she can't imagine how her position might lose—even if it does all the time at SCOTUS, because the conservative justices are hacks. Speaking of conservative hacks, all ready for the Keegan interview?"

"I guess. I've been cramming like crazy—it's like the bar exam all over again. But I'm so nervous. I've never wanted anything this badly."

"I don't blame you. Signing bonuses for SCOTUS clerks when they go to firms afterward are around $300,000."

"I'd love that kind of money," I said. "I could pay off my huge student loans and help out my family too. But it's less about the money and more about . . ."

"The prestige? The status? The love?"

"And other things too. Like the chance to be part of history."

"Yeah," Jeremy agreed. "Former SCOTUS clerks have the best war stories. They love to brag about the famous opinions they wrote—er, drafted . . ."

"It's a great learning opportunity—a chance to work closely with the finest legal minds of our time, drafting and editing opinions on the most important issues."

"I hate the man and his politics, but Aidan Keegan is brilliant. And he works closely with his clerks on revising his opinions line by line, just like my boss. You'll get the experience you didn't get with Christina 'Rubber Stamp' Stinson."

"I'm not going to dignify that with a response."

"Okay. But I'm just agreeing with you that a SCOTUS clerkship with Keegan would be tremendous. And to think: it's yours to lose!"

"Don't say that! You'll jinx me."

"I know the Filipino half of you is superstitious, but rumor has it that your main competition, Lesbia Aroldi, flubbed her interview. Some speculate she was hungover. Or distracted."

"Oh really," I said.

"Coyne, you're a terrible actress. You already knew about Lucia messing up her interview?"

"I heard about it from Judge Stinson. I don't know where the judge heard about it from, though."

"I can't believe Lucia didn't kick ass. I wonder what she'll do now."

"Lucia graduated at the top of her class from Harvard Law, and she's clerking for one of the most respected judges in the entire federal judiciary. If she doesn't get a clerkship with Justice Keegan, she won't wind up homeless."

"Fine. But you have to admit that it's still pretty surprising."

"Surprising, yes. But if Lucia had the poor judgment to get drunk the night before her interview, she probably shouldn't be entrusted with the responsibilities of a Supreme Court clerk, don't you think?"

"Well *hello* there, Ms. Self-Righteous! What did you do with my friend Audrey?"

I laughed.

"Sorry," I said, "I didn't mean to get carried away. But I'm not going to shed tears for Lucia. So she had one bad interview. She'll be fine in the end."

"True," Jeremy said. "Okay, I have to get back to work, but if I don't talk to you before you fly out, good luck!"

"Thanks Jer."

I returned to reading—or, more accurately, rereading—my favorite opinions of Justice Keegan. His fiery dissents, full of vivid, vigorous, sometimes almost colloquial language, were my favorites. I thought about how much fun it would be to work together with him on polishing these opinions to a high gloss.

Before too long, I found my mind wandering again. When my iPhone lit up with an incoming text, I was glad for the distraction.

It was from Harvetta: "Oh baby, so sorry about Keegan."

What did she mean by that? I hadn't bombed my interview; that was Lucia. Or, speaking of Lucia, maybe he had hired her, filling his last opening and shutting me out? But how would Harvetta know that? Maybe from the network of Wilson clerks?

I did what any puzzled person would do. I hopped onto Google and entered "Justice Aidan Keegan" into the search box. And there it was, from the Associated Press:

"Justice Aidan Keegan Dies at 79."

I cycled through news websites—the *New York Times*, the *Wall Street Journal*, the *Washington Post*—in disbelief. It was true. The legendary Justice Keegan—one of the most brilliant minds on the current Court, its finest writer, and a huge personality and great storyteller, which he chalked up to his Irish American heritage—had died, of a ruptured brain aneurysm. It came as a shock, but the news reports did point out that he had multiple risk factors: he was elderly, had high blood pressure, and was a longtime smoker.

I wanted to cry—partly for him, and partly for myself. I would never even get to meet Justice Keegan, much less clerk for him. It seemed like a cruel joke by the universe to take him away at this precise point in time. Part of me wanted to cry, but I was determined not to. I thought of how pathetic Amit looked when he cried in front of me over Beneath Their Robes, and I thought of Judge Stinson's words to me from just the other day: "There is no more potent weapon in any profession than a woman with a feminine exterior and a will of steel."

"Audrey."

I turned around. It was the judge. She wasn't crying, but I could tell she was distraught. I stood up, and we hugged.

"I'm sorry to hear about Justice Keegan," I said. "I know he was your friend."

"A great friend, and a great judge," she said, her voice cracking slightly. "And he would have been a great boss. I'm sorry too, Audrey."

32

Eating Häagen-Dazs chocolate chip cookie dough ice cream straight from the pint requires skill. You need to strategically dig in your spoon to capture the optimal balance of ice cream and cookie dough chunks. The chunks are unevenly sized and distributed, so you can't just eat blindly; you need to canvass and calculate as you go along. This was how I was spending my Tuesday evening, after Judge Stinson told me to go home early for the first time during the clerkship, and I was happy to accept her offer. I planned to finish the entire pint.

I was watching a rerun of *The Bachelor*. The death of Justice Keegan was all over the news, but I had no desire to watch the coverage. Nor did I want to talk to anyone about the news—which was why I had not responded to the numerous text messages and phone calls I had received from James, Harvetta, Jeremy, Lucia, or my mother. Not even my mother. I would have more than enough time to contemplate my future after getting to the bottom of this pint and the end of this episode of *The Bachelor*.

In my sugar-induced stupor, I took a while to realize: someone was knocking at my door. The doorbell hadn't worked since I moved in, and I hadn't bothered to get it fixed, since I spent so little time at home and rarely had visitors.

I ignored the knocking. Whoever it was could wait until tomorrow. I'd finish this pint of ice cream, get an obscene amount of sleep, and start with a clean slate tomorrow morning.

My caller would not be ignored. The polite knocking turned into insistent banging.

"Girl, I know you're in there. Get your skinny white ass to this door!"

Harvetta. Attention must be paid. I got up to answer the door because otherwise she'd break it down with her bare hands.

"My half-white ass, for the record," I said. "I'm proud of my Asian heritage too."

"White or black or purple, your ass will be as big as mine if you keep eating like that," said Harvetta, looking down at the pint of Häagen-Dazs I still held in my hand.

I walked across my small studio, defiantly eating an extra-large spoonful of ice cream as I returned to my spot on the couch. Harvetta sat down next to me.

"It doesn't help to eat your feelings," she said.

"I wouldn't eat my feelings if they didn't taste so good."

"You'll get over this. You'll make it through."

"I'm still in shock. I can't believe it. I was supposed to be interviewing with him this Friday. I had a really good shot at getting it."

"It's just a job. There are other jobs."

"Easy for you to say—you already have your Supreme Court clerkship. And you know as well as I do that it's not just a job. It means so much more than that."

"Does it? I want to do it because I love the law, I love Justice Wilson's jurisprudence, and I want to help him turn that mother *out*. But even if he hadn't hired me, there are other jobs out there that would let me get my law groove on."

Harvetta wanted to clerk for the Court because it would be intellectually stimulating and fun. Her view of the world seemed so . . . naïve. But I didn't want to get into another argument with her over the importance of prestige, of which she seemed blissfully ignorant.

"Cravath, here I come. While you're drafting Supreme Court opinions, I'll be reviewing documents, sitting in front of a computer and clicking a mouse until my hand falls off."

"It's not over yet. The president has to nominate a replacement for Keegan. And that new justice might end up hiring you."

Strangely enough, that obvious proposition had not occurred to me—I was so caught up in the death of Justice Keegan that I hadn't entertained thoughts of what would happen next. But the consolation it provided was fleeting.

"It's such a long shot," I said. "Whoever replaces Justice Keegan will probably have different criteria for hiring clerks. Or people he already knows that he wants to hire. With Keegan, I was close, so close. It's like the universe conspired to deny me a Supreme Court clerkship."

Harvetta grabbed a throw pillow and slapped my thigh with it.

"Listen to yourself! One of the great justices of our time just died—not a perfect judge, but definitely a major figure in the history of the Supreme Court—and all you can think of is *yourself*, and how *you* lost out on a fucking *job*. What is wrong with you, girl?"

I put down my pint of ice cream and placed my head in my hands.

"You're right," I said. "You're absolutely right. I'm so ashamed."

"I'm sorry, I didn't mean to be so hard on you. I came by tonight to support you, not to whoop your ass."

Harvetta reached out to hug me. I gave in to her embrace.

"Trust me," she said. "Everything's going to turn out fine in the end."

I had my doubts. But I knew better than to argue with the indomitable Harvetta Chambers.

33

The next morning, shortly before noon, Judge Stinson summoned everyone into her office for a meeting.

"What do you think this is about?" Larry asked, as we walked across chambers from the clerks' side to the judge's domain.

"I'm guessing it has to do with the passing of Justice Keegan," I said.

"Thanks for the brilliant insights," Amit said. "You're real SCOTUS clerkship material."

I glared at him, my tolerance for snark running low that morning.

The judge didn't waste any time, starting to speak before we were all even seated.

"As you know, my good friend Justice Keegan passed away very suddenly yesterday. I am leaving immediately for Washington, to attend the funeral this Friday. I expect to remain in D.C. through the entirety of the following week, possibly longer. The reason for my extended stay must not leave this chambers."

She looked around the conference table slowly, making eye contact with each of us. All of us, the four clerks and Brenda, nodded solemnly.

"I have been informally advised by a contact in the White House counsel's office that I am on President LaFount's shortlist for the vacancy created by Justice Keegan's passing. The president does not plan to start interviewing his candidates until next week, and he will not announce his nominee until the week after that, out of respect for Justice Keegan. It would not make sense for me to fly out to Washington for the funeral, return to the West Coast, and then fly back again to meet with the president. So I will remain on the East Coast and work remotely."

"I have an urgent project for all of you," she continued. "Around the holidays, each of you—well, except for you, Larry—prepared detailed dossiers on different aspects of my judicial track record. I need that research updated, with all of the mentioned cases printed out, highlighted and tabbed, and put into binders. Then FedEx the binders to me in Washington—Brenda has the address—for delivery by Friday. I'm going to spend this weekend poring over them."

"Judge," Brenda asked, "what should I say to people who call and ask about your whereabouts?"

"If anyone happens to inquire, please advise them that I went to Washington to attend the services for Justice Keegan and then decided to stay on the East Coast for a few days on personal business. If anyone should ask about the nature of that 'personal business,' please say you don't know. If anyone, including anyone from the media, asks about rumors that I am being considered for a seat on the Court, please decline comment."

Judge Stinson looked around the table sternly once again, like a mother about to leave on a trip and telling the kids not to throw a party in her absence.

"If this news somehow gets leaked, I will immediately fire the party responsible. That's all."

We filed out, silently. Once we returned to the clerks' side of the office, we grabbed our lunches and repaired to the chambers library to discuss—well, to gossip about—what we had just learned.

"So does she have a real chance?" asked Larry, while munching on his turkey sandwich.

I remained silent, not wanting to be mocked by Amit for my "brilliant insights."

"Definitely," Amit said. "She has the prestige, the pedigree, and the politics. And she has demographics on her side, as an Asian American woman. President LaFount would love to see the Democrats try to vote against a conservative woman of color. It would be just as futile as when they tried to shoot down Justice Wilson."

"Does she have the right pedigree?" James asked. "She graduated from Boalt Hall. I'm very proud of my alma mater, but I feel that when it comes to SCOTUS, they're always looking for Ivy Leaguers."

"Boalt's perfect," Amit said. "It's an elite law school, but it's not an Ivy. That's a plus factor—there's been a lot of bitching lately about how there are too many Harvard and Yale grads on the Court. And the fact that Berkeley is a public law school is great. It plays into Stinson's up-from-the-bootstraps narrative—modest upbringing, immigrant heritage, daughter of a taxi driver from China, blah blah."

"What happens to us if she makes it to the Court?" Larry asked. "I'm kind of over this whole 'clerking' thing. I don't want to have to do it all over again."

As if Justice Stinson would even hire you, I thought to myself. Maybe a Ninth Circuit clerkship can be given away to further a personal relationship, but not a Supreme Court clerkship.

"It depends on whether the judge would take us with her to the Court," James said. "Would she?"

Amit laughed. "I doubt it. The judges who take their clerks with them after becoming justices tend to be the nice ones, the loyal ones, the less status-conscious ones. The more status-conscious judges try to 'trade up' and hire even 'better' clerks after getting elevated. Our boss is not particularly nice, and she's very status-conscious."

I tended to agree with Amit. It wasn't impossible that Judge Stinson would hire one of us to clerk for her on the Court, but it seemed unlikely. Unlike, say, Judge Polanski, Judge Stinson wasn't getting the best of the best as a circuit judge; but as *Justice* Stinson, she'd have access to the nation's most brilliant young lawyers.

Not long after I returned to my desk after lunch, one of those brilliant young lawyers called me.

"Hey," Lucia said.

"Hey yourself. What's going on?"

"My boss is off to D.C. for the Keegan funeral. I'm guessing yours is too?"

"Yup. She just left."

"And how long will she be in Washington for, if I might ask?"

"A while. And what about Judge Polanski?"

"A while too. What's keeping Judge Stinson in D.C.?"

"She's staying there on . . . personal business. And what about Judge Polanski?"

"Personal business too."

We both laughed. We understood each other perfectly.

"Speaking of personal business, have you given more thought to . . . our situation?"

Ugh. I had too much on my mind to be dealing with this. It made me almost angry.

"Lucia, there's no 'situation' between us."

"It happened very recently, so I doubt you could have forgotten it. We kissed."

"We were drunk. Very, very drunk."

"The alcohol might have lowered our inhibitions, but that doesn't mean there's nothing there. I could tell you were into it—and into me."

"I'm sorry if you got the wrong impression, but this is nothing personal against you. I'm straight."

Silence.

"Lucia, I really value our friendship . . ."

"Audrey, fuck you."

Click.

Was I at all attracted to Lucia? No; of that I was certain. At the same time, when I agreed to meet Lucia for drinks that night at Bodega Wine Bar, it wasn't my plan to sabotage her Keegan interview. It happened organically, maybe opportunistically—I saw an opening, and I took it— but it wasn't premeditated.

But even if it *had* been premeditated . . . so what? As Judge Stinson had told me, it was my duty to rise as far and as fast as I could, using everything in my power to get ahead. And I also remembered this other advice from my boss, quite possibly the next Supreme Court justice: "To be a successful professional woman, you need to be a little monstrous."

34

Not long after Justice Keegan's funeral on Friday, news articles started appearing about the search for his successor. President LaFount had reportedly drawn up his shortlist of possible nominees and would be interviewing a half-dozen contenders. Journalists covering the Supreme Court—Robert Barnes, Emily Bazelon, Joan Biskupic, Jess Bravin, Jan Crawford, Tom Goldstein, Linda Greenhouse, Ken Jost, Dahlia Lithwick, Adam Liptak, Tony Mauro, Jeffrey Toobin, Nina Totenberg—floated their own shortlists. Bloggers started dissecting the lists, arguing over the respective strengths and weaknesses of the contenders, and commenters on message boards dug into the blog posts. It was the legal world's version of Oscar season, full of speculation by pundits and campaigning by partisans (including former clerks to the possible nominees).

With Judge Stinson out of town, in a different time zone, and not checking in very much—presumably she was too busy preparing for her interview with the president—my co-clerks and I decided to have lunch outside of chambers. On Wednesday we went to Il Fornaio, an Italian restaurant—a chain restaurant, but an upscale one—in Old Pasadena. I liked that it was reasonably priced, with entrees under $20, and I could take home half of my pizza and reheat it for dinner later.

We luckily landed a somewhat private table near the back of the relatively busy restaurant. This allowed us to gossip about SCOTUS candidates without fear of being overheard. Back when he did Beneath Their Robes, Amit wrote a story about some clerks to Justice Greenberg who were overheard talking about a pending opinion while out at an Indian restaurant in D.C.; after the item appeared, the clerks got scolded by their boss. So we were mindful of confidentiality—especially after the stern talking-to we got from Judge Stinson before she left town.

After our food arrived, Amit started the discussion.

"So," he said, leaning forward with obvious relish, "who's it going to be?"

"Our boss?" asked Larry. Perhaps because Judge Stinson was the only candidate he knew of. His shirtfront was covered with a constellation of focaccia crumbs.

"It would be nice to have a Boaltie on the Court," James said, slicing into his rotisserie chicken. "It would enhance the value of my degree. And the value of a Stinson clerkship."

"I don't know," I said, adopting my usual protective pessimism—discounting the likelihood of a desired outcome so as not to jinx it. "There seems to be a lot of talk this time around about it going to someone who's not already a judge—a senator, a governor, a cabinet official."

"That's just talk," Amit scoffed. "Every time there's a vacancy, everyone says, 'Oh, the president should nominate a politician! We need political experience on the Court!' But it hardly ever happens—it hasn't happened in years—and for good reason. The Court has political elements, but it's primarily a legal rather than political institution. And the people best positioned to serve on a legal institution are people with legal rather than political experience. It's also more risky to nominate a politician. Why go for a politician when you have so many qualified jurists already serving on the circuit courts?"

"Well, among judges, Steve Collins of the Eighth Circuit is getting buzz," I said. "People like that he's from the midwest rather than the Acela corridor. Joan Biskupic and Tony Mauro think he has the edge."

"He's well regarded," said Amit, "but young. The same goes for Jeff Stuart and Ray Kelton on the Sixth Circuit, and Neal Gosford on the Tenth Circuit. Brilliant former SCOTUS clerks who come from flyover country—coastal qualifications, heartland appeal. But they need more judicial experience. LaFount might want to save them for later—like when Hannah Greenberg's seat opens up. At least that's what Jan Crawford thinks, and she has very good sources in conservative circles."

"So who does Crawford think is the favorite?" asked James. He had neatly segregated the rosemary potatoes that came with his chicken and was barely touching them, keeping with his low-carb diet.

"Her sources say Rashida Williams of the D.C. Circuit," I said. "Currently on the most prestigious circuit court, previously on the California Supreme Court. Smart, African American, a woman . . ."

"And unconfirmable," Amit said. "I agree with Jeff Toobin: put a typewriter in front of her and she turns into a loose cannon. Hard-core libertarians support Williams because of all these speeches and articles of hers criticizing the New Deal, but there's no way she gets past the Senate. If a D.C. Circuit judge gets it, Brent Kirkpatrick is most likely."

"How about that Latino judge in the Fifth Circuit?" asked James. "He's on a lot of the shortlists."

"Ramon Guerrero," Amit said. "I have a law school classmate clerking for the Fifth Circuit who tells me Guerrero is gay."

"Who cares?" asked Larry, between mouthfuls of his sausage and broccoli rabe pizza. "Does that crap still matter?"

"To the religious right it might," James said. "And they have a lot of sway on judicial issues."

"The hard right might care if Guerrero were out, but he's not," Amit said. "His main problems are that he's a little old and he has some random dissents and concurrences in his past—affirmative action, abortion—that could come back to haunt him."

"What about Judge Polanski? Could he get it over our boss?" I asked. My vegetarian pizza was delicious—and because I was still upset over losing out on the Keegan clerkship and stressed over whether I'd get another shot at clerking for the Court, I didn't care about the carbs.

"He has some advantages," Amit said. "He's more brilliant than the judge. He has the Polanski Mafia working behind the scenes for him—they're at the White House counsel's office, and the Senate Judiciary

Committee, and the Office of Legal Policy at the DOJ. But he has disadvantages too. Some people view him as less predictable than Stinson, less consistently conservative—occasionally he 'libs out' on some issue he gets a bee in his bonnet over. We know how unreliable he can be when it comes to en banc votes."

"Judge Polanski is conservative but principled," I said. "He 'libs out' when he feels the law requires a liberal result."

"Presidents prefer predictable over principled in SCOTUS nominees," said Amit. "And Polanski's a white male, which doesn't help."

"So it sounds like our boss has a good shot?" said James. "As conservative as they come, but with the whole 'attractive half-Asian female' thing going for her?"

James talking about attractive half-Asian females caused me to look down at my pizza and study the positioning of the eggplant slices.

"The problem is that she's seen in some quarters as being insufficiently conservative," Amit explained. "Look at some of the conservative blogs and message boards—Red State, Free Republic, Bench Memos. There's distrust of her among the social conservatives."

"Why would that be?" James said. "I don't think I've ever seen a 'liberal' vote from her. You could even argue that she's *too* conservative."

"It's purely a perception problem," Amit said. "Some conservatives think of her—mistakenly, of course—as a 'California' conservative. It might be because the Ninth Circuit's liberal reputation as a court has rubbed off on her, even though she's one of the judges trying to keep its excesses in check. It might be because she's an Asian woman, and people expect an Asian woman to be liberal—Polanski doesn't have the same problem, even though he's a Ninth Circuit judge too."

Amit paused, enjoying his conversational authoritativeness, and speared some fusilli with his fork.

"But again, it's pure perception," he concluded. "Nothing that one good opinion couldn't fix."

35

"So I'm guessing you would all like to hear about my interview with President LaFount at the White House."

Judge Stinson grinned girlishly. We had completed the business portion of the Monday meeting and had reached the point where we would normally recount how our weekends had gone. But nobody was interested in what movie Larry had seen on Saturday night or how far James had run on Sunday morning.

"It went very well, knock wood," said the judge, rapping her delicate knuckles against the conference room table twice. "I met last Wednesday with White House staffers, the vice president, and the president. The meetings lasted for about six hours in total, including an hour with the president—a very gracious and personable man, far more charming than the media gives him credit for. I had met him before socially, through Robert, but only briefly. This was my first extended interaction with him."

"What did you talk about?" Amit asked.

"Mainly my background and upbringing. President LaFount seemed favorably impressed by my life story."

"So you didn't talk about the issues?" said Amit.

"Not with the president. I had the sense that he wanted to know about me as a person—my values, my character, my journey through life. After the interview, he gave me a tour of the family quarters of the White House. He showed me a handwritten copy of the Gettysburg Address and the Lincoln Bedroom—which Robert and I had stayed in years ago, although I didn't mention that to the president. A real treat."

"And he didn't ask you any questions about your judicial philosophy?" asked Amit, with almost impertinent aggressiveness.

"No, not at all. When I met with the vice president and the White House counsel, they asked me some general questions about my judicial philosophy and my approach to deciding cases. But nobody asked me about specific issues like abortion or affirmative action or gun rights. It was clear to me that they were already very familiar with my jurisprudence and my track record on the bench. And I don't think they would want to create a record of having any kind of 'litmus test' for a nominee."

Amit nodded, seemingly satisfied.

"Now let me ask some questions of you," Judge Stinson said. "I'm sure you've all been following the media coverage of the possible nominees. What's being said about me?"

"The coverage of you has been very positive, Judge," I said. "People seem impressed by your qualifications, your judicial experience as both a trial and appellate judge, and the diversity you would bring to the Court as an Asian American woman."

"And what about the criticism? What should I watch out for? My husband hired a political consultant to advise us, and this consultant suggests that—contrary to what one might expect—the greatest danger to my nomination comes from the right, not the left. His research seems to indicate that my biggest challenge would be getting the nomination over the objection of the hard right—and that if I can get the nomination, I would then have smooth sailing."

"I totally agree," Amit said. "The biggest concerns about you seem to be coming from conservatives, social conservatives in particular. Libertarians and the business community seem comfortable with you, and progressives seem to think you're about as good as they can expect from LaFount. But social conservatives are worried that you don't have much of a track record on the issues that matter most to them. They like your immigration rulings, especially *Hamadani*, but they don't like your silence on abortion, religious freedom, gun rights . . ."

"My silence? I wish they understood how these things work. I can decide only the cases and controversies that come before me. I can't just call up the clerk of court and say, 'Cathy, send me an abortion case!' Hopefully the public can be educated during this process."

"Some people don't like that you're married to one of the biggest talent agents in Hollywood, which screams 'liberal' to them. Some conservative bloggers found pictures of you and Robert attending the Vanity Fair Oscars party."

"Well, at least I look fabulous in those photos!"

"And some of them don't like the time you represented an Asian American theater group that was facing eviction. It could end up being an asset in winning support from the left, but eviction defense work for an ethnic theater group doesn't sit well with the right."

Judge Stinson sighed.

"That was pro bono work, performed for the Asian Pacific American Legal Center, a respected civil rights group," she said. "In the end, the theater company vacated the premises—but because their lease was being terminated prematurely, they were entitled to compensation, which we helped them negotiate. All we did was help them assert their rights under a lease. Don't conservatives believe in the validity of contracts?"

"Judge, that makes sense," Amit said. "I think the case—the distorted account of the case, that is—just played into their existing concerns over whether you're too close to the entertainment industry."

"If I'm lucky enough to be chosen by the president, *I* would be the nominee, not my husband. This entire process is quite absurd. But it's the toll that must be collected, I suppose."

"Did the president mention when he'd announce his nominee, Judge?" James asked.

"Within the next three to six weeks, it seems—which strikes me as very soon, but which historically is on the slow side. Since we're in the middle of the term rather than the summer recess, there is some time sensitivity. But President LaFount views Supreme Court appointments as a very important part of his legacy and does not want to rush the process."

She rose from her seat at the head of the table, signifying the end of the meeting.

"Remember: this all stays within chambers. The fact that I interviewed with the president is now public, thanks to the *New York Times* and the *Washington Post*, but anything beyond that should be kept confidential. And Audrey, I'd like to speak with you for a moment."

After everyone else left, the judge and I adjourned to the sitting area of her office. She took her usual position in the club chair, and I perched on the couch.

"Where are we on *Geidner*? I'd like to get that opinion issued as soon as possible."

"We're still waiting on Judge Deleuze's dissent. We circulated our draft majority about two weeks ago, before you left for Washington."

"Marta Marta Marta," sighed the judge. "The member of this court least likely to assist me. If she knew I wanted this opinion out quickly, I wouldn't put it past her to deliberately delay her dissent."

"Judge, I've heard through the clerk grapevine that Judge Deleuze is actually eager to get the opinion out as well. Apparently she believes that her position will be vindicated, whether by an en banc court or the Supreme Court, and she wants this case decided as soon as possible, for the sake of all the couples it would affect. So her dissent might come more quickly than a typical dissent in a case of this importance."

"That's good to know. But I do wish we could speed this up even more. See what you can learn through this grapevine of yours."

The grapevine, the grapevine . . .

"I think I have an idea for how to accelerate the process. But it might require talking a bit about your interview with the president, as well as a little . . . misdirection."

"Do whatever you think best, Audrey. I trust your judgment."

Upon returning to my office, I picked up the phone and called my main conduit to the grapevine.

"What's the good word, Miss Audrey? Is Justice Stinson about to be inflicted upon this helpless nation?"

"Her interview with President LaFount went quite well," I said, before providing a capsule summary of what the judge just told us about her White House meetings—and stressing how well they went.

"Ugh," Jeremy said. "It sounds like Judge Stinson should start ordering up some new robes. She's what, a size six?"

"Don't insult her—size four, tops."

"I need to start looking into moving to Canada. Our country does not need Justice Christina Wong Stinson—as big a conservative hack as Keegan, only without the brilliance."

The comment angered me, but I held my tongue. I had a mission to accomplish.

"Well, I wouldn't pack your bags for the Great White North just yet. Judge Stinson has a decent shot, but there are still . . . concerns."

"Like what?"

"She's worried about *Geidner*. Same-sex marriage is such a hot button issue, and she could be vilified by the left for issuing an opinion upholding Proposition 8. At the very least, it could complicate matters for her nomination—and right now the last thing she wants is controversy."

"Interesting . . ."

"So she's hoping that she can just wait it out and get nominated before she has to issue the opinion. She wouldn't have long to wait—apparently the president wants to announce his nominee in the next few weeks."

"I told you earlier, Deleuze wants *Geidner* out quickly."

"That's a concern. But it's a major, complex case. We probably won't get Deleuze's draft dissent for a few weeks. Then we'll have to revise the majority opinion to respond to the dissent, and she'll have to revise her dissent to respond to our revisions—you know the drill. It wouldn't be hard to run out the clock on this."

"I think you're wrong," Jeremy said. "Underestimate Judge Deleuze at your peril."

36

My plan worked perfectly. On Wednesday afternoon, Judge Deleuze's draft dissent sailed into the chambers email account. Minutes after it arrived, before I even had a chance to read it, Judge Stinson called me into her office.

"Audrey, I presume the prompt appearance of Judge Deleuze's dissent is your handiwork."

"I might have had something to do with it," I said with a smile.

"I don't know what magic you worked, but whatever you did, thank you. Now we just need to finalize the opinion. In a normal case I'd want to revise our majority opinion to respond to the dissent's best points, but right now time is of the essence. So let's keep substantive revisions to a minimum, especially if the arguments in the dissent are already implicitly addressed in the majority. Your main focus should be reviewing our opinion and proofreading and double-checking everything—the case law, the citations to the record, the grammar and spelling—everything. We have the original trial record in chambers, correct?"

"Yes, Judge. It's that tower of boxes in my office."

"Check the record citations against the original record. Don't rely upon photocopies or scanned documents. Everything having to do with this case needs to be perfect. And it needs to be done by tomorrow."

I returned to my office, closed my door, and plunged into what I knew would amount to hours of work. I began by reading the dissent. It was powerful, persuasive, and passionate, as to be expected from Judge Deleuze. But after reading it multiple times, I concluded that there was nothing in it that absolutely required any changes to the majority opinion. Cases like *Geidner*, about politically charged issues implicating fundamental principles of constitutional law, were like that. They weren't going to be solved by legal legerdemain—the artful parsing of precedent, the stitching together of dicta, or the discovery of a dispositive, previously overlooked subsection in a statute. The relevant cases and concepts were limited and known to all. Deciding a case like *Geidner* was simply a matter of framing the issues and weighing the values; those processes, resting on disagreement over basic assumptions, did not lend themselves to endless back and forth and dueling in the footnotes. Judge Stinson would speak her piece, Judge Deleuze would speak her piece, and that was that.

I then turned to reviewing our majority opinion, closely and carefully. At this point in the process, the substance of the opinion was fairly set; I was mainly looking for errors to correct, knowing that this opinion would be the most widely read of Judge Stinson's entire career. I caught two typographical errors and tightened a few case parentheticals, but nothing more.

Finally, around midnight, I turned to double-checking the factual record. I fixed a handful of citations to the trial transcript but otherwise found little requiring amendment. I was about to close the document and head home for the night when I remembered: I should also check the timeliness of the notice of appeal once more. I had checked it when I originally drafted the opinion, and the clerk's office always checked the timeliness of the notice of appeal during the intake process. But the judge had instructed me to check everything again, against the original documents, and I intended to follow her instructions.

Judge Nathanson's order denying the defendants' motion for a new trial was filed on July 11. The defendants had thirty days from that date in which to file their notice of appeal, meaning that their deadline to file was August 10. I dug around the files, found the notice of appeal, and checked the date.

The piece of paper was slightly crumpled, as if it had been chewed up somewhat by a machine, and not easy to read. The notice of appeal had been filed via fax—who knew that people still used fax machines?—and that didn't help legibility.

But I could still read the date in the motion itself and in the fax transmittal line well enough: August 11. The document had been file-stamped at the top with an August 10 date—perhaps because the person in the clerk's office who had received it had forgotten to advance the date on the stamp—but the notice had clearly been filed on the 11th. August 11 was the date in the body of the document, and the fax transmittal line showed it went through at 2:25 p.m. on the 11th.

Was I certain about the deadline for filing the notice being August 10? I counted the days again. And again. And again, out loud, like a child. I wasn't great at math—how else did I wind up in law school?—but I was now certain. The notice of appeal in *Geidner* was not filed until *31* days after entry of the order denying the defendants' motion for a new trial. The notice was late, meaning the Ninth Circuit had no jurisdiction over the case, meaning that the appeal in *Geidner* must be dismissed—before the judge could issue her blockbuster opinion.

How had this escaped everyone's notice? The erroneous file stamp probably bore much of the blame. Out of curiosity, I went online and pulled up the electronic, scanned version of the notice of appeal. In the electronic version, where the blurriness of the fax transmittal was further blurred by an imperfect scan, the mentions of "August 11" looked a lot like "August 10," due to a fuzzy "1" morphing into a "0." I could now understand how this jurisdictional defect had been overlooked—but that didn't change the fact that it *was* a defect, and that the case had to be dismissed.

Judge Stinson had been wise to instruct me to double-check everything against the original documents. But I wasn't sure how she'd receive the news that *Geidner v. Gallagher*, her vehicle to the Supreme Court, had broken down.

37

I approached the doorway to Judge Stinson's office with trepidation, my arms heavy with the *Geidner* bench book and all the documents I needed to prove my case, including the original notice of appeal, a copy of the scanned version with the blurry dates, and printouts of the monthly calendars at issue for counting the days. But why was I so nervous? There was really only one possible option: the court had to dismiss *Geidner* for lack of jurisdiction. And if anyone would understand the need to dismiss for lack of jurisdiction, it would be Judge Stinson. I remembered her law review article about jurisdiction as an important limit on judicial power, how she eloquently discussed the importance of jurisdiction during my clerkship interview, and how Janet Lee had warned me in the chambers orientation about how Judge Stinson was a stickler for jurisdiction—a "juristickler," as the judge had memorably put it during the *Geidner* oral arguments.

Seeing me in the doorway, burdened with my small tower of documents, Judge Stinson waved me into her office. She seemed to be in good spirits.

"You certainly have a lot of paper on your hands," she said. "Let's sit at the conference table."

I placed the stack of documents on the table, consciously trying to underscore its heft as I did so, before seating myself in front of it. I waited for Judge Stinson to sit down before beginning.

"Judge, I have some rather significant news about *Geidner*. It appears the court lacks jurisdiction over the case."

The judge pulled her head back and puckered her lips, as if she had just eaten a lemon.

"Come again?"

I walked the judge through my calculation of the days, showed her the original notice of appeal with the erroneous file stamp, and showed her the printout of the scanned version with the smudged dates. After my explanation, she sat in silence for a few moments.

"This can't be correct," she said. "How could the appellants have failed to file a timely notice of appeal in a case this major?"

"Well, they missed the deadline by just a day . . ."

"Missing by a day is the same as missing by a week or a month. What I don't understand is how the multiple law firms representing the appellants blew this deadline."

"I'm guessing the involvement of multiple firms was part of the problem. With Sawyer & Spock, the Marriage Defense Fund, and local counsel here in California all on the case, I suspect that everyone thought that somebody else was going to file the notice of appeal—which is, after all, a rather ministerial task."

"A ministerial task, indeed. Something that could have been done by those trained monkeys we call paralegals. But Sawyer & Spock, one of the best litigation boutiques in the country, somehow managed to screw it up?"

Judge Stinson fell silent, but I could tell she was very displeased.

"Judge, how should we proceed?"

"I need to think about this. Follow me, Audrey."

I trailed behind Judge Stinson as she stood up, grabbed her handbag, and walked out of her office. After telling Brenda that we'd return shortly, she exited chambers. We then started climbing the grand staircase that I remembered ascending way back when I interviewed for my clerkship. When we reached the top floor, we walked down a short hallway and passed through a doorway into another stairwell—a utility stairwell, with gray concrete replacing the colorful Mission-style tiles. We climbed one more flight to a locked metal door. Judge Stinson dug around in her purse, found a set of keys, and unlocked the door.

We were on the rooftop of the courthouse, and it was nothing short of magnificent. The pink-orange bell tower cast a shadow over part of the space, but otherwise it was all light—California sunlight, drenching everything. The wall of terra cotta tiles was frighteningly low, no higher than our knees, so we could see for miles.

"This is my favorite place in the entire courthouse," the judge said. "We're not supposed to be up here—look how low this wall is, it would be so easy to fall off—but the building manager had a crush on me and gave me a key. Take a walk around and check out the views. I'm going to sit down for a moment."

Judge Stinson seated herself on the tile wall, crossing her legs and looking west. I walked around the roof, enjoying the warmth of the sunlight on my arms and the delicate breeze through my hair. After a few minutes, I returned to the judge and sat down next to her. We sat quietly for a few minutes, until she broke the silence.

"We are not dismissing *Geidner*."

"We're not?"

"No. It's too important a case. It must be decided now. It deserves to be decided now—for the sake of California and the country. We are not going to let the barely late performance of what you accurately described as a ministerial act get in the way of something this significant."

"But Judge, because the notice of appeal was filed out of time, the court doesn't have jurisdiction . . ."

"I am familiar with how jurisdiction works. I have been a federal judge for a fair number of years now, at both the trial and appellate levels."

"As you yourself have written, jurisdiction is an important limit on judicial power. For a court to decide a case when it lacks jurisdiction is inconsistent with the law . . ."

"Don't lecture me about the law, Audrey. I have lived and breathed the law for decades now. You were still in diapers when I started my legal career. As I've said before, I am the decider. This is my call to make, and

I have made it."

"Of course, Judge. I just want to advise you of all the risks. Because if it ever comes out . . ."

"And how would it ever come out? You owe me the law clerk's duty of confidentiality. What we've discussed this morning must remain between us."

I didn't know what to say to that. Despite standing on a rooftop, open to the sun and the sky, I felt trapped.

"I should add, Audrey, that I would of course reward you for your dedication and discretion. If I manage to make it to the Supreme Court—which I believe to be a strong possibility, especially after my opinion in *Geidner* gets issued—I will hire you to clerk for me. You have my word. In a few months, you could be with me at One First Street."

Another chance to achieve my dream, a dream so arbitrarily snatched from me by fate, and all I had to do was keep a confidence. Maybe the universe—or God, who I sometimes believed in and sometimes didn't—wasn't conspiring against me after all.

"Look around at all this," Judge Stinson said, gesturing toward the mansions of Pasadena in the foreground, surrounded by palm trees and expensive landscaping, and the San Rafael Hills and San Gabriel Mountains in the background. "This is what the legal world looks like to someone who has clerked on the Supreme Court. All this can be yours, as long as you remain loyal to me. Remember: you are my clerk, and I am your judge."

I nodded but otherwise said nothing. All I had to do was say nothing, and victory would be mine.

"Let's head back downstairs," the judge said. "We have an opinion to issue. And a world to conquer."

38

The *Geidner* opinion went public a few days later, when it was posted on-line late Tuesday morning. It probably could have been issued on Friday or Monday, but Judge Stinson wanted it to go out on Tuesday—a better day for catching the news cycle. Her calculation seemed to be correct; re-actions came quickly. My office phone started ringing less than an hour after *Geidner* went live.

"Congratulations, Miss Audrey."

"On what?"

"The opinion that you and your boss have produced in *Geidner* is good," Jeremy said. "It doesn't *do* good—actually, it does *evil*—but it's a well-done opinion."

"Uh . . . Thanks? You've read it already? It's about 80 pages, counting the dissent."

"I'm a fast reader. And I knew what to expect. I can't say there were many surprises. But I don't know what it will do to your boss's SCOTUS hopes. It could cause problems for her."

Of course Jeremy, an ultra-liberal gay man living in California, would hold that view. I had no intention of disabusing him of that notion—es-pecially since he had been so useful in expediting Judge Deleuze's dis-sent by blabbing to his friends in her chambers about how Judge Stinson wanted to delay *Geidner*, when she in fact wanted the exact opposite.

"We'll see," I said. "As you can see from the opinion, it takes no stand on the merits of gay marriage as a matter of policy. It simply argues that, as a matter of law, the courts should let the people decide."

"Way to stay on message. It sounds like you're ready for your own confirmation hearing. I just wonder if the opinion will stick."

My pulse quickened.

"What are you talking about?" I asked.

"You know what I'm talking about. A case like this is crying out for rehearing en banc. Or might go up to the Supreme Court. You may have won the battle, but you haven't won the war."

Phew. He wasn't talking about the jurisdictional problem. And how would he even know about that? I was being paranoid.

"I gotta run," Jeremy said. "I've been summoned by *le judge*. I'll talk to you later."

A few minutes later, my cell phone rang.

"Hey girl."

"Hi Harvetta. What's up?"

"So I see you guys issued your opinion in *Geidner*."

"Yup. It just went online."

"Congrats. It's a smart-ass opinion."

"What do you mean by that? It's a serious and substantial opinion."

"It sure is! I don't mean 'smart-ass' as in 'wise-ass,' I mean 'smart-ass' as in 'really fucking smart.' I ain't dissing you, Audrey!"

"Sorry, I misinterpreted you. Glad you like it."

"The jurisdictional discussion is especially strong."

Again my heart palpitated.

"The jurisdictional discussion?"

"Yeah, the jurisdictional discussion—the analysis of whether the proponents of the ballot initiative had standing. Elegant treatment of *Arizonans for Official English*. You did draft this opinion, didn't you?"

"Ha ha, yes, of course," I said, feeling stupid but also relieved. "Sorry, I've been working like crazy lately and I'm totally sleep-deprived."

"How do you think this will affect your boss's chances of making it to the big marble palace?"

"The judge's focus is on getting the law right. How this might affect her own career isn't relevant."

"Okay, you can dodge, but I'll give you my opinion. Upholding Prop 8 could seal the deal for her. It's a great way to shore up her support among the social conservatives without pissing off anyone else. No senator, not even a hard-core Democrat, is going to yell at a Supreme Court nominee on national television for *not* striking down a law."

"I see your point."

"That's just how this game is played. Even the biggest liberal activist in the country, when nominated to the Supreme Court, has to do the whole 'judges are umpires' bullshit. It's Justice Keegan's legacy. We are all originalists now."

"Harvetta, I thought you were conservative. You sound awfully cynical about judicial restraint."

"Yeah, I'm conservative, and yeah, I believe in judicial restraint. But it's much more complicated than the sound bites suggest. What pisses me off is how we don't use confirmation hearings to explore these issues because the nominees are too busy puking up platitudes."

"Fair enough."

"Okay girl, talk to you later. Just tell your boss that when she's up there for her confirmation hearings, she should say some shit that's *real*, not this out-of-a-can crap about applying the law to the facts."

After hanging up with Harvetta, I started scouring the web for news coverage of *Geidner*. Most of the mainstream media sites had little more than headlines—not surprising, given the length of the opinion and how recently it had come down. I was about to turn to the blogs when Amit came into my office, sat down, and started talking at me.

"Why are you checking the newspaper websites? You know they won't have anything up on *Geidner* this quickly."

"Well, I wanted to see what the 'official' reactions to the opinion were. I was about to turn to the blogs."

"Already there," Amit said. "I've already looked at SCOTUSblog, How Appealing, Volokh Conspiracy, Concurring Opinions, PrawfsBlawg. Plus a lot of the conservative political websites, like the Weekly Standard, Bench Memos, Confirm Them, Red State."

"And what's the verdict?"

"The right *loves* this opinion. The social conservatives feel reassured about the judge. But even the libertarians who are down with gay marriage as a *policy* matter, the types of people who would vote for gay marriage at the ballot box, respect her *legal* conclusion that Prop 8 is constitutional. As for the liberals, they seem disappointed, but not angry at our boss. They're more focused on the Deleuze dissent and on whether the case might go the other way through en banc rehearing or at SCOTUS."

"Any talk of how this might affect the judge's Supreme Court candidacy?"

"You bet. Tons of it. It's summarized by Ed Whelan's headline over at Bench Memos: 'All Rise For Justice Christina Wong Stinson.'"

All I could do was laugh. Even though part of me wanted to cry.

39

That evening, when I got home, I took out a legal pad and wrote out, in longhand, a list of ten points for consideration.

1. Jurisdiction is an abstraction and a technicality. It does not go to the merits of a legal issue.

2. Whether a ban on gay marriage is constitutional will come before the federal courts eventually; it's only a matter of time. It is better for both California and the country for this important issue to be decided sooner rather than later.

3. I am merely a law clerk. Unlike the judge, who was nominated by the president and confirmed by the Senate, I do not have the power under the Constitution to decide "cases and controversies."

4. As a law clerk, I perform a "clerical" role—not unlike my cousin in the Philippines who works in a shoe store.

5. My paramount duty as a law clerk is to carry out the will of my judge. I am an extension of my judge. Blaming a law clerk for how a case is handled would be like blaming a secretary for errors or false statements in a brief simply because the secretary happened to type it up.

6. As her law clerk, I owe Judge Stinson a duty of confidentiality. Because she has directed me to keep the jurisdictional issue in *Geidner* confidential, I must remain silent unless and until she says otherwise.

7. Some might say that issuing an opinion in a case where there is no jurisdiction is inconsistent with "the law"—but as I've learned during my clerkship, "the law" is simply what judges happen to say it is.

8. The notion of "the law" as pure and objective, as an independent identity—as something divorced from considerations of power, politics, and personality—is a theoretical construct. The real world works in far more complex ways.

9. Judge Stinson is an excellent judge, and she would make an excellent justice. If keeping silent about the jurisdictional defect in *Geidner* would help advance her Supreme Court candidacy, that weighs in favor of silence.

10. I am an excellent law clerk, and I deserve a Supreme Court clerkship. If keeping silent about the jurisdictional defect in *Geidner* would help advance my Supreme Court clerkship prospects, that weighs in favor of silence.

And then I crumpled up the piece of paper and threw it away.

40

About a week later, while I was eating Häagen-Dazs chocolate chip cookie dough from the pint and half-watching the 11 o'clock news, my phone rang. It was the judge. I was tempted to let it go to voicemail—the judge, after all, was the cause of the anxiety I was attempting to eat—but old habits die hard. And given the late hour, I guessed the call was urgent.

"Good evening, Judge," I said, muting the television and putting down the ice cream.

"Hello, Audrey. What are you up to right now?"

"Nothing much. I just got home"—my trying to play the role of industrious law clerk, logging long hours in chambers—"so I'm having a late dinner."

"Excellent. Listen carefully. I need you to pack an overnight bag with two or three days' worth of clothing, including business clothing. Bring the Armani suit we bought for your Keegan interview. I will come to your apartment to pick you up in less than half an hour. That's all."

Click. No opportunity for me to ask questions or object. Feeling sudden shame, as if the judge had somehow seen me stuffing my face with ice cream, I put the lid back on the pint and threw it into the garbage. Which reminded me: after all my stress eating over the past week, could I still fit into that suit?

I remembered how the judge quoted Thoreau when she bought it for me—"beware of all enterprises that require new clothes"—and I approached my closet with anxiety. If the suit didn't fit, there would be no time to get it altered. I said a silent prayer as I gingerly removed the suit from its Armani garment bag and tried on the skirt.

Snug, but wearable. Too bad I couldn't afford Spanx, I thought, as I tossed some ugly underwear purchased at J.C. Penney into my rollerboard suitcase.

I had no idea what to wear for this late-night adventure with the judge. Fearing that jeans might be too casual, I went for a business-casual look, donning gray slacks and a pale blue shirt.

I had just finished packing when I heard a knock at the door. I looked through the peephole and saw a broad-shouldered African American man in a suit.

"Who is it?" I asked.

"Miss Coyne, my name is Reginald. I'm driving you and Judge Stinson to the airport."

The airport? I reached into my bedside table and grabbed my passport—which luckily I had just renewed, in anticipation of a postclerkship vacation—and pocketed it, before opening the door and introducing myself to Reginald. His right hand went immediately from shaking mine to grabbing my suitcase; with his other hand, he grabbed my briefcase-like purse. By the time I turned off the lights and locked my apartment, he was halfway down the stairs. When I reached the bottom of the stairs, my bags were already in the trunk, and Reginald was holding open the rear door of a black Cadillac stretch limousine. I climbed in next to Judge Stinson, who was looking comfortable in jeans—probably $500 jeans, but jeans nevertheless—and we drove off.

"Audrey, I'm sorry I was a bit cryptic on the phone; I wanted to give you the good news in person. Let me put it to you this way: tonight we're flying to D.C."

"So does that mean . . ."

"My family is coming too—Robert and the girls are meeting us at the airport."

". . . you're being nominated to the Supreme Court?"

"Insightful as ever," the judge said with a laugh, "which is why I'll be so glad to have you as one of my first law clerks. And why I wanted to bring you to Washington, to be present when President LaFount announces my nomination tomorrow morning."

"Tomorrow morning?" I looked at the time on my phone; it was almost midnight. "Haven't all the redeye flights left already?"

"Don't be silly—do you think I'd fly *commercial* to accept my Supreme Court nomination? Larry's father is lending us his Bombardier Global Express jet. We'll arrive in D.C. in time for the 11 a.m. press conference."

We stopped at an intersection and I looked out the window. The message board of a Baptist church caught my eye: "Silence Is Consent." I looked away and settled back into the comfortable leather seat. I had never ridden in a limousine before—and I liked it.

In less than half an hour, the limousine came to a stop, and Reginald opened the door for us.

"That was quick," I said.

"This isn't LAX," Judge Stinson said. "This is Van Nuys, the airport for private-jet people. It's less congested and more discreet. Celebrities love it for the anonymity—which suits our purposes today too."

Within minutes of arriving—we didn't have to pass through any metal detector or body scanner, but simply showed identification to a man who looked half-asleep—the judge and I were boarding the Krasner jet. Robert waved to us from the rear of the plane, where he sat with the Stinsons' two teenage daughters, who seemed passed out. Judge Stinson took one of the seats at the front of the plane and directed me to sit next to her.

"Would Mr. Stinson like to sit up here?" I asked. "I'm happy to go to the back of the plane."

"Oh no, he's back there looking after the girls. And he and I see each other enough. I'd rather sit up here with you."

A young blonde woman who seemed entirely too happy for the late hour approached us with a tray of flutes.

"Some champagne, Your Honor? Miss Coyne?"

By this point in the experience, I was not at all surprised that she somehow knew my name.

"Thank you, Amanda," the judge said, picking up one of the glasses. "Audrey, you should have some, so we can toast. And it will help you sleep. We need our beauty rest. Even on a private jet, redeyes can still be rough."

I picked up a flute, and the judge and I touched glasses.

"To world conquest," Judge Stinson said, looking right into my eyes.

I took a sip, a small sip, because I had no intention of getting drunk. I remembered how Lucia and I toasted to "world conquest" before she boarded the redeye that preceded her ill-fated interview with Justice Keegan.

"Isn't this just lovely?" said the judge, sipping from her champagne and reclining her seat. "It makes hiring Larry almost worth it."

41

The next morning, clad in my tight Armani suit, I found myself in the East Room of the White House, waiting for my boss to emerge with the President of the United States. In the past 24 hours, I had experienced several firsts: my first limousine ride, my first flight on a private jet, and my first visit to the White House. Even though I hadn't gotten much sleep on the plane ride, I felt wide awake—due to the excitement of being here, in the White House, about to watch history being made.

The East Room, despite its vastness, put me in mind of an egg: its main colors were white and yellow. The paneled walls and plastered ceiling were a rich cream, while everything else—the chandeliers, candelabra, standing lamps, and heavy curtains—was gold. The light palette made the huge room feel even larger. Perhaps the darkest thing in the room, but surrounded by a gold frame, was Gilbert Stuart's iconic portrait of George Washington, dominated by black and red hues. Walking past it as I entered the room, I couldn't help but shiver in amazement.

Keeping with the color scheme, rows and rows of gilt chairs with white cushions filled the room, facing toward a flag-flanked podium. The podium stood in the doorway that connected the East Room to the central hall. It struck me at first as odd to locate the podium in the doorway, until I thought about it more practically: it allowed for grand entrances, with dignitaries walking down a long red carpet to the podium, and similarly dramatic departures.

Most of us were seated by 10:30. I sat quietly by myself, since I didn't know anyone else there. I recognized several people in the room—the attorney general, the solicitor general, the White House counsel, White House correspondents for several television networks, and even Justice Wilson—but nobody that I knew personally. We had arrived at our hotel—the St. Regis, a few blocks away from the White House—together, but the Stinsons had gone over ahead to meet with President LaFount prior to the press conference.

I was surprised by how noisy the room was. The press conference wasn't starting for another half hour, but given the grandeur of the room and the importance of the occasion, I expected something like the hush of a church before the start of services. Instead, the TV crews were noisily setting up equipment, staffers were rearranging seats to accommodate latecomers, and people were (awkwardly) attempting to circulate among the tight rows of seats, extending greetings to each other. It was exciting to see the attorney general chatting with the solicitor general, then chatting with the White House counsel a few minutes later. Welcome to Washington.

Shortly before 11 o'clock, the room finally quieted. At 11 o'clock on the dot, President LaFount and the Stinsons entered the room. The president took the podium, Judge Stinson stood beside him, and Robert and the girls moved off to the side of the room, where they stood underneath the portrait of George Washington.

"Good morning," President LaFount said, looking like the businessman he once was, in a navy suit and gold tie. "Today I am pleased to announce my nomination of Judge Christina Wong Stinson as associate justice of the Supreme Court of the United States.

"Judge Stinson is one of the finest and most highly respected judges in the country. As a lawyer in private practice, as a trial judge, and as a judge on the United States Court of Appeals for the Ninth Circuit, she has demonstrated both a technical mastery of the law and a deep commitment to justice."

I wasn't so sure about her "technical mastery of the law." As she herself liked to emphasize, she was a CEO, not a technician.

"Judge Stinson is fair-minded and principled, approaching each case with an open mind, and deciding it based on the law—not based on politics or her own personal preference, but the law of the land. These qualities will serve her well on our nation's highest court."

How open-minded was the judge? I thought about her unbroken streak of votes against immigrants in asylum cases—including *Hamadani*, a case involving a journalist with a very strong claim not to be sent back to Pakistan, a case she managed to save from rehearing en banc through behind-the-scenes lobbying of her colleagues.

"Judge Stinson has traveled a long and remarkable road to where she sits today. Born Christina Wong, she grew up in a working-class neighborhood in the Inland Empire region of California. Her father, an immigrant from China, drove a taxicab, and her mother worked as a nurse. But young Christina worked hard and took advantage of our nation's great public school system. She graduated as the valedictorian of her high school before going on to UCLA, which she graduated from summa cum laude, and UC Berkeley's Boalt Hall law school, where she served on the law review. So if confirmed to the Supreme Court, she would add some much-needed diversity—as the only graduate not from the Ivy League!"

The audience laughed, but the point also had some truth to it. The fact that Judge Stinson had graduated from an elite but public law school could only help.

"After graduating from Boalt Hall, Christina made her first foray into government service, serving as a law clerk to the late Judge Jonathan Coppersmith in Los Angeles. She then joined one of America's great law firms, Gibson Dunn & Crutcher, where she made partner. In more than 15 years at the firm, she handled a wide range of cases, at both the trial and appellate levels, and performed a remarkable amount of pro bono work. Numerous organizations recognized and honored her as one of California's leading lawyers.

"Her time at the firm was important for another reason as well: while at Gibson, she met a dashing young lawyer by the name of Robert Stinson, and they eventually married. Robert, as some of you may know, is one of the nation's top talent agents. Maybe he can help find some work for me after I'm done here in the White House!"

Laughter. It was a bad joke, but the first rule of Washington is always to laugh at the president's jokes.

"Robert is here with us today, together with the Stinsons' two daughters, Megan and Alexandra," said President LaFount, gesturing toward them under the Washington portrait. "I'm sure you must all be very proud.

"In 2004, President Bush nominated Christina Wong Stinson to the federal district court in Los Angeles—the court where she began her public service career as a law clerk. Her nomination received bipartisan support. After several years of distinguished service as a trial judge, Judge Stinson was elevated to the Ninth Circuit Court of Appeals, our nation's largest and busiest appellate court, once again with bipartisan support.

"Now, the Ninth Circuit isn't everyone's favorite court. People like me, who consider ourselves *severely* conservative, often find ourselves at odds with some of the Ninth Circuit's decisions. But during her tenure on the Ninth Circuit, Judge Stinson has done her best to curb some of that court's . . . excesses. She has demonstrated, time and again, in opinion after opinion, a passionate commitment to the rule of law."

Commitment to the rule of law? I tried not to think of the *Geidner* case and the jurisdictional defect we were hiding. Thinking of *Geidner* at this moment felt like thinking about sex during church.

"A passionate commitment to the rule of law—a perfect description of the jurisprudence of Justice Aidan Keegan, whose passion you could see in so many of his opinions. He held strong views, which he expressed in strong fashion. It's impossible to replace Justice Keegan, a giant of the law who has had such a major effect on how we interpret the Constitution. But in nominating Judge Stinson as his successor, I have chosen a nominee who shares his passion for the law—and, ultimately, the people ruling themselves through law, rather than being ruled by unelected judges."

By all accounts, Justice Keegan had a passion for the law; it's why he loved arguing about substantive legal issues when interviewing clerkship applicants, or when writing dissents. Harvetta Chambers had a passion for the law; she read law review articles in her free time, after all. I wasn't sure about Judge Stinson—did she have a passion for the law, or a passion for the prestige, pay, and perks associated with success in the law? (I wondered the same thing about myself sometimes.)

"Nominating justices to the United States Supreme Court is one of a president's most important responsibilities. I gave a great deal of thought to this nomination, and I considered several very fine contenders. What ultimately put Judge Stinson at the top of my list was a decision you might have heard of, in a recent case called *Geidner v. Gallagher*."

So much for trying not to think about *Geidner*. In that moment, I was glad I hadn't eaten breakfast.

"The *Geidner* case involves a challenge to California's Proposition 8, a ban on same-sex marriage that was supported by a majority of the people of California. Now, same-sex marriage is a highly controversial and important issue. If you read Judge Stinson's superb opinion in *Geidner*, which I urge you to read if you haven't done so already, you will see her passionate commitment to the rule of law, her deep understanding of the proper role of judges in our nation, and her recognition that a judge's job is to interpret the law—not to make the law, or to reach out and decide things that judges have no business deciding."

Like, for example, cases where they lack jurisdiction?

"I'm confident that the United States Senate will be as impressed as I was by Judge Stinson's impeccable record, judicial temperament, and unmatched honesty and integrity. And I urge the Senate to act swiftly on this critical nomination, especially since the Supreme Court is in the middle of its term—a very important term, filled with many cases with profound implications for our country.

"Judge Stinson, thank you for agreeing to serve, and congratulations on your nomination."

President LaFount stepped aside, and Judge Stinson took the podium.

She was wearing the dark charcoal Armani suit that we had picked up together—the one that she liked because it was "conservative, not California"—and it was perfect for the occasion.

"Thank you, Mr. President. I am deeply honored by your nomination to serve on the Supreme Court. And I am deeply humbled to be nominated to the seat once held by Justice Aidan Keegan—a dear friend of mine, whose loss we all still feel, and one of the greatest justices of our time. He truly was a giant of the law, as you noted, and I believe the full extent of his influence on the law will not be known for decades to come.

"I am also humbled by this nomination because, unlike several of the current justices, my legal career is not deeply steeped in the Court. I have held the Court in the highest reverence, but from a distance. While I have been blessed by the friendship of justices—Justice Keegan, of course, and Justice Wilson, whom I see here today—I have never had the privilege of clerking on the Court or arguing before it.

"My origins could not be farther from that great marble palace at One First Street. My father was an undocumented immigrant from China, smuggled here illegally, who drove a taxicab until the day he died. My late mother was—Mr. President, my apologies for this small correction—a mere nurses' aide, not a nurse. My childhood was not easy. Even though my parents both worked constantly, we never had any money. My first brush with the law took place when we got evicted from our apartment because my parents couldn't pay the rent—a source of great shame to an eight-year-old girl.

"But what my parents couldn't provide in financial support, they made up for in values. They taught me, their only daughter, the value of hard work—both of them worked long hours, never retiring, working until they passed away—and the value of education. It was through education, they taught me, that I might be able to have a better life. And they were absolutely right. I only wish that they had lived to see this day."

Here she paused, seemingly overcome by emotion. It was the first interruption in her pitch-perfect, polished performance—and probably an intentional one, too.

"I took my parents' words to heart, availing myself of California's great public university system, then entering the legal profession. After clerking, I joined Gibson Dunn & Crutcher as a litigator. This was the 1980s, and it was not easy to be a minority woman in the world of litigation. I would show up to a meeting and opposing counsel would ask me to get them coffee—perhaps thinking I was a secretary, or perhaps knowing I wasn't but trying to intimidate me. It didn't matter. I just followed my parents' advice—always work hard, always keep learning—and I eventually enjoyed great success as a lawyer.

"That success is, of course, a shared success. I share it with my parents, who enshrined in me the values that helped me advance. I share it with my fellow women and minorities in the law, who supported me during tough times. I share it with my many mentors—Judge Coopersmith, the wonderful judge for whom I clerked, and my senior colleagues at Gibson Dunn, who taught me what it means to be a lawyer. I share it with my colleagues on the Ninth Circuit—I might not always agree with them, as the president noted, but the process of working through our disagreements has made me a better judge. I share it with my law clerks, current and former, some of whom are in this room today."

Judge Stinson made quick eye contact with me, and a chill ran up my spine.

"Finally, I share my success with my husband, Robert, and our two amazing daughters, Megan and Alexandra. The three of them make sure that my judicial office doesn't go to my head, constantly reminding me that beneath my robes, I'm just another California mom."

Laughter.

"I come from a galaxy far, far away, called southern California"—more laughter—"but I feel a deep connection to the value inscribed on the front of the Supreme Court building: equal justice under law. This is a value I've worked to advance throughout my career as a lawyer and judge. During my time on the bench, I have always kept in mind my judicial oath. As a judge, I have the duty to interpret the Constitution and the laws of the United States faithfully and fairly, to protect the rights of all Americans, and to do these things with care and with restraint, always remembering the limited role the courts play in our constitutional system."

The limited role the courts play in our constitutional system—constrained by such doctrines as federal jurisdiction. Part of me imagined standing up, in front of the president and all the television cameras, and shouting out the dirty secret of no jurisdiction in *Geidner*. But instead I sat still, in the sausage casing of the beautiful Armani suit the judge had bought for me. Silence is consent?

"I pledge that, if confirmed, I will do everything within my power to fulfill those great and grave responsibilities. I look forward to working with the Senate in the next stage of this process. Mr. President, thank you once again for your confidence in me and for honoring me with this nomination."

42

I spent two days in Washington, basking in the reflected glory of my boss as she attended events in her honor and visited her D.C. friends. Judge Stinson took care to introduce me to everyone—White House officials, Washington power brokers, fellow judges—and always with kind words of praise, calling me "brilliant" or her "most trusted law clerk." It felt like an extended version of our conversation on the courthouse rooftop: "All this can be yours, as long as you remain loyal to me."

I then returned to Pasadena—flying commercial, but on a ticket paid for by the judge—while Judge Stinson remained in Washington, making courtesy calls on the senators who would be voting on her nomination and preparing for her confirmation hearings. This involved poring through binders of material prepared for her by the White House and going through "murder boards"—brutal sessions in which numerous questioners would pretend to be senators, grilling her about her record and legal views, trying to trip her up or make her lose her cool. It sounded like a Supreme Court clerkship interview but worse.

The process of preparing Judge Stinson for her hearings, which was being handled by the White House and the Justice Department, did not involve us clerks. Being back in Pasadena, given what was going on in Washington, felt so irrelevant. We still had work to do; even though the judge wasn't being assigned new Ninth Circuit cases, she did want us to tie up loose ends on pending cases to the extent that we could. But our work was an afterthought for the judge, who hardly called in or emailed to check on our progress. It was like being at home with the National Guard during a war: we were supporting the cause but in a minor way, far from the front lines.

Part of me wanted to be closer to the action, but part of me was relieved. Given my conflicted views about the judge, including the bombshell I knew about her most famous and acclaimed case, I was content to simply be a bystander to history. I remembered what I thought to myself on the roof: all I had to do was say nothing.

One afternoon, a few weeks after my return from D.C., and the day before the start of Judge Stinson's confirmation hearings, James stepped into my office, closed the door behind him, and sat down. This made me nervous. Things had been weird between us for a while and we hadn't had much in the way of one-on-one interaction lately.

"What's up?" I asked, trying to sound as relaxed as possible.

"I was going to ask you that."

"Well, the judge's confirmation hearings start tomorrow, and it seems like things are looking good for her," I babbled. "The Democrats don't seem to have the stomach to challenge an Asian American woman who has lived the American dream."

"I wasn't talking about the judge," James said. "What's up with *you*?"

"Nothing much. I'm just reviewing a case where the judge has to cast an en banc vote so I can make a recommendation. But how she votes is pretty irrelevant, since it seems that Judge Gottlieb has more than enough votes . . ."

"No, I'm not talking about what you're working on. You haven't been yourself over the past few weeks. You seem distracted. Anxious."

"Maybe it's just the excitement of the judge's nomination. Our boss is about to have her Supreme Court confirmation hearings. That's pretty amazing. I guess I've had a hard time focusing ever since coming back from D.C."

"But you were like this even before you went to Washington. Something's on your mind. Something's bothering you."

I looked into his blue-green eyes and quickly looked away.

"Oh, nothing really," I said. "I guess part of me is wondering what kind of justice the judge would be if she gets confirmed."

"Are you worried that she's not brilliant enough to be a justice?"

"No, I actually think she's very smart. Maybe not as brilliant as Justice Keegan, but you can be a perfectly solid justice without being brilliant."

"Do you think that she's . . . too disengaged?"

"Well, I think she'd be more engaged on the Court than she was here. The justices get the biggest and most exciting cases. The judge phoned it in when it came to the little cases. But the Supreme Court doesn't take little cases."

"You're probably right," James said. "So there's no need to fret over what Justice Stinson would be like. No justice is perfect. And it's not like there's anything that one of us could do at this point to change whether she makes it onto the Court."

If only James knew what I knew. The prospect of sharing my secret with him was so tempting. I definitely wanted to get his advice. But I wasn't ready to commit to any particular course of action; I wanted to keep all my options open.

"There is something weighing on me," I said. "But if I share it with you, can you promise that you will keep it a secret?"

"Absolutely. I promise."

I paused. The judge had told me to tell no one. But I couldn't resist the opportunity to unburden myself.

"It's about *Geidner*."

"Ah, *Geidner*! The judge's biggest triumph—and yours. The opinion that got a shout-out from the president when he nominated her. What's going on with *Geidner*? It might get reheard en banc, in which case your opinion goes away. But there's nothing you can do about that. And the opinion already served its purpose, at least as far as the judge is concerned."

"Actually, the opinion shouldn't even exist. When I was doing the final cite-checking and proofreading, I made a discovery: the court lacks jurisdiction."

"That's crazy. How can that be?"

"The notice of appeal was filed one day late. The clerk's office missed it. In the scanned document on the online docket, the date on the notice looks correct. But when you look at the original paper document, as I did in my cite-checking, you can see it was filed out of time by a single day."

"Holy crap. Did you tell the judge?"

I nodded slowly.

"And what did she say?"

"This was back when the president was still mulling over nominees, when some on the right were questioning her conservative credentials as a possible Supreme Court justice . . ."

James paused, but only for a few seconds; he was a quick thinker.

"She didn't—she didn't tell you to ignore it, did she?"

I nodded. For some reason, making James guess what happened instead of telling him directly made me feel less guilty about revealing the judge's secret—even though I felt guilty over keeping the secret too.

"Wow," James said, shaking his head in disbelief. "And to think that she always casts herself as the defender of judicial restraint and jurisdictional limits. But our boss is nothing if not ambitious. You've been keeping this a secret the whole time?"

More nodding from me.

"You have to do something," he said. "You have to tell someone."

"I told the judge. And she made the call to go forward and issue the opinion anyway. That was her call to make. She's the judge."

"Audrey, that's bullshit. Issuing an opinion in a case where the court lacks jurisdiction—and *knows* it lacks jurisdiction—is lawless."

"Lawless? That might be a little strong. The constitutionality of banning gay marriage is an important issue that needs to be resolved. It's going to come through the appellate courts someday."

"Someday, but not today. Don't you think it's hypocritical of the judge to talk so much about how judges must recognize the limits of their role and the importance of jurisdiction, but ignore all of that when it suits her own purposes?"

"I wouldn't call it hypocritical so much as . . . practical. This isn't a case where the judge overturned a law on a whim or because of her own personal political views. The jurisdictional defect here is tiny and technical—a piece of paper got faxed in one day late."

"But here, even if she sustained rather than overturned a law, she *did* brush aside a jurisdictional problem to advance her own personal political views—her conservatism. If a criminal defendant or an immigrant or a plaintiff in a civil case filed their notice of appeal one day late, do you have any doubt the judge would dismiss for lack of jurisdiction?"

I had no rebuttal. We both knew the answer to that.

"Why are you defending the judge so much here? What's at stake for you?"

I shrugged, in what I thought was a casual manner, but James immediately pounced.

"Let me guess: the judge said she'd take you with her as a clerk if she makes it to the Supreme Court. As long as you keep her secret."

I suspected I was smarter than James in a "book smart" way, but he was far more emotionally intelligent than I could ever hope to be.

"The judge likes my work a lot," I offered weakly. "And you could see how she might want a familiar face among her first set of law clerks at the Court."

That almost seemed to anger James. He stood up and moved toward the door, but turned around to face me before opening it.

"Audrey, I see a lot of the judge in you. You share many things—especially ambition. But I trust you to do the right thing."

43

The judge's confirmation hearings were scheduled to last four days. Together with my co-clerks and Brenda, I watched every minute, gathered around the only television in chambers, which was in the judge's office. I honestly wasn't sure how well she would hold up, given her 30,000-feet approach to her judicial duties, delegating vast amounts of substantive responsibility to her clerks. But she actually did well—very well, in fact. She provided just enough legal analysis in her answers to satisfy the senators, but not so much as to get bogged down in minutiae. And, perhaps most important in the age of televised hearings, she looked and sounded great. She never stumbled and never lost her cool, giving her opponents no sound bites to use against her in ads or on the nightly news.

On the morning of her last day of testimony, a Republican senator asked Judge Stinson a softball question about her *Harvard Journal of Law and Public Policy* article concerning jurisdiction.

"Thank you for that question, Senator. As I expressed in that article, I am a strong believer in jurisdictional limits, especially in the federal courts, which are courts of limited rather than general jurisdiction. All too often, courts decide issues that they should not decide—and issues that, in fact, they *cannot* decide, due to a lack of jurisdiction. In the article, I analyze some of the doctrines—rationalizations, really—that judges concoct for blowing past jurisdictional constraints to decide issues they lack the power to decide. If you survey my rulings over the years, as both a trial and appellate judge, you will note my strict attention to jurisdiction and my strong respect for the limits it places upon federal judges."

James gave me a sideways glance. I looked away, but I felt his eyes still on me.

That afternoon, after the close of the confirmation hearings, my mother called. Normally I wouldn't take a personal call in the middle of the workday, but with my boss on national television as a Supreme Court nominee, this wasn't a normal time.

"Hi Mom. What's up?"

"I was watching your boss on the television this morning. Very pretty! *Mestiza* beauty, as they say back home."

"Yes—she's half-Chinese, half-Caucasian."

"And she speaks so well! I don't understand all the law-law stuff she's talking about, but she *sounds* very good. Like a newscaster!"

"You're not the first person to make that observation."

"But, you know, we have a saying: *kung sino ang masalita ay siyang kulang sa gawa.*"

"And that means?" My parents had never taught us Tagalog (or Filipino, if you prefer).

"Whoever talks much never does much. There's a young surgeon here at the hospital, went to Harvard Medical School, did his residency at Mass General, always talking about his education and awards—very *mayabang.* But in the operating room he's very slow, his suturing is sloppy, and the nurses hate working with him because he's so mean."

"I guess prestige isn't all it's cracked up to be," I said. "Reputation doesn't always have a basis in fact. You have to look below the surface."

"So about this boss of yours—would she be a good Supreme Court judge? The newspapers say she is very smart, and she went to good schools, and she looks nice and speaks well. But I don't like how hard she makes you work! Every time I call, you're too busy to talk because you're working. Even though there are four of you! And she doesn't even pay you that much! She should do more of her own work. Does she deserve to be on the Supreme Court?"

"That is . . . a complicated question."

Somehow my mother, lacking any real knowledge of the legal profession, had stumbled upon a number of truths.

"Ay, *hija*, my break is over. I'll call you later. Be a good girl!"

I did want to "be a good girl." I remembered the church billboard I saw on the way to the airport: "Silence Is Consent"—and realized I could no longer consent. I had to do something. But what?

44

The reviews of Judge Stinson's performance in her confirmation hearings were stellar. Commentators praised her poise, polish, and careful, thoughtful responses. I had to concede: even if she didn't often bother with details in her day-to-day work as a judge, when she actually deigned to focus on something she cared about, she could hit it out of the park.

With not much time left before her confirmation vote—because the Court was in the middle of its term, her vote was being fast-tracked—I still hadn't figured out what to do in *Geidner*. Was I delaying because I didn't know what action to take, or was I being cowardly and trying to run out the clock? Did part of me feel guilty about the prospect of taking action that would arguably violate my duty of confidentiality to my judge and derail her Supreme Court prospects?

Early the following week, in an effort to give myself a pep talk about the wisdom of courts exercising jurisdiction with care, I picked up one of my old books from law school, a classic on the subject of judicial restraint: *The Least Dangerous Branch*, by Alexander Bickel, the late, great Yale law professor. There was nothing in it that related directly to the jurisdictional defect in *Geidner*, but flipping through it reminded me of how important proper jurisdiction is to the legitimacy of the courts. Far from being a "technicality," jurisdiction is the foundation upon which judicial review rests.

I came to Chapter 4, "The Passive Virtues," which was also the title of Bickel's landmark *Harvard Law Review* article. Bickel's argument, in a nutshell, was that sometimes courts should refrain from ruling on controversial issues, even if those issues are properly before them, as they wait for societal views to solidify. In other words, judicial passivity can be a virtue.

Passivity as a virtue: that was the ticket. I now knew what to do.

I decided to reach out to Lucia. Her boss, Judge Polanski, was perhaps the one judge on the court who was even more of a stickler for jurisdiction than Judge Stinson. Rumor had it that he would reward any clerk of his who could find a jurisdictional defect by taking that clerk out to a fancy lunch—and considering that the Polanski clerks rarely ate lunch anywhere other than chambers, that was quite a reward indeed. If I could get *Geidner*'s jurisdictional problem in front of Judge Polanski, he wouldn't hesitate to take action.

I picked up the phone and called Lucia. It was ten in the evening, but I knew she'd still be at her desk.

"Hi Lucia. Sorry to bother you, but I need to see you."

"Sorry, Audrey, but you are one of the last people I'd like to see right now. Or ever. I don't know why I even picked up the phone."

"I realize that, well, things didn't end so well with us. But this is very important. It would mean a lot to me if you'd just meet with me."

"I'm not particularly concerned these days with what would or wouldn't mean a lot to you."

"Okay, let me put it another way. I have information that I think you—and Judge Polanski—would be very, very interested in learning."

Silence from Lucia. I could tell I was getting through to her, invoking her conscientiousness as a clerk.

"It's important," I said. "Not just to me, but to the Ninth Circuit. It will take just a few minutes of your time. And you don't even need to talk to me if you don't want to. Can you meet me in the library in five minutes?"

"Fine. But this better be good. And fast."

I gathered up the materials I used to prove the *Geidner* jurisdictional problem to Judge Stinson. I took the legal pad where I had previously laid out the argument, then added at the top—in capital letters, in red marker—"JURISDICTIONAL DEFECT IN GEIDNER V. GALLAGHER." Then I headed down to the library, where I took the table under the Chicago Clock—the table where Lucia and I had had our last intense encounter. This time, though, it would hopefully have a happier ending.

I laid out my materials all over half of the table. The legal pad with the red-marker writing was clearly visible. Also in plain view was the original notice of appeal.

Lucia arrived a few minutes later. She nodded at me in silent greeting.

"Hi," I said. "I just realized: I have to go to the bathroom. Can you keep an eye—a close, close eye—on these materials of mine?"

She gave me a puzzled look. I raised my eyebrows twice, feeling like an inept agent in a spy movie. And then I saw the recognition in her eyes—of course the top graduate of Harvard Law School would be quick on the uptake.

I wandered off for five minutes, meandering through the empty hallways of the first floor of the courthouse. I figured that would be enough time for Lucia to see what she needed to see. When I returned, I noticed that Lucia—who had come down to the library empty-handed—held a sheaf of photocopied materials in her hands.

"Thanks for trusting me with your papers," she said. "You're right. I find them exceedingly interesting. And Judge Polanski will too."

45

A day passed. Then another, and another, and another. No word from Lucia, and no action by Judge Polanski. Had I missed something? Was there really no jurisdictional problem in *Geidner*?

And then the big day itself rolled around: the Senate vote to confirm Judge Stinson to the Supreme Court of the United States. With strong bipartisan support—just a handful of hard-core liberals voted against her—Judge Stinson was confirmed to the Court by a vote of 82–18, as we watched coverage of the vote on the television in chambers.

"Well, congratulations to our boss," James said, an obvious edge in his voice. "The Senate has performed its advise-and-consent function and voted in favor of Judge Stinson. I wonder how informed that consent was?"

I wanted to explain myself to James and to tell him that I *had* taken action, that I *had* brought the *Geidner* jurisdictional defect to the attention of someone I thought would do something about it. And that I had done so in a cleverly passive way, where I could tell myself that I hadn't actively betrayed my boss but had just "accidentally" allowed certain information to get out. But I didn't feel comfortable revealing what I had done.

Fortunately, I didn't have to wait long. The morning after her confirmation vote, Christina Wong Stinson was sworn in as Associate Justice Stinson. That afternoon, Judge Polanski sent around an email to all Ninth Circuit judges—the "All Associates" listserv—unveiling the jurisdictional defect in *Geidner*. His email, clearly based on my research and analysis, left no room for argument. He included an extremely clear copy of the original notice of appeal to his email—presumably a copy that Lucia had made on the evening we met up. His message did not say anything about how he came to learn of the problem.

As a result, a few days later the *Geidner* opinion was vacated—withdrawn, rendered a nullity—and the appeal was dismissed. The proper outcome for the case, as a matter of legal principle, was achieved; the issue of same-sex marriage would be decided in some unknown future case—hopefully by judges more principled than my boss. But none of this affected the confirmation to the Supreme Court of the judge who knew about the mistake and willfully concealed it from public view.

And so justice was done in *Geidner*—but not in terms of Judge Stinson's elevation to the Supreme Court. I wondered to myself: why did Judge Polanski wait to expose the jurisdictional defect in *Geidner* until it was too late to affect Judge Stinson's confirmation?

Shortly after her confirmation and swearing-in ceremony—to which she wore the triumphantly pink Armani suit I picked up with her, as I noticed when I watched on television—Justice Stinson returned to California to straighten out some affairs. She popped into chambers one day, presumably to leave instructions for Brenda and for the movers, and called me in to see her as soon as she arrived.

"Hello, Judge—I'm sorry, Justice."

It felt strange to call her "Justice." But I had to respect the office, even if not the occupant.

"Hello, Audrey," Justice Stinson said, standing up from behind her desk. "Don't sit down. This conversation will be brief. I assume you told Judge Polanski about the jurisdictional issue in *Geidner*."

"Your Honor, I did not speak to Judge Polanski about . . ."

"Spare me the word games, please. I took hundreds of depositions back in the day and I know how to rephrase a question. I assume that you played some role in Judge Polanski learning of the jurisdictional issue in *Geidner*."

I said nothing, but my blushing betrayed me.

"Thankfully, your dishonesty came too late to interfere with my confirmation to the Court."

"Justice, I wouldn't call it dishonesty for a law clerk to . . ."

"Enough," she said, raising her voice and her right hand. "I do not wish to hear excuses for your betrayal. There will be consequences."

I nodded. Even though I knew I had acted properly, I felt bad. I was not used to disappointing, to say nothing of angering, authority figures.

"Your co-clerks will be offered positions with other judges here on the Ninth Circuit for the remaining months of their clerkships, as is customary in these types of situations. But not you. You can resign your position, effective immediately, or we can explore . . . other options."

"You're firing me?"

"Not quite. I am offering you the opportunity to resign. What did you expect, a promotion? Needless to say, I am not taking you with me to the Supreme Court. Nor will I recommend you to any of my colleagues on the Court—ever. You will never be a Supreme Court clerk, Audrey Coyne. And I will never forget what you did to me."

"Your Honor, I'm sorry," I said instinctively—before catching myself and clarifying, "I'm sorry it had to end this way."

"I am as well. I saw so much of myself in you, and so much promise. But that's the end of that."

Justice Stinson sat back down and looked up at me, dismissively.

"Brenda has all the paperwork," she said. "She has already printed out your resignation letter; all you need to do is sign it. Then pack up your personal effects and leave chambers immediately. Don't make me call courthouse security to remove you from the building. They respond extra quickly to requests from Supreme Court justices."

As I packed my few personal belongings—a handful of books from law school that I had brought into the office, a framed photograph of my parents and my sister, an extra suit that I hung on the back of my door— I thought about what had just transpired between me and the judge. I can't say it came as a surprise—I knew the judge would be angry—but, until then, I hadn't really stopped to think through all the implications.

I would never have the privilege of clerking for the Supreme Court. A longtime dream of mine was dashed. At the same time, I would never have the corresponding burdens. And make no mistake about it: being a Supreme Court clerk came with burdens, the weight of high expectations. Within a few years of leaving your SCOTUS clerkship, you were expected to enjoy a certain amount of professional success: a partnership at a major law firm, a tenured professorship at an elite law school, a high government office. If you weren't a federal judge by age 45, people would wonder: what went wrong? And even making it to a coveted, life-tenured seat on the federal bench didn't put an end to ambition. District judges wanted to be circuit judges. Circuit judges wanted to be particularly well-respected circuit judges, such as feeder judges—or, better yet, Supreme Court justices. I recalled what Judge Stinson had told me during my clerkship interview: "I like to be a judge who's going places." Success didn't take you off the treadmill, but simply put you on a different treadmill, at a higher speed and with a steeper incline.

But now I didn't have to worry about any of that. With no hope of a Supreme Court clerkship in my future, I was free to just be an Ordinary Person. It felt liberating to have the weight of ambition lifted from me. Or so I tried to tell myself.

I tried to imagine with pleasure the perfectly normal, boring life that awaited me. I'd go back to Cravath and plunge into the toil of a junior associate. I'd leave after a few years, maybe to work in government or go in-house or join a boutique firm. At some point I'd get married and have two or three kids. I'd keep working as a lawyer, doing competent work in service of my clients, and move a notch or two up the career ladder. My kids would grow up and go off to college and get married themselves. Eventually I'd retire, filling my time remaining on earth with travel, classes, and grandchildren. And then I'd die, having lived a pleasurable, productive, perfectly pedestrian life. My death would be noted not as a news item, with a *New York Times* obituary, but with a death notice paid for by my family.

And who was I, really, to aspire for more than that? Yes, I'm intelligent and accomplished, but not to any extraordinary degree. It would be an exaggeration to call me "brilliant." There are hundreds, if not thousands, of law school graduates and young lawyers just like me. When we're young, overachieving, and unstoppable, we all think we're special. But as we grow older, we reach a more realistic understanding of our place in the world. It happens at different times for different people, but eventually we all come to terms with our own ordinariness.

We can't all become Supreme Court justices, or even federal judges, or even prominent lawyers with noteworthy cases. And this reality is not unique to law. Very few doctors will cure a major disease. Very few actors will win Oscars or Tony Awards. Very few writers will pen best sellers. Very few bankers will become billionaires. Very few soldiers will become generals.

We can't all become part of history; we can't all become stars. Instead, we must serve as members of the chorus, or even the audience, so the true stars can stand out and shine. Indeed, without supporting players or an audience, there can be no stars. The role of being an audience member, while not prominent, is essential. It's the role played by the vast, vast majority of humanity, and it holds no dishonor.

So, in one sense, not getting a Supreme Court clerkship was a great blessing. It gave me freedom: freedom to step off the track, freedom to stop chasing elusive glory, freedom to live a normal life, freedom to just . . . be. Dropping out of the race gave me such sweet relief. I looked forward to watching others pass me by, sweating and panting and struggling mightily—for what?—as I just stood there, breathing deeply and savoring the sky above me and the ground below.

Judge Stinson's confident pronouncement that "there is always somewhere else to go" was simply wrong. You can stop exactly where you are, anytime you want, plant your feet, and declare to the world, "Here and no further." And in that moment, you will have your victory; you will have overthrown the tyranny of ambition.

Or so I tried to tell myself, as I packed up my belongings and left chambers for the last time.

46

I called up Cravath back in New York, where I had an outstanding job offer, and said that I wanted to accept and start work as soon as possible (which I needed to, out of financial necessity). The firm was happy to have me, especially since I was coming off of a clerkship with a judge who had just been confirmed to the Supreme Court, and told me I could start as soon as I liked. I asked to start one week later, which would give me enough time to tie up loose ends—pack up my (admittedly few) things, find someone to sublet my apartment, and say my good-byes.

And my apologies. I began with Amit, whom I asked to meet me in the Little Mural Room, a random room in the courthouse that always seemed to be empty. Back when the courthouse was a hotel, it served as the "morning room," where guests would enjoy coffee and read newspapers. It had a peaceful vibe, thanks to several murals of southwestern scenes painted in soft colors—a vibe that I thought might come in handy in case Amit got upset.

Amit and I had never exactly been friends, so as soon as he arrived and sat down, I got straight to the point.

"I'm leaving town soon to go back to New York and start at Cravath. Before leaving, I just wanted to say I'm sorry. I'm sorry I used my knowledge about your writing Beneath Their Robes to blackmail you into withdrawing your Supreme Court clerkship applications. I was blinded by my ambition, and I acted wrongly. I hope you can accept my apology."

Amit smiled. Was he gloating?

"Apology accepted," he said. "Yes, you acted unethically. But it's also true that I shouldn't have been writing BTR. So in a sense I'm glad that you stopped me before I got in too deep. I shut the site down and was able to go back to my legal career. No harm, no foul."

"That's very gracious of you. I expected you to give me a harder time."

"I was furious with you at the time. But the more I thought about it, the more I didn't want a Supreme Court clerkship. At least, not with the justices that our boss had the power to hook me up with."

"Why is that?"

"I have a confession of my own to make. Remember how uncomfortable I looked at our Monday morning meetings whenever *Geidner* came up, and how I didn't volunteer that enthusiastically when the judge asked who wanted to work with her on it? Or remember how campy and over-the-top Beneath Their Robes was? One reader described Article III Groupie as the 'drag queen of the legal blogosphere.' Audrey, I'm gay."

Ha, I thought to myself, maybe Jeremy was right after all when he said there was a gay in every chambers in the Ninth Circuit. He just should have guessed Amit instead of James.

"Well, just because you're gay doesn't mean you have to disagree with *Geidner*," I observed. "You can think gay marriage is good social policy but still think that states are allowed to ban it without violating the Constitution."

"True," Amit said. "I've been politically conservative my whole life, but it's only in the past few months that I've been starting to come out and deal with this whole 'gay' thing. Doing Beneath Their Robes was helpful to me in exploring this part of me. Anyway, I just didn't want to be working on such a major case about gay rights while I was going through a very personal struggle—one that's not yet over. So I'm actually thankful to you for picking up *Geidner*."

"And look where it got me," I said with a laugh. "Hated by our boss. And persona non grata at the Supreme Court."

"But you acted correctly. I'm not worried about you. I suspect the world hasn't heard the last of Audrey Coyne."

Amit rose to his feet. I stood up too, and he hugged me.

"Whoa! So now that you're gay, you're a hugger?"

"Good luck at Cravath," he said. "I'll be back in New York soon to start at Sullivan & Cromwell. Maybe I'll see you in the city sometime."

That went surprisingly well. Next up was James, whom I texted and asked to come down to the Little Mural Room after Amit left.

"I just bumped into Amit in the elevator," James said when he arrived. "You're like a doctor's office in here."

"I don't have much time. I'm heading back to New York this weekend and starting at Cravath next week. Before I go, I have a lot of surgeries to do—to repair fractured relationships."

James laughed. God, he had a great smile.

"I wouldn't say our relationship is fractured," he said. "I still value our friendship and have so much respect for you."

"That's exactly what I wanted to talk to you about. I wanted to thank you for being my conscience. I don't know if I would have done the right thing if you hadn't urged me to. Yes, the *Geidner* secret was eating away at me, but I did manage to keep it to myself—for weeks. I might never have said anything if not for our conversation. To be honest, I don't want to think about what I would have done—or not done—if you hadn't spoken up."

"But that was because you confided in me in the first place. You didn't have to do that. You could have just kept your mouth shut, clerked for Stinson on the Court, passed Go, collected your $200—or your $300,000 signing bonus, actually."

Mention of the money I had basically given up made me momentarily ill.

"Oh God, don't remind me!" I moaned. "Instead of a six-figure signing bonus, I have a six-figure student loan balance."

"Join the club. But it's nothing that a few years of working at Cravath can't fix."

"Speaking of fixing things—I'm sorry about how badly I ended things with us. It came at a time when I was under an incredible amount of stress, working on the *Geidner* opinion and prepping for my interview with Justice Keegan, and I just snapped. Do you think there's any chance we might someday . . . pick up where we left off?"

James paused—a long, long pause.

"I don't know," he said. "We're going to be on opposite sides of the country. You're going to be in New York, working insane hours at Cravath. I'm going to be up in San Francisco at Morrison & Foerster, also working long hours . . ."

He must have seen the disappointed look on my face, because he quickly changed his tone.

"But look," he said, "I think you're amazing, Audrey. Let's stay in touch—and what will happen will happen."

Vintage James, sensitive as always. Even I, in all my romantic cluelessness, could see what James was doing here: letting me down easy.

"That sounds good," I said. "Let's keep the channels of communication open."

Channels of communication? I sounded like a middle manager ending a team meeting.

We stood up and hugged—a long, long hug. Maybe I was engaging in wishful thinking, but I felt a sense of possibility in the embrace.

My next meeting was with Lucia at the scene of the crime, so to speak: Bodega Wine Bar. It wasn't for another few hours—we were meeting up during that brief window of free time for Lucia when Judge Polanski was driving home—so I decided to walk from the courthouse to downtown, which would give me the chance to clear my head.

Looking back at my botched and brief relationship with James, which was over before it had really begun, I thought about how I had so much to learn about matters of the heart. I was a 24-year-old law school graduate, but I felt like a 14-year-old high school girl in terms of emotional maturity. And perhaps this wasn't surprising: I probably had about as much relationship experience as a high school girl, considering how I had devoted most of my energy over the past decade to my career rather than my personal life. I resolved to focus more on romance upon returning to New York. And even if I'd be working long hours at Cravath, I would at least have more psychological energy to devote to finding a love interest, now that my quest for the immortality of a SCOTUS clerkship was over.

I ran a few errands downtown and still arrived at Bodega half an hour early. I took the same seat at the bar that I had the fateful night that Lucia and I had met up for drinks, saved the same seat for her, and ordered a glass of merlot—but barely touched it, waiting for Lucia.

Lucia arrived punctually, as usual, and ordered a glass of pinot noir. I thanked her for the role she played in exposing the jurisdictional defect in *Geidner,* and we drank a true "law nerd" toast: to jurisdiction. After the toast, I took a generous sip from my glass of wine and plunged right in.

"Lucia, I have a confession to make. And an apology. Remember the night that we came here before your interview with Justice Keegan? When I flirted with you, and urged you to drink more, and we kissed?"

She continued to nod, but I detected a slight darkening of her expression.

"That was . . . dishonest of me. I'm straight—I always have been—and I was never interested in you romantically. I flirted with you and egged you on in terms of drinking that night because, well, I knew you had your big interview the next day—for a clerkship that I badly wanted for myself. And you just seemed so well prepared and so unstoppable, with your Fay Diploma from Harvard and your clerkship with Judge Polanski and all of that. So I, well—I guess you could say I sabotaged you."

As soon as the gush of words escaped me, I felt better—like when I unburdened myself about *Geidner* to James.

But Lucia didn't feel better. Seconds after I finished, she picked up her wine glass and flung its contents at me (yes, she was drinking red). By the time I had blinked the wine out of eyes and wiped my face down with a napkin, she was gone.

I went to the ladies' room and cleaned myself up as best as I could. I was wearing dark jeans, fortunately, but I didn't hold out much hope for my white blouse. And I didn't have time to go home and change before my next appointment at Bodega.

"Miss Audrey, what the hell happened to you? That shirt looks like a modern art project."

I told Jeremy about my meeting with Lucia.

"Hell hath no fury like a lesbian scorned. At least she didn't slug you. Think of it like a spa treatment: she gave you a red-wine facial."

"I should probably apologize to you before you order a drink," I said. "I'm sorry I accused you of envy and bad faith when we argued over Judge Stinson. You were right: she turned out to be, well, a politicized judge."

"In other words, a conservative political hack."

"Yes. One who put her ambitions ahead of the law. But many of her issues were specific to her."

"So you still have faith in 'the law,' then?"

"I do," I said. "There are judges out there who do their best to follow 'the law,' to interpret it as opposed to make it. Maybe not Justice Stinson—and, no offense, not your boss either. But we can both name judges on the court who call cases as they see them. Like Judge Polanski. Or Judge Dennis O'Sullivan, up in Portland. Or Judge Samantha Garber, also in Portland. And a few others, including a lot of the senior judges."

"That's fair," Jeremy said. "I just fear there will be fewer judges like them over time and more political hacks. But I guess we'll see."

"And you were right about another thing: I had a gay co-clerk."

"James?" Jeremy couldn't hide his giddiness.

"No. Amit."

"Oh."

"I stopped by the courthouse to say good-bye to him and he came out to me. And hugged me too."

"I guess that doesn't shock me—that Amit's gay. He could be a bitchy little queen at times."

"It takes one to know one."

"Touché. Now please get Her Royal Highness a drink."

47

My last day in Pasadena, a Saturday, arrived before I knew it. I surveyed my apartment, now entirely empty (I had tossed the IKEA furniture), and admired its cleanliness. But I wouldn't miss the place. It had gotten the job done, being cheap and close to the courthouse, but I had never taken the time to make it my home. I supposed this was typical for law clerks and young lawyers, nomads moving from city to city, chasing one professional opportunity after another.

My luggage, a bulging blue suitcase and the black rollerboard I had taken to D.C., sat by the door. All of my other possessions I had previously packed into boxes and shipped to my parents' place in Woodside, where I'd be staying for a few weeks while I hunted for an apartment of my own. I looked forward to getting my own place—and one that I could plan on living in for more than a year. I'd probably live in Queens, an easy commute to Cravath but significantly less expensive than Manhattan—just not as far out as Woodside, maybe Long Island City or Astoria.

I heard a knock at the door. Who could it be? Harvetta was driving me to the airport, but she wasn't supposed to come by for another half hour or so. (I had asked Pervez to drive me to the airport, for old times' sake, but he had another commitment: a party in honor of his cousin Ahmed, who after losing in the Ninth Circuit had won relief from deportation from the attorney general, thanks to a grassroots campaign and the intervention of some prominent politicians.)

I looked through the peephole: Lucia. Not seeing a wine glass in her hand, I let her in.

"Hi," she said.

"Hello," I said. "You're just in time. I'm about to leave for the airport."

I gestured toward my bags, then toward the emptiness of the apartment—so empty that our voices echoed in the small space.

"I'm glad I caught you," she said. "I'm sorry about the other night."

"I deserved it. Dousing me with wine was nothing compared to what I did to you."

"About that—apology accepted. I can't really be that angry about it because, honestly, I would have done the exact same thing if I had been in your shoes. All is fair in love and SCOTUS clerkships."

I laughed.

"Plus," she said, "it all worked out in the end. I just got hired to clerk for Justice Liotta!"

"Congratulations!"

We hugged. Yes, I was envious of Lucia. But in keeping with the new, better me, I tried to suppress it.

"When are you clerking for her?" I asked.

"This coming term. She was all hired up, but then she had a clerk who asked to postpone the clerkship, due to a family issue. I interviewed with her last week and she made me the offer last night."

"That's awesome."

"I'm thrilled. She's also Italian American—I knew the interview was going well when we conducted part of it in Italian. She's a better fit for me than Justice Keegan. Instead of being the Court's major crusader against gay rights, she's our champion."

"It will also be cool to clerk for the 'swing justice.' She casts the deciding vote in so many major cases."

"Yup. And she uses her clerks a lot as emissaries to the other chambers. It's supposed to be a lot of fun."

Just then, as if summoned by all the Supreme Court talk, Harvetta appeared in the open doorway.

"Hello, ladies! Did I hear some talk about fun?"

"Harvetta, meet Lucia, who's clerking for Judge Polanski now and who will be clerking for Justice Liotta. Lucia, meet Harvetta, who's clerking for Justice Lin now and who will be clerking for Justice Wilson. You'll be clerking at the Court together, so it's great that you're meeting now."

They shook hands. I tried to sound cheery, but inside I was heartbroken. They would be clerking at the Court together—making history, walking the marble halls of One First Street, knowing the outcomes of headline- and history-making cases before the public—while I'd be toiling away at a law firm. Getting over not getting a Supreme Court clerkship would take time.

"Okay girl," said Harvetta, turning to me and grabbing my blue suitcase, "you ready? It's time to ship your ass back to New York."

48

I started up at Cravath that Monday. They didn't waste any time in putting me to work, staffing me on a collection of cases against Credit Suisse related to residential mortgage-backed securities. The hours were long; my first week in the office, I didn't go home before ten in the evening, not even on Friday. But it was fine. I had worked long hours during my clerkship and I was glad for the distraction. Plunging headlong into work would help me get over things.

I also started exercising—partly to help me get over things, and partly to get back into shape. I had about five extra pounds, picked up during the final stressful weeks of my clerkship, that I wanted to lose. I certainly didn't want to gain more weight (which a number of my law school classmates who went directly to firms after graduation had already done).

One morning, a few weeks into my time at Cravath, I was at the gym running on the treadmill, cranked up to level 8. I had the small television tuned into CNN, but I wasn't paying close attention; it was just something to distract me from my effort. Then a news alert flashed across the screen that did grab my attention:

"Justice Hannah Greenberg, Dead at 83."

I almost fell off the treadmill. I immediately slowed the treadmill down to 3.5 and listened in to the broadcast. Justice Greenberg—whom everyone had expected to be the next justice to leave the Court, before Justice Keegan's death—had lost her battle with cancer, after a long and valiant struggle. President LaFount, not even done with the first year of his presidency, would have another vacancy to fill.

That meant another justice on the Court. With four new clerkships to be filled. But not with the likes of me. My former boss, Justice Stinson, would make sure of that.

49

Surprising many veteran Court watchers, President LaFount nominated a second Ninth Circuit judge in a row: Judge Polanski. It was unusual to have such strong representation on the Supreme Court from a single appeals court (other than the D.C. Circuit), but in other ways the Polanski pick made sense. He was a staple of SCOTUS shortlists in a Republican administration, and his extensive network of loyal law clerks, the Polanski Mafia, was advocating for him strongly behind the scenes. And because President LaFount had recently replaced a white male (Keegan) with a woman of color (Stinson), he now had the leeway to replace a woman (Greenberg) with a man (Polanski).

Judge Polanski's swift confirmation to the Court—given his impeccable credentials, many years of judicial service, and reputation as a judge who truly did follow the law—came as no surprise. What did come as a surprise was the phone call I received a few days after his confirmation.

I was in my office at Cravath, munching on a salad I had ordered from my desk, when my secretary, Debbie, took a call for me.

"Audrey, Justice Polanski is on the line for you."

I almost spat out a cherry tomato. I swallowed the tomato, chased it with bottled water, and answered the phone in as composed a manner as I could muster.

"Hello, this is Audrey Coyne."

"Audrey! Frank Polanski here."

I would have suspected a prank call, perhaps from Jeremy, but that

Polish accent was unmistakable.

"Hello, Justice Polanski," I said, trying to sound as deferential as possible over the phone. "Congratulations on your confirmation."

"Thanks, thanks. I detest D.C., but this new job I just got is pretty good, so I'll put up with it. How do you feel about Washington?"

"I haven't been there often, but I've been impressed on the few occasions I have visited. It's a beautiful city."

"I find it cold—not temperature-wise, although I guess compared to California it is—but architecturally cold. All those monuments. Monolithic gray government buildings. Reminds me of my childhood behind the Iron Curtain. Anyway, how would you like to clerk for me?"

"I beg your pardon, Your Honor?"

"Audrey, you're a young woman—a young, brilliant, beautiful woman—so I'm sure you heard me the first time. How would you like to clerk for me?"

"Is that . . . is that an offer, Justice Polanski?"

"You could call it that. What's your answer?"

"Uh, shouldn't I send you an application first?"

"I know all I need to know about you. You applied to clerk for me on the Ninth Circuit, so I know that your paper credentials—résumé, transcript, recommendations—are stellar. I got to see some of your work product during your clerkship year, in terms of opinions and en banc memos you worked on—also excellent."

"Thank you, Justice. But maybe you want to interview me?"

"Nah. I know you're smart enough for me, so the interview would just be to see if you pass the 'dinner test'—as in, can I have dinner with this person and not hate them or be bored by the end? And you already passed that test. As you may recall, we sat next to each other at the law clerk orientation last year."

"Yes, that's right . . ."

"Most important, I know that you're a young lawyer of great integrity. One of my former law clerks, Lucia Aroldi, speaks very highly of you. And let's just say that I know, from Lucia, that you share my concern for the rule of law—especially in the area of jurisdiction."

Lucia must have told him about *Geidner*. I didn't ask for any credit when I clued her in to the jurisdictional problem, but I guess she gave me credit anyway.

"As you may have noticed during your clerkship year," Justice Polanski said, "I am—at the risk of sounding immodest—a very principled jurist. I follow the law where it takes me; I don't twist it to serve my political ends. And I get the sense that you share my views."

"Absolutely, Your Honor. I most certainly do."

"One other thing. Unlike your old boss, I draft most of my own opinions. My clerks help me with research and editing. After they've worked with me for a few months, I let clerks try their hand at a little drafting—but when a clerk drafts something, I edit it to within an inch of its life. I enjoy the law so much that I can't help immersing myself in the nitty-gritty—and I'm a bit selfish, in that I like to keep a lot of the fun of writing for myself. I hope that that's okay with you."

"I'd welcome the opportunity to learn the judicial craft as your apprentice. That was always my vision of what a judge does and what a clerkship should be."

"So, how about it? Don't make me beg. Will you clerk for me, Audrey Coyne?"

"I would be honored, Justice Polanski."

50

The next day I found myself at LaGuardia Airport's Marine Air Terminal, the beautiful old Art Deco building that's home to Delta's shuttle between New York and Washington. Justice Polanski wanted me to head down to D.C. immediately; as I knew from Lucia, everything was an emergency with him. I planned to crash with Harvetta for a few days while I looked for an apartment of my own. After I found my own place in Washington, my parents would drive down with the rest of my stuff.

I was sitting at the Yankee Clipper restaurant, having a coffee and reading the *New York Times*, when out of the corner of my eye I spied a fearsome sight: Justice Stinson, trailed by two guards with earpieces and a pretty, petite Eurasian woman who looked like a 20-something version of Christina Wong Stinson (and, by extension, me).

I froze. Had the judge seen me? When I could move again, I picked up the *Times*, folded it out as expansively as I could, and buried my face in an article about a string of poisoning deaths in Pakistan.

"Audrey?"

I raised my head slowly—a sign of my guilt, I belatedly realized, because an innocent party would have looked up quickly to see who it was—and met the judge's gaze. She was dressed head to toe in bright cobalt blue, in a pantsuit with matching shoes and handbag, which was perhaps why she jumped out at me visually from the drab masses.

"Hello, Justice Stinson."

I rose to my feet, putting the newspaper to one side—slowly, not like how I hurriedly dropped the coffee-table book during my clerkship interview—and reached out for a handshake.

"Audrey, it's lovely to see you. Come here."

Instead of shaking my hand, the smiling judge moved in for a hug. What do you do when a Supreme Court justice tries to hug you? We hugged.

"So you're heading to D.C. this morning?" she asked.

"Yes. What brings you to New York, Justice Stinson?"

"I came up here last night to deliver a speech at Columbia Law School in honor of Justice Greenberg—the inaugural lecture in what will be an annual series—and now I'm going back to Washington. What's taking you to D.C.? A case you're working on?"

"Actually, I'm heading down to clerk for Justice Polanski."

I relished the look of shock that briefly crossed Justice Stinson's face before she composed herself. She then waved over the young woman, who was standing a respectful distance behind the justice.

"Audrey, this is Phoebe, who will be clerking for me at the Court. Phoebe, this is Audrey, who clerked for me on the Ninth Circuit—and who will now be clerking for Justice Polanski. Thanks to Audrey, my record as a feeder judge continues, even though I'm now a justice!"

The judge chuckled at her self-congratulatory comment while Phoebe and I shook hands.

"It's nice to meet you," Phoebe said. "I've heard a lot about you."

"Don't believe any of it!" I said, laughing nervously. A stock response, but I meant it—who knew what Justice Stinson had said about me?

"Audrey, you'll always have a special place among my former clerks. Phoebe, I'd like to chat with Audrey for a moment. Why don't you take the guards and meet me by the gate?"

Phoebe bowed to excuse herself and then left with "the guards." Was this LaGuardia Airport in the 21st century, or some kind of medieval court?

With just the two of us present, and nobody else within earshot in the noisy restaurant, I waited for Justice Stinson's condemnation. It would be unseemly to argue with a Supreme Court justice in public, so I'd have to endure the tongue-lashing as well as possible.

"You know, Audrey, I meant what I just said. You will always stand out among my clerks."

"Thank you, Justice."

"I don't mean it entirely as a compliment," she said icily—followed by a grin, so anyone watching us would think we were having a friendly chat. "We will always be tied together, whether we like it or not. I do admire you for managing to get what you wanted in the end, despite your betrayal of me—or perhaps because of it."

"Justice Stinson, I wouldn't call it a betrayal so much as a . . ."

"You're an improbable person, Audrey, but so am I. We have that in common—along with difficulty in loving or being loved, and ambition—insatiable ambition."

"I didn't do what I did for ambition," I said. "I did it for the law. The rule of law, which I hope to advance while clerking for Justice Polanski—a principled jurist, who exposed the jurisdictional defect in *Geidner*. That's what being a judge requires: upholding the law. It's not about the power and prestige."

The justice waved her exquisite hand dismissively. "So say you, about to start your Supreme Court clerkship. What else is there besides power and prestige? Don't be ridiculous. Everybody wants this. Everybody wants to be us."

"Not everybody is in this for the same reasons. Some just love the law, from its grand doctrines to its minute details. Like my friend Harvetta, who's clerking for Justice Wilson—she reads law reviews for fun. Or like Justice Polanski—he writes his own opinions because he enjoys it so much."

"Oh, you and your beloved Justice Polanski. You'll find working for him to be . . . interesting. He does love the law, and he is a great legal mind, but you will soon find that he has certain . . . idiosyncrasies. You will come to know them if you haven't seen them already."

The way she said it seemed calculated to unnerve me—and it did—but

I concealed my anxiety, not wanting to give her the satisfaction.

"I know Frank very well," she continued. "We've been rivals at times, yes, but colleagues and friends too. I know things about him that very few people know—things I've kept to myself over the years, even when the FBI came sniffing around just now as part of his Supreme Court vetting. Suffice it to say that you will find him as a person to be quite . . . unique."

"I'm sure I'll learn a lot from clerking for Justice Polanski," I said.

"But not as much as you learned from clerking for me," Justice Stinson said with a smile. "Anyone can teach legal doctrine or legal writing. I taught you about how things work in the real world. I taught you about power—how to get it and how to use it. Don't ever forget the lessons I taught you."

"I will never forget them, Justice Stinson."

"And remember this: regardless of our differences, I will always be your judge, and you will always be my clerk."

I nodded, slowly and solemnly. She was right about that, at least.

"Well, Audrey, it was very nice seeing you, but I really must be going," Justice Stinson said, looking down at her jewel-encrusted Patek Philippe. "I will see you at the Court."

"Yes, Justice Stinson. Have a safe trip to Washington."

She leaned in, enveloping me in the scent of Chanel No. 5, and we hugged again.

"Remember," she whispered, "there is *always* somewhere else to go. Always."

Acknowledgments

Thank you to my editor, Jon Malysiak, without whom I could have never finished this book. I first had the idea for *Supreme Ambitions* back in 2005, but it wasn't until Jon entered the picture that I started to make any real progress. Throughout the entire process of turning a concept and some rough sample chapters into a finished work, Jon was not just an (excellent) editor, but also a cheerleader, therapist, and friend.

Thank you to Jon, Tim Brandhorst, and Bryan Kay for their willingness to take on an unusual project and to support it with unflagging enthusiasm. Thank you to Rebecca Bender and Kelvin Kelsey for great copyediting that went well beyond copy, Elmarie Jara for her elegant and eye-catching cover design, and Neal Cox and Sonali Oberg for their contributions on the publicity front.

Thank you to all my friends, more folks than I can possibly name here, for more than I can possibly mention here. My gratitude includes, but is not limited to, their taking an interest in this project; their wise advice on writing, editing, and promoting a book; their comments on parts of the manuscript; and, most of all, their friendship.

Thank you to all my colleagues at Above the Law and Breaking Media, especially Elie Mystal, Staci Zaretsky, Joe Patrice, and John Lerner, for being such fun to work with and so supportive of my literary endeavors (which occasionally took me away from my day-to-day duties on ATL).

Thank you to Mark and Jane Shemtob for making their beautiful lake house in the Berkshires available to me as a writer's retreat—and, more importantly, for being such a wonderful presence in my life over the past few years.

Thank you to Brianne Gorod, Judge Richard Posner, and Zachary Baron Shemtob for their insightful comments on early drafts. And special thanks to Zach for putting up with me during this long and sometimes stressful journey (and, of course, more generally).

Thank you to Chief Judge Alex Kozinski for being an early supporter of my writing career, dating back to Underneath Their Robes, and for his comments on the manuscript.

Thank you to Judge Diarmuid F. O'Scannlain for being such a superb boss, role model, and mentor. Thank you to my co-clerks—William Birdthistle, Ryan Bounds, and John Demers—for making my clerkship year so memorable, as well as for their continued friendship over the years.

Thank you, finally, to my family, scattered across continents but united by love. Special thanks to my parents, Emmanuel and Zenda Lat, and my sister Charlene—I owe them everything, and to them I dedicate this book.